D1199525

Cryptography:
InfoSec Pro Guide

About the Author

Sean-Philip Oriyano is a 20+ year veteran of the information technology field, where he is an instructor, author, cyberwarfare expert, and security researcher. Over the years he has worked with many clients, including all branches of the U.S. Military as well as several international clients, and has been sought to instruct at the U.S. Air Force Academy and Naval War College. He obtained his knowledge through a combination of apprenticeships and experience over the years, attaining over 50+ certifications and licenses along the way. Sean has published several books and training videos, and he has authored a dozen research papers on topics such as hacking, forensics, and encryption.

Sean spends most of his time instructing for both public and private clients all over the world. He has consistently received praise for not only his unconventional instructional methods but also for his ability to present complex topics in an easy-to-understand way.

Sean holds many certifications and qualifications that demonstrate his knowledge and experience in the IT field, such as the CISSP, CNDA, CEH, and Security+. He is also trained in Incident Command and Management from FEMA and has earned a MEMS Badge for his efforts.

Outside of work Sean enjoys hiking, skydiving, flying, playing ice hockey, and following the greatest sports franchise ever, the Montreal Canadiens.

About the Technical Editor

Jason McDowell has had a varied government career, stemming from 11 years of service in the U.S. Air Force and then transitioning his commitment to a career as a civil servant with the Department of Interior. During his time as an active-duty member of the Air Force, Jason contributed to many different projects that immersed him in the industrial controls field as well as deployable field communications arena. Additionally, Jason performed as a unit Communications Security (COMSEC) officer, which enabled him to experience cryptography at a grassroots level. His involvement in the deployment, protection, and destruction of both Secret and Top Secret cryptographic keying materials gave him a newfound respect and appreciation for cryptography and the policy surrounding it.

Finishing his military service as a system administrator for a combat communications unit, Jason transitioned his skillset to the civil service workforce. His first position was with the Bureau of Land Management (BLM) in Las Vegas, Nevada. During his two years as an Information Technology Specialist for the BLM, Jason expanded his breadth of experience and knowledge working in a freshly built enterprise environment. He was integral in various projects that impacted the health of the company infrastructure, as well as the protection of physical and logical assets. While at the BLM, he played a lead role in upgrading perimeter security systems to meet the stringent federal facility requirements set forth by Homeland Security Policy Directive-12 (HSPD-12). He also had the opportunity to edit and generate numerous company policy documents, including the Continuity of Operations Plan and Site Security Plan.

Jason's next and current position settled him into an IT Specialist role with the U.S. Fish and Wildlife Service (FWS). Maintaining his commitment to the Department of Interior, Jason's role with the FWS has greatly expanded his scope of work and has tasked him as an IT Project Manager for multiple federal construction projects. He acts as the primary technical consultant for all ongoing Southern Nevada projects, and is working daily at a ground level with project contractors, ensuring consistency and adherence to organizational policy. Jason continues to reeducate and renew his skillset through training and course content development. His appreciation of the information technology field and all its facets has enabled him to grow his skillset through both certification and in-field application. Jason currently holds the A+, Net+, Security+, MCSA, CEH, and CISSP certifications.

Cryptography:
InfoSec Pro Guide

Sean-Philip Oriyano

New York   Chicago   San Francisco
Athens   London   Madrid
Mexico City   Milan   New Delhi
Singapore   Sydney   Toronto

Cataloging-in-Publication Data is on file with the Library of Congress

McGraw-Hill Education books are available at special quantity discounts to use as premiums and sales promotions, or for use in corporate training programs. To contact a representative, please e-mail us at bulksales@mcgraw-hill.com.

Cryptography: InfoSec Pro Guide

1 2 3 4 5 6 7 8 9 0   DOC DOC   1 0 9 8 7 6 5 4 3

ISBN   978-0-07-179425-1
MHID   0-07-179425-5

Sponsoring Editor   Amy Jollymore

Editorial Supervisor   Patty Mon

Project Manager   Nidhi Chopra,
Cenveo® Publisher Services

Acquisitions Coordinator   Amanda Russell

Technical Editor   Jason McDowell

Copy Editor   Bart Reed

Proofreader   Vicki Wong

Indexer   Ted Laux

Production Supervisor   George Anderson

Composition   Cenveo Publisher Services

Illustration   Cenveo Publisher Services

Art Director, Cover   Jeff Weeks

Cover Designer   Jeff Weeks

I first and foremost would like to dedicate this book to the memory of my father, who passed away during the writing of this book. Dad, you are gone, but never forgotten. Thanks to my mom for encouraging me to go into this field in the first place. Without her support I don't think I would have made it this far.

And in the spirit of this book, I also have a coded dedication for someone special out there—you know who you are.

SIAAQKIIMTNPGLYWJYKCLVNCXUEWZKYACVHPWELNGQYVOAMFN
QBNQVEGQBLLGIYUVEHKVCLZRISHJFQNSWLHWXMGDZW
APXUNBREUQGQBWPPEOUVEJSJRXUZMEMTMVPLZPCW
JYGXGITQXBRFUVVEAOFPZGIXROILVNWOF

XRRBBMIIFPKUKKHMULAYMRBVIGUMMSEAZQMFPTRP
MAGATRIAVYTDSLYITYCXPD

Duty, Service, Honor

Contents

Acknowledgments

Amy, thanks for giving me the opportunity to write this book and making the experience as low pressure as it could be. Also thanks for keeping my "scatter-brained" head focused.

Amanda, thanks for your help and input during the writing of this book. It is much appreciated and kept me on track.

Jason, your input was invaluable, and thanks for keeping me honest and not pulling any punches in your comments. Don't worry, I don't hold grudges that long.

Katrina, thanks for the support and words of encouragement during my work on this book. Your smile was enough to give me the tailwind I needed.

Cryptomuseum.com, thanks for the use of your images and your help.

To my classmates: I would love to thank each of you personally and tell you how much I appreciate and value the support you gave me in my personal life after my father passed.

Shigeru Miyamoto, thanks for letting me borrow Hyrule for awhile.

Mark, thanks for your support and for making sure I had the gear I needed to get things done.

Mick, thanks for encouraging me to take breaks from writing and get my butt to the gym.

Jennifer, your expertise and encouragement were invaluable.

Introduction

This book is a beginner's guide to the world of cryptography and will give the reader a basic understanding of the science. The reader will learn the terminology, processes, and the mechanics of cryptography, and how to put those skills and understanding together to gain knowledge of even more complex systems. This text will allow the reader to learn how to use each cryptosystem by experimenting with some of the leading examples through puzzles and code-breaking sessions.

Why This Book?

This book is intended to get people thinking about the world of cryptography without having to become a mathematical genius to understand everything.

Who Should Read This Book

I recommend this book to anyone interested in the field of cryptography who has been confused or intimidated by the formulas and science they encountered. I have attempted to make this book cover the essential details in a fun way that builds a foundation for later exploration.

What This Book Covers

This book covers the history, mechanics, categories, applications, and future of cryptography.

How to Use This Book

This book is intended to be an interactive journey, giving readers the ability to see the algorithms and systems in action as well as use the systems themselves.

How This Book Is Organized

This book is arranged in such a way as to introduce you to the basics of cryptography and then take you through increasingly more complex concepts. Toward the end of the book we look at the more cutting-edge technologies and the future of cryptography.

Chapter 1: The Language of Cryptography   Cryptography has a language that is all its own. Although the language is complex, it is understandable and plays an important part in understanding the world of cryptography. In this first chapter, you learn the language of cryptography.

Chapter 2: History of Cryptography   Cryptography is not a new technology and has been with us for quite a long time. In order to better understand the present and the future, we take a look back at how the technology has evolved and what this means for the future.

Chapter 3: Components of Cryptography   Although you can sit back and listen to the music of an orchestra, you learn much more by understanding the various instruments. In this chapter, you learn about the components of cryptography and how they relate to one another to make up the final picture.

Chapter 4: Algorithms and Ciphers   Every design has a blueprint, and in this chapter you learn about the blueprint or design of a system that makes it work.

Chapter 5: Hashing and Message Digests   Not all cryptography deals with keeping information secret, and in this chapter you see and understand the world of hashing and how it preserves information in its own way.

Chapter 6: Cryptanalysis and Code Breaking   Every time someone has a secret, someone else is likely to want to know it. In this chapter, you learn about how codes can be broken through an analysis of the famous Enigma machine and other techniques.

Chapter 7: Public Key Infrastructure   Cryptography comes in many forms, with asymmetric and Public Key Infrastructure (PKI) being just two examples. In this chapter, you learn the value of PKI and how it relates to many of the technologies you use every day.

Chapter 8: Steganography   Hiding in plain sight—this is the power of steganography. Hiding information in such a way that someone can look right at it and not know it's there is something that only steganography can offer.

Chapter 9: Applied Cryptography   Once you have learned about cryptography and the rules involved, you must then think about how to apply the techniques in the real world. In this chapter, you see how cryptography has been applied to many of the items and systems you use every day without realizing its presence.

Chapter 10: Quantum Cryptography   The story of evolution is ongoing, and in our world part of that evolution is quantum cryptography, which uses the power of quantum mechanics to enhance existing systems in ways never imagined.

Chapter 11: The Future of Cryptography   Finally, this chapter discusses where cryptography is going and how it will play an increasingly larger role as technology becomes more advanced, more information is generated, and the legal system imposes stricter laws regarding privacy and protection.

About the Series

I worked with the publisher to develop several special editorial elements for this series, which we hope you'll find helpful while navigating the book—and furthering your career.

Lingo

The Lingo boxes are designed to help you familiarize yourself with common security terminology so that you're never held back by an unfamiliar word or expression.

IMHO (In My Humble Opinion)

When you come across an IMHO box, you'll be reading my frank, personal opinion based on experiences in the security industry.

In Actual Practice

Theory might teach us smart tactics for business, but there are in-the-trenches exceptions to every rule. The In Actual Practice feature highlights how, at times, things actually get done in the real world (that is, exceptions to the rule) and why.

Your Plan

The Your Plan feature offers strategic ideas that can be helpful to review as you get into planning mode, refine your plan outline, and embark on a final course of action.

CHAPTER 1

The Language
of Cryptography

We'll Cover

● Fundamentals of cryptography

● Key concepts in cryptography

● Key terms and terminology

Cryptography is a field that has a language all its own—and a complicated and unique language it is. When you first delve into the field and dip those toes into the pool of knowledge known as cryptography, the terms may be overwhelming and intimidating.

Don't let the idea of formulas, algorithms keys, and the like scare you off and make you feel like you aren't smart enough to understand them, however. The science is very accessible and digestible at a basic level, but obviously can quickly spiral into complex mathematics—which is something we will not being doing in this text.

In fact, we should think not in terms of formulas, mathematics, logic, and that D we got in math class in 12th grade (long story). Instead, we should think in terms of applications. Where can cryptography be applied, and why should we care? Well, the reality is that the knowledge is applied everywhere you look and frequently in places you would not even guess or be aware of. Some of the places where encryption is used range from the obvious to the not so obvious, as the following list shows:

● **Hard drives**   In today's world, with the abundance of portable computing devices such as laptops that are easily stolen, drive encryption has become a large part of routine security in the mobile space. Many different products have arrived in the last few years that work to ensure that the thief cannot violate the confidentiality or integrity of the data.

● **Digital signatures**   More and more e-mails are being digitally signed to validate the identity of the sender and to ensure that the information is as the sender intended it to be.

● **E-commerce**   For the last decade, an increasing number of transactions (such as banking and shopping) have taken place online. Without encryption offering the protection needed to keep these transactions secret and authentic, e-commerce would not be possible—or at least not in its current form.

● **Cell phones**   Cell phones make widespread use of cryptographic technologies to authenticate devices as well as protect data and other items. Additionally, many financial transactions are now being completed via mobile devices such as tablets and smartphones. This makes cryptographic operations an integral daily activity for a vast number of customers.

This is just a short (very short) sampling of the applications of cryptographic technologies in today's world and marketplace and is just the beginning of the many real-world applications of the art. Hopefully, by the end of this book you will look at current technologies and applications with a new perspective that includes the concepts we will discuss.

Your Plan

When reading through the following chapters, take the time to observe the world and the technologies around to see if you can identify places where cryptographic technology may be used. This is a great exercise because it will get you in the right mindset to understand and possibly implement the technologies later, or at the very least be able to identify them in the software or hardware you purchase.

Fundamentals of Cryptography

So what is cryptography? Well, in the broadest and truest sense, it can be referred to as the science and art of creating, studying, breaking, and working with techniques that secure communications. In more simple or layman's terms, it is the science of securing communications of all types. In the past, the term mainly focused strictly on the process of encryption, but now it has expanded out to cover all the items mentioned here in this text, plus many more.

LINGO
The word **cryptography** comes to us by way of the Latin language and translates into English as "secret writing," which quite accurately describes what we will discuss in this text.

Encryption gets the most attention in the field of cryptography, so let's focus on this first and expand our understanding outward from there. Encryption provides a very important tool to the modern world, much like it did in the ancient world, and that is to keep specific information secret to prevent exposure to those who aren't supposed to see it. How it does this is something that will be discussed in more detail later in the book. Right now we are just concerned with concepts and getting oriented.

IMHO

Encryption, the most widely encountered component of the cryptographic suite, is at the heart and center of many of the commonly performed tasks, including e-commerce over the Internet. Due to clever design and implementation, encryption has enabled the level of secrecy needed to carry out this activity and at the same time maintain the simplicity and transparency needed to make it practical and usable. If either of these last two points was not the case, then the Internet as we know it and the transactions that take place on it would look like a complex mess of unidentifiable characters and symbols—far different from what we are used to seeing today.

Encryption is a process that converts unencrypted information from a clear and open state to a secure and relatively protected state intended to keep the information safe from prying eyes. While the information may be digital, analog, or just written down on paper, the concept is still 100 percent the same: What comes in is unscrambled, and what goes back out is scrambled. Regardless of the medium used, the fundamental and overarching concepts still remain: Plaintext (unencrypted) information is fed into the cryptographic process, and encrypted secured data exits. A simplistic food-based example (I like food) is the meat grinder. Solid meat is fed into one side, on the opposite side out comes ground beef. My apologies to any vegetarians! That ground beef is now in an encrypted form. In other words, there is no way to tell exactly what cut of beef was originally fed into the grinder. Grilling up a fat juicy patty with that ground beef would be a form deciphering that encrypted "message," but that's another section.

Is the process that simple? Yes and no. At a conceptual level, it is just like what's stated here, but at an ever-increasing technical level, it is much more than this. Figure 1-1 shows what encryption looks like at a very fundamental level.

Encryption has been used for thousands of years, but even though the art has taken many forms during this long history, the underlying concepts have remained essentially unchanged, although greatly expanded upon. Even when our cave-dwelling ancestors and others used primitive means to obscure their intentions from outsiders, the basic concepts were the same as they are today.

Note

Cryptography plays an important role in information security and is often mentioned in the context of something known as the "CIA triad" in this field. CIA doesn't refer to a shadowy government agency in this case; rather, it refers to the elements of *confidentiality*, *integrity*, and *availability*. Although encryption cannot help you with preserving the availability of systems or information, it can preserve the first two elements (confidentiality and integrity) very effectively.

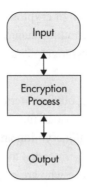

Figure 1-1   The encryption process

In Actual Practice

So what is encryption good for? Just about anything that requires a level of "secrecy" benefits from encryption. Real-world applications range from the simplistic cave drawings to the mathematically complex algorithms of some of today's highest bit-encrypted ciphers. In actual practice, we use a wide range of encryption functions on a daily basis, and it's quite amazing to realize just how integrated into our daily lives encryption really is. It has become a technology that we as a society would not be able to safely operate without. Consider all of your online banking transactions, your debit card purchase at the grocery store, that birthday present you purchased online, or the vacation hotel reservations you made last summer. All these products rely on some form of encryption to secure your information and ensure it gets to the intended party. Strictly speaking, encryption is a very effective and relatively easy means of keeping information away from prying eyes and restricting it to those parties who are intended to possess it. The process and technology is effective at keeping information secret, but it does have limitations like anything else, and knowing these limitations is an important piece of information to have handy.

When speaking about encryption as a means to keep something secret, it is important understand that this need not necessarily keep information from being altered. In fact, information that is secret can be altered; therefore, a means of preserving the stated information is also important.

However, the history and evolution of cryptography and encryption is a discussion for later. Let's strive to get the language and mechanics correct first. We'll get things started by focusing on the core items that cryptography and encryption attempt to protect and preserve:

- **Confidentiality**   This is the most obvious item that is preserved by encryption and is the one most will think of when discussing the topic. The need to keep something secret was an early requirement of encryption and the one most widely enforced. When encryption does its job the way it is intended to, information that is meant to stay secret will stay that way to all except those who are meant to view it. In fact, the information will look like a scrambled "mess" and be essentially impossible to view or use in any other way.

- **Integrity**   Not something that you may commonly associate with science and art, but one that is nonetheless important. Integrity simply refers to the need to ensure that information is not altered and is in fact in the same form that the creator or sender wished it to be in when it is received. This element is a relatively new feature of the art, as there hasn't been a genuinely effective and easy way of ensuring this element until the modern era and the introduction of hashing and message digests (both discussed in a later chapter). Remember when we discuss integrity later on, however, that any time integrity is preserved, it is distinctly different from preserving confidentiality. Integrity is very much the domain of the cryptographic function known as hashing.

Your Plan

When considering any situation in the real world, where you believe encryption or cryptography is the answer or the "magic bullet," you should be able to answer the following questions:

- ❑ Am I trying to *prevent* others from *accessing* or viewing my data?
- ❑ Am I trying to *prevent* information from being *altered* without my knowledge?
- ❑ Am I trying to positively *identify* who the sender or party is that sent a message or carried out an action?
- ❑ Do I need to be able to *verify* that information came from a *trusted source* and no one else?

- **Authentication** This is a vital supporting element and feature covered by encryption. Simply put, information must be trusted in regard to who created it and/or who sent it. Authentication is very important when verifying data, a person, or even software such as drivers. Applications of cryptography that support authentication include digital signatures and hashing, both of which are discussed in the following pages and chapters.

- **Non-repudiation** A fascinating, but little thought of, element preserved by cryptographic elements is *non-repudiation,* or the ability to positively identify the source or origin of an action or an item of data. Essentially it provides the ability to definitively prove who and where an action or piece of information came from. Non-repudiation should also, in theory, eliminate or substantially cut down on what is known as *spoofing,* or the impersonation of another party, if the system is kept secure. A great example of a non-repudiation supporting application of cryptography is the use of digital signatures, which will be discussed in detail later.

> **LINGO**
> Authentication can and is an incredibly important benefit to have in today's digital world. In today's digital world, it is easier than ever before to claim that a piece of information is true and correct. **Authentication** provides the ability to verify data in regard to its source.

> **LINGO**
> **Non-repudiation** is a huge benefit in today's world because it can limit a lot of the situations where an individual or party claims they didn't do something, but really did. For example, with non-repudiation features in place, such as with a digital signature, it is possible to definitively state that a message originated from someone. To help you understand the term *non-repudiation,* let's consider its root. To "repudiate" means to "deny the truth or validity of" a claim; thus, non-repudiation simply means the *inability to refute or deny a truthful and proven claim.* In essence, you can't lie your way out of this one!

Each of these elements (plus more) will show up again and again in later chapters, so learn to recognize them in any of the many forms they take. Remember that the elements seen here can exist separately or be used together (as they often are) to create a substantially more powerful solution for a particular application.

IMHO

I always recommend that newcomers to the field always think of the first two letters of CIA and what they stand for as well as the supporting elements of authentication and non-repudiation as a way to help smooth the understanding of the art. You can do this, too, by thinking about which elements are preserved by a particular cryptography function or feature. For example, when hashing is discussed later, try to think of what element or elements of CIA it is preserving.

Things to Know Upfront About Encryption

So before we go much further, let's clear up some misconceptions about cryptography. To make sure you don't get sidetracked or confused about the process, let's take a look at some erroneous ideas:

- *Encryption is unbreakable.* This is a commonly held misconception—that encryption, when performed properly, is unbreakable. This statement is simply not true at all, because encryption is actually breakable in just about every case. You may be wondering at this point whether this is indeed true, as you may have heard otherwise. However, I assure you this is the case.

- *All encryption is created equal.* This is also a misconception that has widespread appeal among common users. As you will learn later, many aspects of the encryption process can affect its strength, effectiveness, and usability in the real world.

- *Confusing means encrypted.* Encryption and its parent art cryptography provide a systematic and intensely logical approach to securing data. As you learn more about encryption and its subsequent functions, you will quickly appreciate the preciseness and exactness of this integral system.

- *Encryption can only be understood if you're a mathematician.* As stated before, the nitty-gritty details of encryption are based on very complex mathematical algorithms; however, as students and practitioners of cryptography, we respect the complexity for what it is and simply rely on these intricate algorithms as a foundation and framework to the actual encryption functions. In other words, we don't build the engines, but we do drive the cars.

In just about every case, encrypted data can be revealed if enough time and effort is put forth by the curious party. The idea is that by the time the information is revealed, it will be useless or, as would be the case in many situations, the attacker will have decided to give up and move on.

In Actual Practice

In a later chapter we will encounter several awesome examples of cryptography and cryptographic systems, one of them being the Enigma system. Although we won't worry about the details here, as they are covered well enough later, I can say that the system shows us the concept quite nicely.

The Enigma was a simple pre-computer-era system that was a collection of simple wires and rotors, but was so powerful that some messages that were encrypted by it didn't get broken by brute-force methods until much later (for example, 2001).

- *Encryption requires computers.* This seems to be another misconception by the newbie to the field, which is that something so complex must require tons of processing power to carry out. Frequently people envision big powerful computers—on par with the HAL 9000—that perform the encryption and decryption process. This is entirely untrue because great cryptosystems were created before the advent and introduction of computers into the field.

In Actual Practice

Another great example that is coming up in a later chapter is a famous system known as the Vigenère cipher. This cipher, although broken now, was used for a considerable length of time, up to and including the U.S. Civil War, for a period of around 300 years. The Vigenère cipher used a complex system to replace the contents of the original message with coded content. Although the system was complex and tedious, it did not require the powerful computing systems that came later.

- *Encryption is hard.* This is a subjective opinion for the most part. Encryption is without a doubt complex when you move into the higher-order mathematics and logic, but not everyone needs to be at that level. In fact, for the vast majority of us that information is unnecessary to know. What may be hard is choosing from all the options available, but I can help you with that in this book. With a basic understanding in hand, you, too, can choose the best option for a given situation and be ready to go.

Note

I don't want to give the impression that just anyone can do encryption—or specifically that anyone can author an encryption algorithm, which is something different from what we will see here altogether. Encryption algorithms are extremely complex, high-order mathematics and are the exclusive domain of mathematicians and scientists with labels such as Ph.D. after their names.

Although the mathematics and formulas are very complex in this field, we do not need to know the intimate details at that level to understand encryption and the larger body of knowledge known as cryptography. As such, I will try to refrain from formulas in this text—they are unnecessary. As Stephen Hawking once said, "Every mathematical formula in a text cuts book sales in half."

- *Newer technologies eliminate the need for encryption.* This is also a common, but erroneous thought to have in mind. Encryption is only one part of a solution, and in many cases it addresses problems that other technologies cannot. For example, encryption cannot take the place of a good firewall or anti-malware application, nor can it take the place of common sense. It is only one member of a cast of characters designed to protect and safeguard information and other items from those who would wish to view or alter them without permission.

IMHO

Never forget that encryption may also protect you or your company from other threats, such as the threat of legal action. In the state of California, for example, encrypting a hard drive on a laptop can lessen the legal penalties in the event the laptop is stolen and personal information is compromised. If the encryption of the drive is not undertaken, the legal ramifications can be harsh, with fines and other penalties available to the prosecutor. The law in the state is known as SB 1386 and covers encryption as part of its scope.

The Process of Encryption: A Closer Look

Before we get into the mechanics, terms, and other fine details of encryption, let's take a brief look at some of the cast of characters and what each does for the process. We'll get started by looking at some basic terms and processes and then we'll put them together.

Encryption

As was stated earlier, encryption is the process of converting something from one format to another that is unreadable by normal means, thus keeping the data secret or confidential. Encryption takes information and transforms it using a mechanism that is mathematical or logical in nature and outputs the end result that is then delivered to the recipient who can then "unpack" it using the correct methods and processes.

Note

In the cryptography field, it is not uncommon to use the names Alice and Bob to refer to the parties involved in the encryption process. However, this naming is not a hard-and-fast standard, and in this text I will use different names to refer to the parties involved.

Consider a sample situation where we have two parties: We'll call them Link and Zelda. These two parties need to share something—it doesn't really matter what—and keep it secret. In our scenario, Link creates a message and before sending it to Zelda runs it through a process that encrypts or scrambles it and then transmits the message. Link also tells Zelda how the message was encrypted along with some instructions on how to decrypt the message.

When Zelda receives the message from Link, she starts the process of reversing, or *decrypting,* the message. When receiving the message, Zelda uses the instructions to decrypt the message and then view its contents.

If done correctly, this process only allows Link and Zelda to know what is being said or transferred, with everyone else left to wonder. This is the goal of the process of encryption. Figure 1-2 shows this process and how it looks conceptually.

Plaintext

In Figure 1-2, the input and output are labeled simply as "plaintext" and "ciphertext," respectively. *Plaintext* is simply the information that enters the encryption process to be

Figure 1-2   The encryption process conceptually, in its simplest form

scrambled. Plaintext—and I must stress this point—can be literally anything and not just text, so don't get hung up on that term. Plaintext can be text, binary code, or even an image that needs to be transformed into a format that is unreadable by anyone except those who possess the secret to unlocking it.

Plaintext is not only what goes into the encryption process but what comes out of the decryption process as well (more on that in a moment). Remember that you can read plaintext; this is the element of the process you are trying to protect.

LINGO
The term **plaintext** is used when referring to information that has not been transformed by the encryption process into another form. Is either term more correct than another? No, there is no difference between the terms plaintext and cleartext, and either can be used interchangeably with the other at any time. The choice is really yours, just be sure that whatever term you decide to use you stick with it, because changing back and forth could confuse others.

Ciphertext

If plaintext comes into the process of encryption to get converted into a scrambled format, the resulting format is called ciphertext. *Ciphertext* is nothing more than plaintext that has been operated on by the encryption process to render a final product. This final product actually contains the original message, albeit in a format that is not retrievable unless someone knows the correct means or can break the code.

In Actual Practice

Ciphertext can indeed be broken using the techniques contained in a body of knowledge known as cryptanalysis. Cryptanalysis includes a myriad of methods that may be employed in an attempt to break a message. We will explore these methods and concepts much later in this book after we have explored the techniques in encryption in more detail and have a solid foundation.

Algorithms and Ciphers

Probably the trickiest and most mysterious part in the encryption process is something known as the *algorithm* or *cipher*. This component sounds complex (and it is), but we don't have to get into it that far. In fact, the algorithm or cipher is nothing more than a formula that includes discrete steps that mandate how the encryption/decryption process is to be performed in a given instance. For example, let's look at a method used by a process discussed later to understand this relationship. In this upcoming sample letter, the characters in a message are shifted a certain amount of spots to the right, thus yielding an encrypted message or ciphertext. Conversely, the algorithm would specifically state that to decrypt the information, the individual characters

LINGO
Algorithm and **cipher** are used interchangeably in just about every case you will encounter. To some the terms refer to distinctly different processes, while others will insist that the processes involved are the same, just with a different name. Although we won't argue the semantics here, it is worth pointing out that the terms are intertwined and closely related, with ciphers being components of an algorithm.

would be shifted the exact same amount to the left. In other words, the process is reversed, and by abiding by the rules of the encryption process used, you can convert the ciphertext back to plaintext.

So are all algorithms created equal? Absolutely not; they are in fact very different, but they can generally be broken into one of three types, each working in their own separate and unique way. Keep in mind that each of the types of encryption are covered in depth in later chapters. I mention them here to start to distinguish between each and to set up later discussions.

IMHO
Two of these encryption types mention a special item known as a "key," which I will discuss in a moment, and how it pertains to the encryption process itself. Let's first worry about the types of algorithms, how they differ from each other, and why you should care.

- **Symmetric encryption** This is the oldest and most widely used type of encryption. Symmetric works by using the same combination to encrypt as to decrypt. The combination used is known as the *key*, and the same key that is used to encrypt will be used to decrypt. This method is both simple and quick and relies on the sending party both generating a key and finding a way to provide the same to the receiving party. Figure 1-3 shows what the symmetric encryption process looks like conceptually.

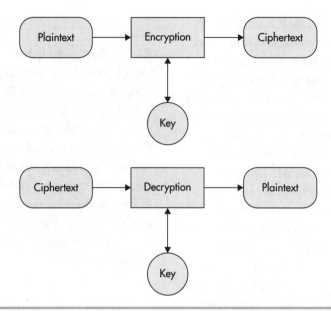

Figure 1-3 Symmetric encryption. Note the same key is used for both encryption and decryption.

Tip

Symmetric encryption is simple to remember if you think of the word "symmetric" as conveying a sense of balance. In this case, the same key is used to perform decryption and encryption, which gives a sense of balance as both keys are exactly the same or equal.

- **Asymmetric encryption** This is one of the newest forms of encryption, and one of the most interesting when examined closer. In essence, the asymmetric encryption process boils down to using one key to encrypt and a totally different, but related one, to decrypt the information. Asymmetric algorithms are ideally suited where non-repudiation and integrity are both needed. Generally, these types of algorithms are not used to ensure confidentiality, simply because of performance reasons (more on that later). Figure 1-4 shows what the asymmetric process looks like.

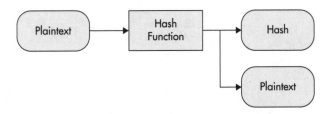

Figure 1-4   The asymmetric encryption process. Note that a separate key is used for encryption and another for decryption.

Tip

Asymmetric encryption is also sometimes known as "public-key cryptography." This name comes from the fact that one key is held exclusively by a single individual or party while the public key is available to the masses. Stay with me here; these concepts will be explained later. Just remember at this point that the "public" key is asymmetric and is different than the "private" key. Keeping things simple, the private key is, well, private. The public key is, yep, you guessed it, public. That being said, in this particular algorithm, you should always protect that private key!

● **Hash functions**   Any algorithm that fits into this category is unique in how it operates and may confuse your thinking a little. Whereas the previous two types of algorithms are designed to spit out ciphertext that is intended to be reversed, this one does not strive to provide us this. In fact, this type of algorithm takes input and generates a piece of information that is unique and cannot be reversed (or cannot be reversed easily). Hashing is unique because it provides integrity features, but it does not provide confidentiality. Figure 1-5 shows the hashing process in action.

LINGO

In the real world, **hashing** can produce a fixed-length value known as a "hash" or a "message digest." The two terms are indeed interchangeable, but at the same time should not be confused with ciphertext, as that is entirely different. Ciphertext is intended to be reversible whereas a hash is not designed to be so.

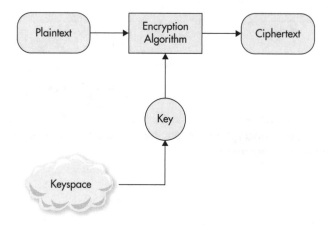

Figure 1-5 The hashing process. Note the output of both the original plaintext and the hash.

Each of the algorithm types introduced here are intended to be used for a specific purpose, and each will provide good levels of protection for the information that is entrusted to it if they are used within these constraints. Using an algorithm outside of what it is designed for may not only be less than optimal, it may provide no protection at all— and, even worse, it will also foster a false sense of security in those using it.

In Actual Practice

In the real world, it may seem that algorithms need to be kept restricted lest the secrets as to how data is encrypted be revealed to the outside world. This may seem to be the case, but it is not. In reality, an old but well-known concept known as Kerckoff's Principle is an important but interesting piece to the puzzle. Kerckoff's Principle states that algorithms do not need to be kept secret and, in fact, may actually suffer if they are kept as such. The principle goes on to state that the strength of a system is largely dependent on the key that is used, not the algorithm itself.

Keep in mind, however, that Kerckoff's Principle is not some sort of law; instead, it may be thought of as a general guideline or suggestion. In fact, the National Security Agency (NSA) in the United States is one of the many such agencies and organizations that develop algorithms and do not make them public.

Working along with algorithms are something known as *ciphers,* which are nothing more than a set of instructions used during the encryption and decryption process. Although the actual functioning of ciphers varies as much as the algorithms, we will discuss later that they still essentially perform the same processes. In the real world, two main types of ciphers are in play: stream ciphers and block ciphers. They both provide protective services to information.

Keys

Let's move on to the important and frequently complicated subject of keys. Keys are incredibly significant for us if we are to understand the encryption process fully.

In the strictest and most technical sense, a *key* is a discrete piece of information that enacts a specific result or output for a given cryptographic operation. Sounds confusing, but it doesn't need to be if we look at this the right way. A key in the cryptographic sense can be thought of in the same way as a key in the physical world—as a special item used to open or unlock something (in this case, a piece of information). In the encryption world, the key is what allows access to secured information, thus creating a meaningful result. Without this key, access and translation of the information would not be possible.

IMHO

Another helpful way to think of a key is as the combination for a combination lock. A hundred combination locks of the same model may be purchased by you, but they typically will all have different combinations if they are preset by the manufacturer. Although it is theoretically possible that you may acquire two locks with the same combination, it is intended to be highly unlikely.

I personally like the lock analogy in relation to keys because it helps when thinking of the overall encryption process later.

Similar to how a lock of any type will define the parameters of the key or combination that may be used on it, such is the case with encryption keys. Encryption keys are defined by the algorithm in use at a given time. The algorithm is like the design of a lock, which dictates all the different types of grooves, cuts, and other features of a key.

Think of it this way: Let's propose a theoretical combination lock, much like the one you would use to lock up a bike or a gym locker. This hypothetical lock needs (in our case at least) to have a combination of eight digits that will be used by an individual to unlock the lock in order to open their locker or bike. In this case, we can we can write down the parameters of the proposed key in a pseudo formula as such:

- **Combination length:** Equal to 8
- **Valid usable digit range:** 0 to 9

With this information in hand, we can see that the combination must be eight digits in length and each digit can only be in the range 0 to 9, inclusive. If we look at the numbers and amount of valid combinations, we can calculate that there are 100 million possible arrangements of digits, given the information we have.

Is 100 million a lot? Well, it is and it isn't. In human terms, the number of keys is a lot, but in the digital world not so much. In fact, many of the stronger algorithms include a substantially larger number of keys than is possible with our simple example. In cryptography, all the potential key types possible with a particular algorithm are commonly known as the *keyspace*. Algorithms are designed to provide the greatest amount of protection; as such, modern algorithms are designed to have a vast amount of potential keys in order to thwart guessing or brute-force attacks (which you will learn about much later).

IMHO

If it helps you understand the value of having a large keyspace, consider a different approach to the situation. Envision a trench that is one mile deep and one mile across that stretches from Sacramento, California to Los Angeles, which is a distance of about 400 miles. Take that trench and fill it up with ping pong balls and somewhere in this process pick one ball at random, paint it red, and toss it in the trench. Although someone could dig through the trench and perhaps find the red ball, they probably won't be able to do so quickly. Although statistically one may find the red ball first or maybe find it halfway through, it is likely they will be digging around for a good period of time. In this analogy, the trench would represent the keyspace, the ping pong balls would represent all the possible keys, and the red ping pong ball would represent the one correct key for any given encryption sequence.

Let's not get too comfortable by thinking that the number of keys is a potent defense against attack, because it is not the only factor. Another factor is key length or size. Basically, as a key gets longer, it offers stronger protection against attacks. Key length together with key size combines to form a stronger solution and defense against many types of key weaknesses, both by design and through outside attack.

So do longer keys make a given particular encryption scheme stronger? Well, this can be debated, but the answer is that the length of keys can have a substantial impact on the power and strength of an encryption system. For instance, a cryptosystem developed only 40 years ago with 56-bit keys would now be viewed as much weaker in the face of stronger computing systems. In fact, over

LINGO
Key length or **size** refers to how "long" a key resulting from an actual algorithm may be, but there is another term referring to length of which you should be aware. This term is *bits*, as in a key is a 40-bit or 1024-bit key, for instance.

the last 30 years as computing power has increased thousands of times, algorithms have had to be developed and strengthened to increase the length and number of keys available in any given system.

So how much does key length make a difference? Well, this can be a tricky question, and an even trickier problem to get your head around, so let's look at this in a matrix format. Table 1-1 shows the relative strength of keys compared to one another as well as how long it would take to break each one on different hardware, whereas Table 1-2 shows the relative value of each key length.

In Actual Practice

As increased computing power showed up on the scene, key lengths had to be increased with more bits being added to the scheme. So how much power does an extra bit add to a scheme? Consider a 56-bit key: Adding a single bit (that is, changing it to a 57-bit key) doubles the strength of the system, and adding 10 more bits (making it a 66-bit key) makes the key 1,024 times stronger than the original 56-bit key.

In the mid-to-late 1990s, computing power that had the ability to break many of the shorter keyed cryptosystems became widely available to the public, when they had been solely the domain of governments and corporations before. Moving forward to today's world, we can see that commodity hardware (hardware that can be purchased off the shelf) is much more accessible and available than ever before. In fact, many of the computers available today to the consumer are able to process at a minimum 50,000 56-bit keys per second, or more.

Power	40 Bit	56 Bit	64 Bit	128 Bit
Individual	1.4 Min	73 Days	50 Years	10^{20} Year
Corporate	2 Sec	35 Hours	1 Year	10^{19} Year
Government	0.2 Sec	3.5 Hours	37 Days	10^{18} Year

Table 1-1 Times to Break a Key of a Given Length on Different Types of Hardware

Looking at Table 1-1 and 1-2, it would seem that a longer key would automatically equal a greater amount of protection, and in many cases this is true. However, there are tradeoffs in the name of performance. A longer key generally equates to longer encrypt and decrypt times. Additionally, the old axiom that says "more is better" is proven wrong here in relation to key length and protection. In fact, the length of the key will only result in a stronger algorithm up to a point, and anything after that will slowly plateau and result in the aforementioned increased processing time.

One more factor that enhances the effectiveness and security of a key is a technique known as a *cryptoperiod,* the objective of which is to define the specific period of time a cryptographic key may be used before it is pulled from usage in favor of a new key. The cryptoperiod, when used as intended, dictates that after a defined period has expired, the key is no longer to be used to encrypt or decrypt any information, and will either be relegated to an archive or discarded altogether.

When a cryptoperiod is in use, the actual timeframe for key usage is defined by a myriad of factors, dependent on the organization itself. Factors that can impact the time a

Key Length	Value
40	Of no use to companies and governments; effective at stopping casual attackers.
56	Used for privacy. Vulnerable and has been broken. DES is the best example of a broken 56-bit encryption scheme.
64	Considered safe, but still is vulnerable and has been broken.
128	Considered generally unbreakable, but some newer technologies and implementations have been vulnerable.
256	Impossible to break with today's technology.

Table 1-2 Subjective Values of Each Key Length

In Actual Practice

Key lengths may also be impacted by export laws that fall outside the scope of the cryptographer—and the scope of this book for that matter. When we discuss key lengths and export laws, we'll refer to the United States and the laws that were in place for a period of time. In the United States the laws that were in play for a while absolutely forbad the export of any encryption technology that exceeded 40 bits in length. Anyone who chose to run afoul of this would quickly find themselves in trouble with the U.S. government and in the same category as those who would export weapons technology to foreign powers. Although these laws were intended to prevent the technology from getting into the hands of hostile powers, it also impacted, tremendously, the flow of strong encryption technology outside the U.S. Although such controls still exist, they have been substantially relaxed, and the export of stronger encryption is allowed more than it was before—but restrictions still exist.

key is valid are key compromises of any type, cost of replacing a key to include decrypting and re-encrypting with a new key and business requirements. Factors that effect the cryptoperiod include incidents such as the loss of a key or other types of compromise.

Putting It All Together

Now that you know the key players and terms, let's put everything together to form a complete picture of the encryption/decryption process. First, it is important to clearly understand what is needed prior to the encryption or decryption process occurring.

In the case of encryption, here's what's needed:

- **Plaintext**   In other words, you need to have the information on hand that you are going to put through the encryption process.

- **Encryption algorithm**   This is the mechanism that will perform that actual encryption process and is responsible for being the "mechanism" that transforms the information.

- **Key**   The item responsible for setting the specific options or configuration, if you will, of the mechanism at a specific point in time.

In the case of decryption, here's what's needed:

- **Ciphertext** This is the previously encrypted information that needs to be manipulated to once again reveal its original contents.

- **Decryption algorithm** This is a mechanism capable of reversing the encryption process, allowing the original information to be viewed, provided the right key is used.

- **Key** This is the item responsible for configuring the decryption process to allow the ciphertext to be viewed.

Note

The key is not any random key—it must be the corresponding key or the same key used to encrypt the data in the first place. If a random key or incorrect key is used, the result will be information that is not useful.

Let's now look at the encryption process again. Let's say that, hypothetically, Link wants to send Zelda another message. Knowing what you know now, the process would look like what's shown in Figure 1-6.

In Figure 1-6, the original message would be represented by the plaintext being fed into the algorithm as input. Together with the plaintext into the algorithm is a key selected out of the keyspace defined by the algorithm in use. Along with the plaintext and algorithm, a key is also selected after which they are combined to produce ciphertext.

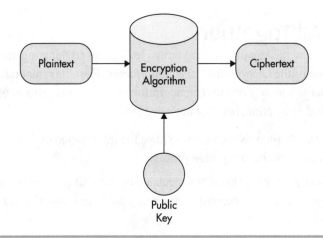

Figure 1-6 Encryption process using a key

Note

In Figure 1-6, the keyspace looks like it is separate from the algorithm when in fact it is defined by the algorithm, and the user is free to choose whatever key they wish from the keyspace. In the diagram, the two (the keyspace and algorithm) are illustrated separately to make things a little clearer to visualize.

So the encryption process is simple; nothing that we haven't seen before or discussed. Let's look at the decryption process, as defined in Figure 1-7.

In Figure 1-7, the decryption process is shown, which is simply a reverse of the encryption process, but with a little tweak here and there. First, if we assume that the message from Figure 1-6 is being decrypted here, then it means that Zelda received the message from Link and had the instructions (the algorithm) and the combination (the key) provided to reverse the encryption operation. Because Zelda already would know the key as provided by Link, she doesn't have to worry about selecting a new one; in fact, a new key wouldn't help. All Zelda needs is the ciphertext, the key, and the algorithm to begin the process.

Both encryption and decryption, as defined in Figures 1-6 and 1-7, are simple and effective, but they are only a small part of the process. In fact, the process shown here only covers symmetric, as the same key is used to encrypt and decrypt. What about asymmetric encryption? Let's look at that process as well.

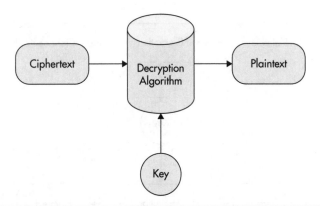

Figure 1-7   The decryption process

Note
In this opening chapter, we will only discuss the basic functioning of asymmetric encryption just to set the stage for later discussions. If the details seems a little confusing, don't worry. We will clear this up later—just note the differences between the two types, symmetric and asymmetric, right now.

In asymmetric encryption, the process changes just a little because two keys exist that cannot be used to encrypt and decrypt the same piece of information. With this in mind, let's look at the process a little more closely to understand how this works.

Suppose Link and Zelda wish to exchange information once again. This time, Link wants to send information to Zelda that only she can view. With symmetric encryption algorithms, this is trickier because Link not only has to encrypt the information, but he also has to send the encrypted data to Zelda along with the key used to decrypt. This presents some interesting problems because Link must now figure out a way to get both to Zelda without the key being compromised. This is where asymmetric encryption comes in. In Figure 1-8, you see how asymmetric encryption works.

Note
Further explanation of asymmetric encryption will come in later chapters; however, just remember from our previous explanation that the "public" key is readily available and not a secret part of the process.

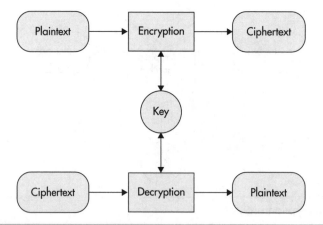

Figure 1-8   The encryption process using asymmetric methods. Note the public key.

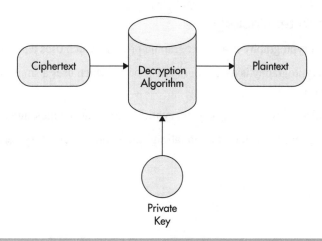

Figure 1-9   The decryption process in an asymmetric system. Note the private key.

Of course, every encryption process must have a decryption process (see Figure 1-9).

Asymmetric decryption is simple in concept. However, keep in mind that the private key is a critical and sensitive piece of this process. You will realize just how important when we dig deeper into the nuts and bolts of this methodology.

As you can see, two different encryption methods can be used to protect the secrecy of information. Both of these methods will be discussed more in depth later in the book.

We've Covered

Fundamentals of cryptography

- Cryptography is used to secure the integrity and confidentiality of information.
- Cryptography is the science of protecting information in all its forms from prying eyes and unauthorized modification.
- Cryptography is applied in everything from cell phones to hard drives.

Key concepts in cryptography

- Keys are used to determine the settings used for a particular encryption or decryption sequence.
- Algorithms are formulas used to determine the mechanism of encryption and decryption.
- Plaintext is information that has not been encrypted.
- Ciphertext is information after an encryption sequence has been performed.

Key terms and terminology

- Asymmetric cryptography is a cryptographic process which uses a public and private key.
- Symmetric cryptography is a cryptographic process which uses a single key for encryption and decryption.
- Hashing is also known as one way encryption that creates a message digest.
- Legal issues prevent particular applications and export of cryptosystems.

CHAPTER 2

History of Cryptography

We'll Cover

- History of cryptography

- Cryptography in the ancient world

- Modern cryptography

- Future directions for cryptography

- Historical users of cryptography

Cryptography is the body of knowledge that relates to the safeguarding of information either by keeping it secret or by keeping unwanted changes from being detected. Contrary to what many think, the art has been around for a very long time and has evolved much over the years, moving from a curiosity to a science that is in found in many aspects of technology. Although it may never be known exactly when the art appeared, it is almost assuredly sometime after man learned to write down information that the need to conceal a meaning arose. Since the time the science came on the scene, changes have been made to how it's done, and the mechanisms have advanced to a high degree.

The science of cryptography provides unique abilities not attainable otherwise or as easily. Crypto provides three key fundamental functions: confidentiality, integrity, and non-repudiation. *Confidentiality* is the concept of safeguarding data or information from any unauthorized outside party viewing or accessing it in any way. In addition, *integrity* is provided through a mathematically complex and intensive mechanism known as *hashing*. Finally, *non-repudiation* is also provided by the art of cryptography and gives us the ability to prevent a party from denying their part in initiating an activity.

> **LINGO**
> **Hashing** is a process that converts a message or input into a fixed-length encrypted string of information typically in an alphanumeric format. The length of a hash will always be the same no matter what the input may happen to be, although the actual characters in the hash will be different.

For most, cryptography is an unknown and is something that is the stuff of secret agents, spies, puzzles, and games and mentioned in areas such as national security matters. Heck, most of the public would not understand the role that cryptography plays in their lives when they perform online banking or store their health records online, for example. Consider for a moment the individual who writes a letter to his friend; this individual puts the letter in an envelope then drops it in a mailbox. This individual typically considers the envelope all the protection he needs, but does not think of the fact that someone may be able to see the letter through the envelope or even go through the extra step of replacing the letter with one of their own. Although this may seem far fetched with a traditional letter, such things are possible with the new generation of e-mail. The general public usually doesn't think about possible security problems with e-mail and that there may be many mechanisms at work behind the scenes to keep their messages private and confidential in cyberspace.

Cryptography Overview

Let's start with a brief overview of what cryptography is offering us as users and readers of this text. Simply put, the goal of cryptography is to preserve confidentiality, integrity, and non-repudiation by performing each individually or in combination. When applied with the appropriate skill and knowledge, cryptography provides levels of protection that would be near impossible to achieve using other basic methodologies. Confidentiality is the ability to protect information from unauthorized disclosure; information is prevented from being viewed by those not authorized to view it, which is the primary function of encryption. In addition, integrity is provided through the cryptographic mechanism known as hashing, which employs a robust mechanism for allowing detection of changes to the information's original form. Finally, non-repudiation is provided via the science of cryptography and enables the prevention of the sending party denying the origin of the information in question. Through the application of cryptographic protocols, information can be protected both in transit and in storage.

IMHO

I think it is always helpful to consider one of the cornerstones of security when talking about cryptography, which is the CIA triad. CIA refers to Confidentiality, Integrity, and Availability, which are the three central areas in security. Although cryptography only indirectly supports availability, it deals heavily with the other two components—and non-repudiation as well. Using these elements as a set of guideposts—for they apply to cryptography—helps me (and hopefully you) focus on the true impact of cryptography on you and your data.

> **Note**
> You may be picking up this text because you are a security professional or just because
> you are interested in the topic. For those who are professionals in the security field,
> understanding how cryptography works is essential to being able to properly carry out
> your job. Although you do not need to know all the nuts and bolts that may exist under
> the hood, the basic functions and how they are applied are important. If you are one
> of those who are just interested in the field, you will find an exploration of the topic
> stimulating and perhaps exciting and intriguing.

What Is Cryptography?

Let's put a finer point on what cryptography is and what it does for us before we move
on to how it has evolved. Cryptography is the science and practice of safeguarding
information through the use of special tools, techniques, and other methods. This has
evolved over time, as you will soon see, to not only describe how information is changed
from one form to another but also how to create new systems and defeat existing ones.
In fact, the field of cryptography has broadened substantially through necessity and has
continued to increase in complexity, covering older traditional methods and the new high-
technology digital methods and systems.

Encryption is what gets the most attention and may be considered the nice "romantic"
technology that everyone thinks about when they hear the word *cryptography*. Encryption
is the heavyweight of cryptographic processes in terms of frequency of use, but it is not
the only one. Within the field are numerous technologies and protocols that work to keep
information secret as well as detect possible modifications to the original data.

This study, cryptanalysis, has been used almost as long as encryption and
cryptography itself, largely due to the fact that whenever something has been written
in code by one party there have been other parties trying to find out hidden secrets.
The ability to break these codes is known as *cryptanalysis* and is a hot issue for every
government as well as those seeking protected information because it allows secrets to be
uncovered.

Early cultures have shown us some of the fundamentals of cryptography, but not
everything that we need to know. So what is cryptography anyway? Well, when the
science and art is carefully applied, it is extremely useful and is an effective tool in
protecting all sorts of information from compromise. Cryptography can keep information
secret through the careful and thoughtful application of seemingly simple techniques that
together form more than the sum of the individual parts. Such systems can be designed to
be relatively simple or can quickly evolve into the complex variety based on what is being
protected. Some simple and ancient applications include the protection of information

such as hunting routes and messages to the gods, as the Egyptians did. Other more current applications are more complex and involved, such as those used to protect credit card information, e-mail, and other similar types of information.

As with the Egyptians, one of the most widely used applications of cryptography is in the safeguarding of communications between two parties wanting to share information. Guaranteeing that information is kept secret is one thing, but in the modern world it is only part of the equation. In today's world, information must be kept secret, and provisions to detect unwelcome or unwanted modifications are just as important. In the days of Julius Caesar and the Spartans, keeping information secret was not as challenging a task as it is today and in fact was substantially difficult. In the days of yore, keeping a message secret could be as simple as writing it in a language the general public didn't understand or was unlikely to understand. Later forms of encryption required that elaborate systems of management and security be implemented in order to safeguard information.

Is the body of knowledge relating to cryptography only concerned with protecting information? Well, for the first few generations of its existence the answer was yes, but that has changed with the knowledge being used in systems such as those for authenticating individuals and validating that someone who sent a message or initiated an action is indeed the right party.

The knowledge contained in the field has even made some of the everyday technologies you use possible. In fact, one area that owes its existence to cryptography is e-commerce. The practice has reaped tremendous benefits from the field, allowing for the secure exchange of financial information as well as preventing exposure of and authenticating access to that information. In fact, the case could be made that e-commerce would not exist in anything resembling its current form without the backing of cryptographic science.

Now you may be tempted to think of cryptography as operating strictly within the domain of computing, but this is simply not true. It is used in many other areas very different from what the Egyptians, Greeks, and others had ever even thought of. One area that has benefited tremendously is that of cell phones and mobile technologies. The evolution and advancement of cryptographic science and its processes in these fields has led to a number of threats being thwarted, such as the cloning of devices and the decrease of identity theft. Specific to cloning, mobile technology has implemented increasingly advanced cryptographic measures to prevent malicious duplication of a device, the potential for running up thousands of dollars in fraudulent charges, and eavesdropping on another party.

So what are the key concentrations of cryptography? We've touched on a few of them already, but there are more you should be aware of. There exists the possibility for this knowledge to be applied in any one or more of five areas, including those relating to confidentiality, integrity, authentication, non-repudiation, and key distribution. Each of these benefits is something that must be understood to put the tools and techniques in their proper context. Some additional protections and usage are

- A prominent role of authentication can be found within the actual authentication process used to log in to most systems and services. Authentication has become commonplace in many of our normal, daily activities. Consider the information used to authenticate and validate a credential such as an ATM card or a computer login at work. Our PINs and passwords must be kept absolutely secret and protected to prevent inadvertent disclosure to unauthorized parties. Another fundamental example of cryptography's role in authentication is in the hashing of passwords, which allows a method of authenticating a party without the need to transmit the password itself over a network (the hashes themselves are instead).

- Non-repudiation is another area that the science of cryptography provides to the modern world. Non-repudiation, simply stated, is the ability to have positive proof that a particular party or entity is the one who originated an action. For example, in many corporate environments the application of a digital signature to e-mail is used as a potent means of asserting that a certain party transmitted the message. The possibility of the specific party not being the one who transmitted the message or carried out the action raises other legitimate security concerns, such as the compromise of the sender's system access (for example, did they lose control of their credentials and not say anything?). With this mechanism in place, it is possible now to have strong accountability for every action within an organization, allowing for the tracing of actions back to whomever initiated them. Non-repudiation should also, in theory, eliminate or substantially cut down on what is known as *spoofing* (impersonating) another party if the system is kept secure.

- Finally, one other critical aspect of any effective cryptosystem is key distribution. Arguably one of the most valuable components of a cryptosystem is the key, which represents the specific combination or code used to encrypt or decrypt data. This "combination" must be kept absolutely secret and accessible only to authorized parties; failure to do so severely weakens and many times compromises the entire system.

Consider this example: If an individual is required in their work environment to set a 12-character complex password, but then writes that password on a sticky note and places it on the lid of their laptop, the system is compromised no matter how strong the password may be otherwise. Another example would be the soon to be covered Caesar's system : If a message encrypted with this system is considered secure, that security is severely compromised if the key is sent along with the message, kind of like locking the front door to a house and then taping the key to the it.

History of Cryptography

While cryptography may seem like a new technology to many, it is in fact much longer lived than many realize. Cryptography has been around for a long time and has a rich and interesting history that goes back at least 4,500 years, if not more. So let's set the "Wayback Machine" and take a look at the origins of cryptography and trace it up through modern times.

Cryptography is more than likely one of the oldest bodies of knowledge that we can find evidence of. Although the original systems may not actually be in use for the most part anymore, each one adds something to today's technology and body of knowledge. The knowledge associated with encoding and hiding information is still very much considered mysterious and much like a "black art," as few truly understand all the logic and mathematics behind the scenes. In fact, it is this veil of mystery that led the science to be considered a black art and, by some, a way to communicate with spirits or the devil itself.

For many of you, it is possible that the first time you saw an encrypted message was when you set eyes on Egyptian hieroglyphics. This intricate and complex system of writing was used for religious and spiritual purposes. Although 4,500+ years ago the Egyptians most likely were not trying to keep secrets for the same reasons we are today, there is evidence that suggests they were trying to keep the ability to commune with their pantheon of gods somewhat controlled. In fact, it is believed that only members of the royal family and members of the religious orders could fully understand how to read and write the complex designs (although this has not been proven either way). The knowledge needed to read and write this beautiful and complex system was so restricted that when the last person capable of writing it died, over a thousand years ago, the knowledge was lost until a French soldier unwittingly uncovered the key to deciphering hieroglyphics in 1799. Figure 2-1 shows an example of hieroglyphics in an Egyptian tomb.

Figure 2-1 Egyptian hieroglyphics in a nobleman's tomb

In Actual Practice

Hieroglyphics, and arguably the best example of cryptography, began in or around 2000 B.C. in Egypt, where they were commonly used to decorate the tombs of deceased rulers and kings as well as other VIPs. The pictures served as a way to illustrate the story of the life of the deceased and proclaimed the great acts of their lives. It seems that the writing was intended by its designers to be purposefully cryptic; however, they did not intend to hide the text. To researchers now it seems that the writing system was designed to provide an additional sense of importance or regal appearance. As time went by, the developed writings became ever more complicated, and eventually the public turned to other pursuits and lost interest in deciphering them.

(continued)

In the eighteenth century, scholars in Europe were in the midst of making several attempts to decode the ancient Egyptian language. The common belief at the time was that the ancient culture held secrets both scientific and mystical that were encoded in the language represented by these strange writings. Confusion about decoding them was abound, with the prevailing wisdom being that the glyphs represented actual ideas as opposed to sounds as in other languages. The symbols, despite the work of scholars, stubbornly held onto their secrets for many more years, much as they had for a thousand years and more before.

The missing piece to understanding hieroglyphics turned out to be the famous Rosetta Stone. This stone was discovered by a soldier in the French Army in 1799. The stone was eventually transferred to English control after they defeated the French Army in Egypt. Due to the work of experts, and 20+ years of hard work, the ancient language was decoded and reintroduced to the world. The language could be read once again, and the world could enjoy the culture that had been lost. The Rosetta Stone went on to become a household name, even today, with the stone itself having a home in the British Museum. Figure 2-2 shows the Rosetta Stone.

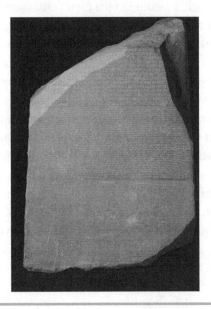

Figure 2-2   The Rosetta Stone

One of the earliest examples of the art is considered by some to be the paintings that early man used to render ideas on cave walls. Although this may be a bit of a stretch, it is not hard to see how anyone looking at a cave painting would assume that only the ones who drew them knew the meaning behind them. Because it is likely that only members of a tribe or clan would be the ones in the know, all outsiders would be barred from gathering any knowledge because they would not know how to read them.

IMHO

On a recent trip with my girlfriend to the Valley of Fire State Park in the great state of Nevada, I observed many petroglyphs on rock faces within the park. The glyphs were drawn by the inhabitants of the Valley one thousand to two thousand years ago, and now their meanings are lost. It isn't hard to imagine them in the same context as an intentionally encrypted message in today's world. Looking at these glyphs, I could only wonder what the ancient people were saying and whether there is a key someplace that would unlock the meanings of the pictures.

Of course, not all encryption techniques were meant to hide secrets relating to life, death, or military information. Others were meant to hide more taboo pieces of information, such as those that were sexual in nature. Although the text is known as containing a lot of information relating to the erotic arts, there is other information contained in the text that recommends how to live a life with a family and other aspects of love. Past all this information is a section on what is known as the mlecchita-vikalpa, or the art of secret writing, which was put forth to assist women in the concealment of the details of their liaisons. One of the techniques, in fact, involves a process that has come to be known as a substitution cipher, which is still in common usage today.

Another ancient civilization that was excellent at hiding information in creative and unique ways comes from China. The Chinese were known to use the unique nature of their language to obscure and transform the meaning of messages for those not intended to see them. Such transformation of messages through language could easily hide the meaning of a message to those not privy as to its true meaning, thus keeping privacy intact. However, although the practice of transforming the content of messages was known to the Chinese, it never saw widespread use, and evidence indicates that it never saw major use outside of private purposes. In fact, although it may seem logical that leaders such as Genghis Khan would have used such techniques during their conquests, no evidence has ever shown this to be the case.

IMHO

I'll add that the prevailing wisdom seems to indicate that Genghis Khan not only didn't use encryption to obscure messages, he really didn't need to. Why use cryptography when you have a fast moving army that can descend upon a city quickly? In other words, why send an encoded message when you have an army that could be on top of an enemy so fast it wouldn't matter anyway.

Other civilizations such as India made use of cryptography and did so more than the Chinese people did at the same time in history. In India, it was known that the government at various times used special codes and ciphers to communicate with their spies who were part of their early intelligence network. Although the codes were simplistic compared to those in use today for the same purpose, they were very effective at concealing the meaning of messages from outsiders.

Note

It is fascinating to note that the early Indian ciphers consisted largely of what are now known as simple substitutions based on phonetics. Essentially, this method is similar to what is now known as "Pig Latin," where the first consonant is placed at the end of the word and followed by the sound "ay." This method may seem simple to any child who has spoken Pig Latin on the playground with friends, but it still was effective at the time.

Another one of the more well-known encryption techniques from the ancient world comes by way of the Mesopotamians. Much like in Egypt of old, this culture used specialized symbols (known as cuneiform) to convey information, and after this knowledge was lost, the writings stood as an enigma to travelers in the Middle East. Complicating the deciphering of the language was the lack of a key which meant incorrect assumptions were being made. In the case of cuneiform, the deciphering process was simpler than that of the earlier example involving the Egyptians, but it still took some time.

Potentially complicating the picture even more was that the writing technique was around for so long. For the many centuries the script was in use, it evolved dramatically, meaning that the symbology changed and reflected different meanings in some cases. Figure 2-3 shows an example of cuneiform writing.

A little known example of cryptography known as ATBASH comes courtesy of the Hebrew language and the Bible. This cipher was simple in design and concept, but in implementation it was straightforward compared with later ciphers. Essentially the design of the technique flipped the characters of the alphabet, with the characters at the

Figure 2-3   Sample of cuneiform writing

end replacing the ones at the beginning. Once this was done, the letters were substituted accordingly. The following shows how this process looks in the English language:

ABCDEFGHIJKLMNOPQRSTUVWXYZ

ZYXWVUTSRQPONMLKJIHGFEDCBA

IMHO

Some have cited the ATBASH cipher as the possible inspiration for what is known as the Bible Code. The Bible Code is purported to be the way the creators of the Bible hid messages and prophecy within the work. Whether or not this is the actual case is still the source of some debate, but the idea is intriguing, to say the least.

One of my personal favorites comes from the Spartans and Scytale (rhymes with *Italy*). This method is markedly different and unique among all the methods mentioned so far. It approaches the problem of how to encrypt by replacing an algorithm with a wooden dowel. To use this encryption method, all parties would have to agree on the diameter of

the dowel prior to exchanging messages. Next, the sender would take a strip of leather
or parchment and wrap it around their dowel and inscribed the message in several lines
across the parchment, rotating the dowel as each line was completed. After the message
was inscribed, the parchment was unwrapped and sent to the intended recipient, who
would wrap the parchment around their dowel, which is of the same diameter, and read the
message. This method of encoding messages, although simple, was popular in a handful
of ancient civilizations, including the Greeks and in particular the Spartans, who used it to
transmit messages on the battlefield. Figure 2-4 shows a diagram of Scytale.

Another personal favorite, and one we will revisit later, is the Caesar Cipher, which
is a simple-but-effective process that has been around for over 2000 years. Julius Caesar
used this process to encrypt or encode his messages to his commanders in the field for
the same reason the military today does—to keep sensitive information private. Although
the cipher is simple, it is still in use today, and in fact is the one that most school children
would be familiar with because it has appeared in countless puzzle game books and cereal
boxes over the years.

Simply put, the process Caesar used shifted each letter three places further in the
alphabet (for instance, Y becomes B, and R shifts to U). Although the process could
use any shift amount, Caesar settled on a shift of three spaces. Although simple, it was
effective at keeping secrets at the time because anyone encountering the message would
most likely assume it was in a foreign language—if they could read at all. As shown here,
the first row represents what is known as plaintext, and the second row is the equivalent
ciphertext if a shift of two was used instead of three:

ABCDEFGHIJKLMNOPQRSTUVWXYZ
CDEFGHIJKLMNOPQRSTUVWXYZAB

Figure 2-4   A diagram of a Scytale system

Let's move forward a bit in time to take a look at some of the techniques that emerged during the Middle Ages. Much like before, and definitely like the times that came after, cryptography was mainly focused on protecting the secrets of diplomats and military types. During this time period, the first truly new ciphers came from Italy, specifically Venice, where a new organization was created in 1452 to deal with the issues involving cryptography.

One figure who emerged from this time period is Leon Battista Alberti, who later became known as the Father of Western Cryptology. Alberti was responsible for the development of a technique known as polyalphabetic substitution. This technique is still widely utilized by many modern-day processes and mechanisms. Essentially, this process relies on substituting different characters for the same unencrypted symbol. This technique came into being after Alberti reviewed how other existing ciphers were compromised or broken and then envisioned a technique that could thwart these methods. Don't worry too much about polyalphabetic substitution at this point because it will be discussed further in a later chapter.

LINGO
Leon Battista Alberti is known as a **polymath**, or an expert in many fields. In Alberti's case, he was an author, artist, architect, poet, priest, linguist, philosopher, cryptographer, and humanist polymath.

Alberti's technique was essentially simple in concept, but powerful in practice. The initial mechanism as designed was simple, being nothing more than two copper disks with the entire alphabet written upon each of them. To encrypt a message, the encrypting party chose a letter on the outer ring and lined it up with the inner ring. The outer ring represented the letters in the unencrypted message, and the inner the encrypted message. By matching up the unencrypted letters with the ones on the inner ring, one could quickly translate a message into another form that was unreadable without knowing the settings used. Making the process even more complicated is the fact that the settings were redone after every so many letters in order to make the mechanism that much more robust. Because the settings were changed every few words, the cipher changed enough to blunt the overall effectiveness of known code-breaking methods. Even though this technique, when explained, seems very weak, at the time it was considered to be very strong. Also, the idea of rotating the disks to change the process every so often was a major step in the field of cryptography, one that is also still used today (albeit in a different form).

Of course, Alberti and the Italians didn't come up with all the advances in the field of cryptography: There were many others, one of which was made by the German Abbott Trithemius. Trithemius was responsible for authoring a series of books that came to be known as *Polygraphia*. At the time, the books were viewed by some to be heretical and related to the occult due to their extensive use of tables and codes. It wasn't until much later that research showed that what had been documented and devised was a complex and effective method of encrypting information. The process worked like so: To encode and convert a message, each letter of the plaintext in the first row of the table is swapped with the letter in the same position in the second row, with the same process being repeated for the each letter within the message. The result of this process is a message where each letter is replaced at least once before a letter is reused.

Note

Much like other ciphers in use, the Trithemius technique was improved by later followers, such as Giovan Belaso in 1553. The technique that Belaso introduced used whole phrases to encrypt plaintext instead of a single letter. This technique will be visited more later, but I wanted to mention it now just to put it into context.

A later development, and a significant one at that, is known as the Vigenère cipher. The Vigenère cipher is much more complex than Alberti's cipher in that is uses 26 unique and distinct alphabets as opposed to Alberti's two. Each alphabet is the same, except each one is shifted by one letter. Essentially, each row is a representation of the Caesar cipher and represents a shift of some given number, with row number 1 representing a shift of 1, row number 2 representing a cipher alphabet with a shift of 2, and so on.

To use this method, a different row is used to encrypt each letter in a message. In other words, the sender of the message would encrypt their message, with each letter being encrypted by a different row. In order to decode the message, the recipient must be aware of which row of the matrix was used to encrypt each letter. In turn, there must be a way to agree how the switch between rows will occur. This agreement is achieved via the selection of a keyword.

The evolutionary leap this represented was huge because it rendered the many forms of frequency analysis moot. In fact, it wasn't until much later that this cipher was routinely broken, albeit slowly.

In Actual Practice

In 2010, a glass vial was discovered that contained a message written during the Civil War. The coded message was authored by a Confederate commander outside Vicksburg the day the city fell to Union forces.

The message offered no hope to the Confederate officer, one Lt. Gen. John C Pemberton. It clearly and unambiguously stated that reinforcements would not be arriving. The message was a short six lines and was dated July 4, 1863, which also was the day the General surrendered to future U.S. President and then Union General Ulysses S Grant. The surrender represented a major turning point in the war in the favor of the Union.

The glass vial sat alone and undisturbed in a museum dedicated to the Confederacy in Richmond, Virginia until experts were able to recover the message and decrypt it. The message when it was decrypted stated the following:

Gen'l Pemberton:

You can expect no help from this side of the river. Let Gen'l Johnston know, if possible, when you can attack the same point on the enemy's lines. Inform me also and I will endeavor to make a diversion. I have sent some caps (explosive devices). I subjoin a despatch from General Johnston.

The significance to our story is that the message was rendered into its encrypted format via the Vigenère cipher.

But let's not focus just on techniques; let's also consider some of the historical events cryptography played a role in, such as the life, and death, of Mary Queen of Scots. Poor Mary, who was eventually executed in 1587 on the orders of her cousin Queen Elizabeth I of England, used cryptography in the events leading up to her eventual demise.

Prior to her execution, Mary had thrown herself upon the mercy of the Queen after she had been coerced to give up the Scottish thrown to her infant son James in 1567. Following the abdication, an inquiry had determined that she had colluded with her third husband, the Earl of Bothwell, to murder her second husband, Lord Darnley. As a result, Mary was held in prison as a long term "guest." Not content with this situation, Mary's own supporters, and Mary herself, made other plans. In the years between 1571 and 1586, a handful of plots were put forth to free the Catholic Mary and place her on the throne, supplanting Protestant Elizabeth. Elizabeth was not naïve, however, and knew that such plots were in the works, but was reluctant to move against Mary and accuse her of treason without proof. As fate would have it, later events would unfold that provided the proof Elizabeth needed to seal Mary's fate.

In July of 1586, Mary was a prisoner under the ward of Protestant, Sir Amias Paulet, at Chartley Castle in Staffordshire when she received a letter from Sir Anthony Babington, asking for Mary to approve "the dispatch of the usurping Competitor," which meant that permission was being sought for the assassination of Elizabeth.

Mary was able to communicate with her network of allies by smuggling encrypted messages in and out Chartley within casks of ale. The messages were kept secret, or so Mary thought, through use of an encryption mechanism that relied on substitution. Mary's code substituted symbols for letters of the alphabet and also some words. The cipher also included some additional tricks known as "nulls," or symbols which represented nothing at all, to confuse any code breakers trying to decipher the letters.

Where did Mary's plan fall apart? Well, unbeknownst to Mary, the courier who carried the messages back and forth, Gilbert Gifford, was a double-agent who worked for Elizabeth—specifically, for Sir Francis Walsingham. Sir Walsingham, the head of intelligence at the time, had the messages intercepted and monitored in an effort to gain evidence, which was about to pay off. Everything that Mary sent to Babington was intercepted and later passed to Walsingham's expert code breaker Sir Thomas Phelippes. Phelippes was a master of his code-breaking craft and was fluent in six languages. He was able to see clues to break many a code. In this particular case, a method known as frequency analysis was used to look for patterns that could reveal the underlying message.

To make things even more interesting, the messages were not only broken, but they were altered. In an effort to root out all the conspirators in one swift stroke, Phelippes added a postscript to the message asking Babington to provide the names of others involved in the plot. With this resulting reply in hand from Babington to Mary, the conspirators were rounded up and their heads made an untimely separation from their bodies.

Elizabeth herself was presented the evidence by Sir Thomas Gorges with the following comment:

> "Madame, the Queen, my mistress finds it very strange that you, contrary to the pact and engagement made between you, should have conspired against her and her State, a thing which she could not have believed had she not seen proofs of it with her own eyes and known it for certain."

On the heels of the discovery, Mary found herself taken to Fotheringay Castle and subsequently tried in October 1586. Despite her denials, the evidence was too much, as Mary was done. Elizabeth now had what she needed and formally signed a death warrant calling for Mary's execution in February of 1587. Mary lost her head, and the case was closed on the tale.

> Although she didn't actually live to see it, Mary did have the last "laugh" in the whole affair. Mary, of course, never replaced Elizabeth, but her son James VI of Scotland was crowned James I of England in 1603. The succession was the result of Elizabeth never having a child of her own to take the throne.
>
> Interestingly enough, James himself was the target of a famous assassination plot known as the Gunpowder Plot, involving the famous conspirator Guy Fawkes.

At the same time all of this intrigue was going on, a new organization called "Black Chambers" showed up in Europe in many different countries. This entity was commonplace throughout Europe during the 1700s forward, but what did it do? Simply put, the Black Chambers were put in place to investigate and break codes as their primary responsibility. Many of these organizations were in place all over Europe, with one of the most famous in Vienna. In fact, this particular Black Chamber was so well organized and thought out that it was reportedly able to intercept mail destined for foreign embassies and then copy, alter, and reseal the contents before sending them back to the post office later the same morning.

Of course, the Austrians weren't the only ones involved in the code-breaking field: The British had something to say about it, too. The English had their own code breakers and had numerous victories in the field. They were known at times to decrypt and process over 100 letters a day—amazing considering that no computers were used. In fact, at least one individual was granted the title of "Decypherer" after demonstrating extreme skill in breaking foreign diplomatic codes.

The original 13 colonies were also involved in the code-breaking game, but without the centralized mechanisms that were present in Europe. In fact, the colonies' encryption efforts were carried out through the dedicated work of clergymen and other religious types. Significantly, the colonies had a major code-breaking coup early in the war when a coded message from Dr. Benjamin Church was intercepted. It was suspected of being a message sent to the British, but without it being deciphered, this could not be confirmed. Solving the code was a somewhat unlikely and little remembered individual by the name of Elbridge Gerry. Gerry provided the skills necessary to break the code and show that Church had tried to work with the Tories, a crime he was later exiled for. Later code breaking saw individuals such as Benedict Arnold implicated in crimes against the colonies. Additionally, the Colonists employed their own code during the war as well. General George Washington was supplied with a tremendous amount of information about British forces around New York City. Additionally, the Continental Army utilized a process known as steganography in the form of invisible ink to conceal messages even more.

Note

Elbridge Gerry was better known for being the vice president of the United States under the fourth president James Madison. Another fun fact is that Gerry lent his name to the practice of Gerrymandering, or the redrawing of districts to support a political party (I would explain more, but politics is a code I can't break).

In early American history, several fascinating tales came as the result of code breaking and similar techniques, all worthy of the best spy novels. During the Revolutionary War, James Lovell, a Colonist, became the father of American cryptology. His work led to the breaking of many ciphers, including many that led to victories for the colonies. In particular, one of the most important messages that was broken actually set the stage for the final showdown in the Revolutionary War.

After the war, the intrigue didn't stop. Two men, Aaron Burr and James Wilkinson, along with cryptography, found themselves at the center of another storm. As the two men explored the Southwest for the United States, confusion as to whether the ambitious Burr was doing it for the U.S. or himself arose. Wilkinson, as a undercover Spanish agent, altered Burr's encrypted letters to make it seem as if he was claiming the territory for himself instead of the U.S. This letter later found its way into the hands of President Thomas Jefferson, which led to Burr being tried and acquitted, but with his name tainted nonetheless.

Speaking of Jefferson, he had something to say about cryptography himself. In fact, Jefferson invented a system known informally as the Wheel Cipher, but he never used it much himself in practice. However, the system was successfully used by the U.S. Navy for several years. The system itself consisted of a set of wheels, each with random orderings of the letters of the alphabet. The system was used by reordering how the wheels are placed on an axle. The message was encoded by aligning the letters along the rotational axis of the axle, such that the desired message is formed. Without knowing the orderings of symbols on the wheels and the ordering of wheels on the axle, any plaintext of the appropriate length is possible, and thus the system is quite secure for one time use.

In 1811, another interesting footnote to the story of cryptography occurred—the phasing out of a system known as the Great Cipher, which was at one time used by King Louis XIV of France. This cipher was used to encrypt many messages by the royal for years, but was finally pulled out of service in 1811 in favor of newer techniques—and not to mention the loss of the key. When it was pulled out of service, it immediately led to thousands of diplomatic messages becoming unreadable. Also, interestingly enough, it also had a part to play in one of the more well known stories of all time. The Great Cipher code was broken in the 1700s in France, and one of the messages that was cracked referred to a unique and mysterious prisoner who was later known by the identifier the "Man in the Iron Mask."

Up to this point, cryptography could be said to be of limited interest, with only certain parties having need of the technology. However, about 50 years later, in 1844, something changed the landscape: the invention of the telegraph. The telegraph made communication between remote parties much quicker and quite convenient, but what it didn't bring was security. To secure the transmissions and make the system safer for its users, special ciphers were needed. Seemingly at the same time the general public's interest in the technology grew substantially, with many individuals taking a stab at creating their own unique ciphers designed to protect their information. Making the situation with the telegraph even more of a big deal was the fact that the military used the technology to transmit communiqués between locations. In fact, the invention of the telegraph system was the first time in history that the commander of an army could be in near instantaneous contact with troops and commanders in the field.

All good things must come to an end, though, as some of the older ciphers started showing their age and were routinely broken. During the Civil War, one of the ciphers used a great deal was the old-school Vigenère Cipher—the same cipher from three hundred years before, but virtually unchanged from its original incarnation. When the Confederacy decided to encrypt messages, they relied on this system, which led to a tremendous amount of messages being broken by the Union. The Confederacy made the job even easier for the Union by reusing codes, especially three phrases: "Manchester Bluff," "Complete Victory," and "Come Retribution." When these codes were discovered by the Union cryptanalysts Tinker, Chandler, and Bates, the South's messages were regularly deciphered by the Union. General Grant commented that at one point the Union had gotten enough intelligence from the decrypted messages that it may very well have shortened the war.

In 1863, things got even more serious when a way to break some of the more common mechanisms of the day was discovered. Cryptanalysts discovered relatively simple and repeatable methods that could analyze many of the popular ciphers of that day and break them. The fact that a method could be used to break the main type of ciphers in use meant new types would have to be developed if secrets were to be kept intact and safe.

Modern Cryptography

As the world became more complex and mechanical methods—and later computerized and digital methods—were brought into play, new cryptographic systems needed to be developed and researched. The older methods would not stand on their own and, as such, needed to be either upgraded, complimented, or replaced with methods more suitable and durable for the modern world.

Prior to the twentieth century, cryptography was mainly focused on the patterns formed from linguistic and other similar based systems. However, from the beginning of the twentieth century forward, the situation changed with newer systems introducing number theory, algorithms, algebra, and other high-end mathematics that had not existed in the systems before.

As processing power increased, so did other technologies that indirectly drove the need for increased strength and complexity in ciphers. Just as the earlier invention of the telegraph drove the need for improved ciphers and management, so did later inventions such as the radio and, later still, the digital age and the Internet. With radio the need for privacy was even great than before. In the telegraph there was some degree of security due to the transmissions being sent over a long cable, but in the radio age waves could go anywhere and be intercepted without restriction.

As the twentieth century and its turbulent times approached, cryptography was the subject of more research and emphasis than ever before. The modern round of cryptographic research could be said to have been accelerated by events in Europe, where war was on the horizon and most felt imminent. England decided that in light of the current political climate it was probably wise to invest in research in this area, so if and when war did start that they would be ready to break enemy codes. From this desire a special group was formed that came to be known by the ambiguous name "Room 40," after the room number that initially housed the group. When war broke out in 1917, the group was prepared for the challenge of code breaking enemy ciphers. During the war, they had tremendous success in unraveling the German naval ciphers. Of course, the Germans didn't help their cause by using code words that were nationalistic or political in nature and frequently signaled when the code words were being changed.

The French also jumped into the game in World War I by intercepting German radio signals using the many antennae that dotted the French landscape. Due to the code structure and format that the German military chose, the French were able to intercept many codes and break them regularly.

In 1917, the United States was not yet in the war, but they did form a cryptographic organization that was known by the name MI-8, under the leadership of Herbert Osborne Yardley. The group was able to regularly analyze coded messages of all types, including all types of encryption and special inks. The group saw action only a short time later during World War I and was successful in their code breaking as well. The group was still functional after the war and functioned all the way up to 1929, when Herbert Hoover closed the group, deciding it was unethical to have such a group that could read other's messages. Now out of work and in the middle of an economic crisis, Yardley wrote a book about his experiences titled *The American Black Chamber,* which went right to the top of the best sellers lists. At the same time, a famous husband and wife team—William Frederick Friedman and Elizabeth Smith—became famous in the field breaking codes and creating new ciphers. They developed ways to break existing ciphers using new forms of frequency analysis and other means.

It was during this same period of time that technology introduced machinery to assist in the cryptographic process. Cryptographic devices were a game changer in the making, and they impacted both cryptography and cryptanalysis as a whole. Intricate and elegant machines were that could perform complex encryption processes that used to take substantially longer to do by hand. The early machinery devised at the beginning of the twentieth century was simple; many were either never used or were curiosities, while others still were proof of concepts. No matter what they looked like or their relative complexity, the encryption process was more or less the same as it had always been, just a little more advanced.

One of the first machines able to carry out encryption reliably was made in the early decades of the twentieth century by Lester S Hill. Hill's device utilized a system different from the ones in the past because it used special polynomial equations (don't worry, there won't be a test later) to complete the encryption process. Hill employed a series of matrixes to make the process easier, but then went one step further and constructed a machine that could perform the calculations and processes necessary to encrypt a given piece of information. By today's standards, the machine was (and is) woefully simple and easy to defeat, but it represented a shift in how the process could be performed.

In Actual Practice

Lester Hill never really got many accolades for the machine he invented and he himself was only remembered for his application of mathematics to design and analyze cryptosystems. His machine only saw very limited service in the encryption of radio traffic before being relegated to the curiosity section of the history books. Interestingly enough, Hill also developed methods to detect changes in transmissions, which was one of the first examples seen that supported the concept of information integrity.

During the Prohibition era, alcohol was transported into the United States by illegal smugglers who used coded radio transmissions to control illegal traffic and help avoid Coast Guard patrols. The rum runners developed their own code and ciphers intended to protect information on deliveries and drop-offs. The codes were so successful that the Coast Guard had to hire their own cryptanalyst to decipher the messages and enable the rum runners to be captured.

A few years, later one of the landmark items of cryptography was introduced in the form of the Enigma machine. This machine has emerged as one of the more famous examples of a cryptographic device, which has been praised as well as loathed due to its association with the Nazi party. The Enigma machine was nothing more than a simple mechanical encryption device that was widely used from the 1920s forward. The device was actually used by multiple governments, but it achieved a certain level of notoriety as the Nazi party used it both before and during the war. The device resembled outwardly an old-school typewriter, but inside had complex inner workings consisting of rotors, dials, wires, and such that came together to form an extremely strong and effective system.

Although, in theory, Enigma was an incredibly strong system, it had to be used strictly "by the book" and certain protocols had to be followed. However, the users of the system did not find themselves so disciplined, especially later in the war, which led to the reuse of some of the combinations of codes. This, in turn, led to the system being compromised, and messages that were thought to be secret were actually being intercepted and read by the Allied powers. Figure 2-5 shows an image of the Enigma machine.

Figure 2-5   The Enigma machine

The Enigma machine also provoked other events during the war, namely the breaking of the system by the Allies. Enigma was initially broken in 1929 by a group of three Polish mathematicians, led by Marian Rejewski. This group was to provide the foundation for the later coup of German intelligence and cryptography.

Although it has not been definitely determined how the Polish group was able to get their information regarding the German military-grade Enigma, they did do so. One story puts forth the idea that the Polish were able to intercept a large volume of German messages, which was coupled with the French supplying captured training manuals for the Enigma device. The Poles were able to use this combined information to build an Enigma machine in mid-1933. Once the machine was built, the team was able to use mathematical equations to determine the configuration of the system.

Over the course of the war, the Poles learned how to almost routinely break the messages that the Germans were transmitting. At the same time, the Germans made modifications to the system by adding additional rotors and more configurations to the machine, making the task of code breaking that much harder.

In Actual Practice

Enigma and the accompanying cipher was the backbone of the German military, being used both in land and naval operations. Invented in 1918, the system was originally designed to be used in financial communications, such as those in banks, but never achieved much success in that area. The German military, however, did see the value in the system and adopted it for communications.

The Germans believed the system to be unbreakable and therefore never even considered the possibility of it being compromised. This way of thinking was very reasonable considering the extreme complexity of the system. It has been estimated that the odds against breaking the system were at least 150 million to 1.

The Nazis were completely unaware that the system, which was currently undergoing tests for its effectiveness in the field, had already been cracked as of 1932. At the time, the Germans didn't even change keys all that often in the system, and only later changing them daily as the war erupted. The Poles passed their collected information over to the British and French in 1939. This handing over effectively made the Allied code-breaking effort successful. It has been said that the code-breaking effort used by the Allied forces would not have been successful if not for the actual working Enigma machine.

With the machine in hand, the Allied code breakers were able to closely analyze the system and exploit a flaw in it. Unknown or unaddressed by the Nazis was a simple, but important flaw—the inability for a letter to encrypt to itself. This meant that a message that contained an *S* could not have the same letter encrypt to an S in the final message. This flaw gave Allied analysts enough to unravel messages. Errors in messages sent by tired, stressed, or lazy German operators also gave clues. In January 1940 came the first break into Enigma.

To speed up the deciphering process, a system put forth by Polish analysts was implemented. The result was the Bombe, a machine that could rapidly break the keys the Germans used to analyze messages and discover the daily keys used by the German military or navy.

In Actual Practice

The British unit responsible for breaking Enigma was based at Bletchley Park and was codenamed "Ultra." The unit was highly secretive and only was talked about many years after the war, in 1967. Due to the secretive nature of what the unit performed, many of the former workers that are still alive will not even speak of their activities to this day.

During the course of the war, several countries possessed their own organizations intended to break codes. One of these was formed by the Swedish in 1946 and employed 22 people when the war started. The group was divided into different groups, with each having a specific language as its specialty. The Swedes became highly skilled at breaking the messages of the different warring nations. Adding to their success was the fact that using cryptography effectively requires discipline, which the layman does not really understand, and as such many systems were broken due to sheer laziness on the part of the user.

IMHO

An interesting footnote to this story, in my opinion at least, is the role of British honor after the end of the war concerning the activities at Bletchley Park. At the end of the war, the brass in the British military were told that they were never to reveal that the Enigma had been cracked. The British felt that their vanquished enemy could claim that they had not been fairly beaten.

Of course, the Americans also employed their own code-breaking effort that proved invaluable in several conflicts, including Midway and Pearl Harbor. Prior to the events of December 7th, 1941, the United States had been regularly decrypting Japanese codes. In fact, the United States had decoded the Japanese declaration of war several hours before the Japanese embassy had even decoded it. At the time preceding the attack, the United States was already actively reading the Japanese diplomatic codes and already were well aware the night before the attack that something was going to happen within the next 24 hours. Furthermore, the messages that were intercepted and decoded indicated that the attack would be on American interests somewhere. Adding to the information was the fact that the Japanese carrier fleet was conspicuously missing and could not be located. Other intelligence that was gathered showed that the Japanese were transmitting messages to their diplomats asking as to which ships were currently in Pearl Harbor. Even more interesting is the fact that some messages were even sent over commercial telegraph systems instead of secure ones, and these messages were missed. Such failure to put the information together into a coherent picture is a massive failure of intelligence.

It has been theorized that there was so much chatter at the time from the Japanese that such messages were overlooked. In other words, the problem became one of separating the good information from the sea of irrelevant or deceptive information. Many opportunities were missed and not re-evaluated until after the attack had taken place. Many other messages may have been missed because there was a lack of Japanese translators available at the time. So, in retrospect, much of the intel that could have been gathered was hidden in plain sight because there was no one present to read it or detect a problem. Interestingly (or ironically) enough, the U.S. had more information on this single attack than any other attack before or since and missed the opportunity to act.

The code the United States broke was known as JN-25, which was used by the Imperial Japanese Navy. The code was named this because it was the 25th separate code identified by the U.S. The code evolved several times after its introduction in 1939 and was updated just prior to the Japanese strike on Pearl Harbor. The version that was introduced on December 4th, 1941 was the version that was completely broken by the U.S. code breakers and led to the events later on in 1942. This code allowed the U.S. to get forewarning of the upcoming attack on Midway Island.

A little background on the JN-25 code: The Japanese Imperial Navy came up with the secure code with the intention of passing command and control information to their fleet. The Japanese developed a very strong code that relied on secure and complex algorithms. The code was frequently updated by the Japanese, which amounted to almost an entirely new system each time. This obviously was a code that, when discovered by the Allies, had to be used to protect something extremely sensitive.

The Allies launched a coordinated effort to break the code and reveal its secrets. After the events of December 7th, 1941, radio communications between members of the Japanese navy increased as their aggression increased across the Pacific and Asia. With this increased radio traffic, the Allies were able to collect transmissions that made analysis much easier and the eventual breaking of the code possible.

IMHO

An interesting footnote to the breaking of the Japanese codes is the role courtesy played. The Japanese people were known for their unerring adherence to formalities, which actually provided the code-breaking teams with the ability to see patterns and predict parts of a message reliably. The Japanese tended to use phrases such as "I have the honor to inform your excellency" as well as formal, stylized titles, which were known to be at the front of messages every time.

Admiral Chester Nimitz had at his disposal a team at Pearl Harbor that had broken the JN-25 code. In early 1942, the U.S. intercepted numerous messages that stated the Japanese would move against a target only known by the code "AF." Since this codename was unknown, the U.S. had to figure out what it was to avoid another surprise attack it could ill afford. To reveal what the location was, a trick was used to supplement the cryptanalysis that was being performed. The base sent a special transmission out that stated water was running low at the base over a method that the Japanese were known to be monitoring. The Japanese intercepted this message as expected and shortly thereafter started to transmit messages to their forces stating that "AF was short on water." This coupled with the fact that the Japanese were slow in getting their secret codebooks updated meant that the U.S. also had time to decode other messages, almost right up to the time of the attack.

The result of the battle was decisive due in no short measure to the misuse of encryption and the careful application of cryptanalysis. The broken code had allowed the U.S. Navy to know the size, strength, and general direction of the attacking force. Admiral Nimitz was even able to use the broken messages to understand the tactics that would be employed against him. Using his own force, carefully deployed to work against the Japanese weakness, the Americans were able to win the Battle of Midway.

IMHO

Yes, at the end of the day it was the skill and daring of the U.S. Navy that ultimately won the Battle of Midway, but code breaking and encryption figured into the equation. Without the code-breaking efforts of the men at Pearl Harbor as well as the mismanagement by the Japanese, the story may have been different—we will never know for sure.

In this book, we can say our journey starts when the current phase of the modern era began, which is about 1949. It was during this year that Claude Shannon published a paper titled "Communication Theory of Secrecy Systems" in the *Bell System Technical Journal,* which included results from his WWII work. This paper, along with others, as well as a book on the topic, formed a base of theoretical work for both cryptography and cryptanalysis. Shortly after Shannon's work was published, cryptography stepped into the shadows and became the domain of three-lettered agencies such as the NSA and CIA. In fact, from 1949 until the 1970s, no major work was published in the United States, but when it eventually was, the entire game changed.

In the middle part of the 1970s, a new technique was published in encryption that was known as the Data Encryption Standard, or DES. The first public acknowledgement of the technology was in fact made in March 1975, when IBM submitted the technology to the government for adoption as a new standard. The idea was that this new standard would be used to protect the increasing amount of electronic communications. The technology was accepted by the Federal government after certain adjustments requested by the NSA were made. Because the standard was publically and formally approved by the NSA, the result was substantially increased interest by the academic community and the public in general.

DES lasted a long time and was only showing its age in the early 1990s. In fact, the Data Encryption Standard was eventually broken routinely during the 1990s. As such, a replacement was sought to compensate for the increase in computing power and the march of technology. Toward the end of the 1990s, a competition was put forth to determine the successor to DES. The competition eventually came up with two winners: one being a derivation of DES, known as Triple DES (more on this later), and the other being AES, or Advanced Encryption Standard. Both were formally recognized by the NSA and were seen as replacements for DES. They have been widely used ever since.

Another major advancement that debuted in the latter half of the twentieth century is now known as *public key cryptography*. The system was first published in 1976 by Diffie and Hellman. The system was huge and pushed a new type of cryptography not seen or envisioned before. This system distributed keys in a unique way and was so revolutionary that it even spawned a new class and name: *asymmetric cryptography* (another topic we'll discuss later).

This development of public and private key cryptography represented a major addition to the field because all previous systems had been symmetric in nature. Prior to this development, one key was used to encrypt and decrypt. All of the electromechanical machines used during the intervening years were symmetric, such as the Caesar and ATBASH ciphers, as well as essentially all cipher and code systems throughout history.

With the explosion of computing power and the ever more complex cryptosystems available in the twentieth and twenty-first centuries, the face of the field has changed substantially. The tools currently available have made high-quality cryptographic power available to non-governmental institutions, thus leading to systems that are very tough to break. In light of this, the government and other groups have gotten into heated debates time and time again over public safety and privacy. On one side, the argument is that systems that are publicly available should not be so strong that they cannot be broken by government and law enforcement. On the other hand are those who believe that the systems should be strong regardless of whether you are in the public world or not.

In one of the landmark events of the last couple decades, an individual named Phil Zimmermann argued for strong systems to be made publicly available. Zimmermann made a system known as Pretty Good Privacy, or PGP, that was released way back in 1991. The response he got was a little more than he had hoped for, with the U.S. government providing lots of pressure and threats of prison, causing him to distribute a new version that was different and not as strong as the original. The U.S. government's main beef was that the version, as released, had run afoul of export laws and thus landed Zimmermann in a lot of hot water.

> **LINGO**
> **Asymmetric cryptography** uses two items known as *keys*. They are related by the process they support, but are totally different from one another. This system is different from previous systems that used a single key.

> **LINGO**
> **Export laws** in the context of cryptography are something that has to be considered whenever a company exports cryptographic technologies to another country. Before such laws were relaxed, anyone exporting technology offshore of the United States had to get approval or face harsh fines or even prison time. In fact, from the end of World War II until about 1996, cryptography was considered to be in the same class as military equipment, and export of the technology was treated as such.

In the United States, as in other countries, cryptography is legal for domestic use by companies and individuals, but this does not mean that there has not been controversy over its use.

One of the biggest issues in the United States concerns the NSA and cryptography. The NSA has been both confirmed and rumored to exert influence over the use of cryptography. In fact, the NSA was confirmed to be involved in the development of the DES protocol at the very least. It was said due to the NSA's direct involvement, the protocol was made stronger and resistant to cracking.

Yet another controversial development occurred in 1993 when the NSA proposed the Clipper Chip. Almost from its inception, the program was widely criticized and vilified. The chip was designed to be embedded in electronic devices and would have allowed the NSA to decrypt communications under specific circumstances. The classified cipher caused concerns that the NSA had deliberately made the cipher weak in order to assist its intelligence efforts. Ultimately, the controversy as well as other factors shelved the program.

We've Covered

History of cryptography

- Cryptography is an old technology that has been around in various shapes and forms for over 2000 years.

- Cryptography most likely emerged at the same time that messages were conveyed between different groups.

- Cryptography has evolved dramatically over the years.

Cryptography in the ancient world

- How ancient societies used the power of cryptography to not only safeguard information, but how they were able to utilize it and break it as well.

- Symmetric key encryption has been in use for thousands of years.

- Public key encryption is a new development in the cryptographic field.

Modern cryptography

- How cryptography has been used in the modern era since World War 2 and the new mechanisms that have developed.
- Cryptography has evolved from primitive forms to advanced stages that compensate for improvements in security.
- Modern cryptography will move to more complex systems as technology advances.

Future directions for cryptography

- What cryptography is doing now and what it may be doing in the future will be dependent on new advances in technology.
- Quantum cryptography is a future form of cryptography.
- Cryptography will evolve based on future needs.

Historical users of cryptography

- Julius Caesar used cryptography to deliver messages to his commanders within his army.
- The Spartans used the system called Scytale to deliver messages between different units and were able to keep messages secret.
- Mary Queen of Scots used a cryptographic system to deliver messages to her fellow co-conspirators.

CHAPTER 3

Components of Cryptography

We'll Cover

- Components of cryptography

- How the various components fit together

- The role of keys

- Algorithms and ciphers

- Managing keys

When talking about cryptography, it is important to understand how things fit together from a high level. The first couple chapters discussed the key (no pun intended) terms in the world of cryptography. We have explored the diverse and exciting history of cryptography (at least to me it is, and hopefully by the end of this text you will be fired up as well) to see how the technology has been applied over the years.

As we know, cryptography is both an art and a science that deals specifically with protecting and preserving information, both in the area of integrity and confidentiality. With the technology in play, any individual unaware of the method used to transform the information cannot alter or view the content. We have also seen that the information being encrypted can be anything—it's just a matter of how we transform the information using our desired method.

The basic components of cryptography (or at least the key terms) were discussed in the first chapter, but what we didn't talk about is how everything fits together. I gave you the terms and the background history of the art so you could get a sense of the diverse ways it has been applied as well as an understanding of the events it has been involved in over the years.

This chapter explores the various components of cryptography, discusses how they fit together, and provides examples. It also explains what each component means and why you should care.

Cryptography: Taking a Look Back and Looking Forward

Throughout our journey into cryptography, we start at the basics and then move to complex topics before noticing just how simple things really are—or, as I like to say, we go "there and back again" during our journey. Although cryptography, as you will learn, is used for many different things and in many diverse applications, it uses the same basic parts we discussed back the first chapter. Thanks to popular culture, encryption is one of the best known (although only somewhat grasped) techniques by the public, but the mechanics are not well understood. Nor does the majority of the public even know just how much lurks behind the scenes.

IMHO

Although I enjoy a good movie, don't get the idea that the stuff you see in movies or TV is anything close to what you will enjoy in this book. I will do my best to make things interesting and exciting, but it won't be as dramatic as in the movies. You may have seen characters such as "Q" from the *James Bond* series or heard hacking terminology used in TV series such as *Warehouse 13,* but it just doesn't portray the technology the correct way with more emphasis on drama than the science itself. The way encryption is depicted makes for great entertainment, but nothing more. I know that most of you won't have any aha moments from reading this book, but I just felt it was my place to point this out to dispel any misconceptions.

This is where you, my friend, start on your journey—by gaining an understanding of the components (and minutiae) that make up the world of cryptography. Along the way, you will gain an understanding of how confidentiality and integrity of all sorts of information are preserved by the different aspects of crypto.

IMHO

Cryptography means "secret writing" in Latin, and the body of knowledge is concerned with just that—writing in code as well as concealing and guarding information. Far too often people hear "cryptography" and think of encryption. Although that thinking is partially correct, it does not cover everything in the field, as you will learn.

Encryption

Encryption, as you now know, takes information and converts it to an unreadable format that can be reversed. This process can only be reversed under a very specific set of conditions that will allow the encrypted information to be decrypted. If the information cannot be readily reversed when you are given the correct instructions and combination, then it isn't very useful.

Note

How information is specifically transformed from one format to another is a discussion we will have later in this book. What we want to concentrate on first is the mechanics of the process and what goes into making encryption a reality for us. I'm sure you're asking yourself, "Why wait?" The answer is simple: You should understand how the process and components work together at a high level before we dive down deep and explore how everything functions.

Encryption is absolutely ideal for protecting information from unauthorized disclosure if it is used correctly.

So now that you know what encryption is, you need to fully understand what it can and cannot do. I think this is an important subtopic to discuss before we start putting the pieces together. I want you to keep in mind the strengths and weaknesses of each system we discuss so you understand where you may effectively use a system and where you may not.

Your Plan

In this chapter, you should remember what each component does because the terminology I use here is the same as in earlier chapters. I also want you to focus on what these pieces do when they are all placed in front of you and assembled into a solution. Focusing on each of these components will provide you several benefits, but in particular I want you to think about each of the following components:

❑ **Name**   What is the formal name for the component? This is important because a lot of the terminology is standardized, so locking in the name to the component early on is extremely beneficial to you.

❑ **Function**   What does the component do? Always try to think clearly about what each component does—both by itself and within the overall process. I want you to think about what alterations to an individual component does to the overall system.

❑ **Importance**   How important is this component to the overall process? I want you to think of the significance of each individual part to the overall process and what a given weakness in that part will do to the process as a whole.

Additionally, I want you to think of the following points when considering of the encryption process and the components that comprise it:

❏ Encryption is meant to conceal information from parties that may wish to see it but are not otherwise authorized to view it. This is the strength of the technology, but it can also be its weakness if used incorrectly. For right now, just remember that it is good at concealing information from prying eyes.

❏ Concealment doesn't mean information is entirely hidden. Just because something is encrypted does not mean that an attacker or curious party cannot do some snooping and glean some information that may be useful. Details such as the length of a message, when it was sent, who it was sent to, and who (or what) was the intended recipient may reveal something useful. The problem is that all, some, or none of these details may be exposed.

❏ Not all change is good. In other words, just because something is encrypted does not mean I can't change it if I wanted to. Essentially, I can change your encrypted message even if it is just ciphertext, even though I may not know what the information actually is or what it was changed to. Although this tampering may be easy to detect if the underlying information is a message that a human being may be reading, it is not so easily detectable if the information is in binary because it is not so easy to detect a 1 or 0 out of place. Rest assured, young apprentice, we will talk later about how to detect changes in information, no matter if you are carbon or silicon.

Keep these points and questions in mind as you go through this chapter (and the entire book), as they will help you focus your thinking and serve you well later. Now, let's get to work, young Padawan.

Visiting an Old Friend

Previously we discussed a system known as the Caesar, or Caesar's Cipher. This system was an only-cryptographic mechanism that was used by Julius Caesar himself, which is where it gained its name. Although the cipher was not originally invented by Caesar, he made extensive use of the process when sending orders to and from his commanders in the field. The process used by the cipher is very simple by today's standards, using a variation of a process known as a substitution cipher. Let's take a look again at this cipher before we delve into things a bit further. Understanding the cipher will reap huge benefits for us later.

IMHO

Something I find extremely cool—or scary, depending on how you look at it—is the fact the Julius Caesar was reportedly able to encrypt and decrypt messages using his cipher in his head. Because the cipher is very simple, this may not seem like that big of deal to you, but you may not be considering everything. Let's just say for kicks that I gave you an encrypted message, any message, and shifted the letters some number of spaces and you knew ahead of time it was three spaces to the left. Now I write you the Gettysburg Address in this code. Would you be able to read the message without pausing or even thinking about it? Could you read the message so easily that if I was listening to you and not looking at the writing I would think it was written in plain English? Maybe some of you out there could, but that doesn't take away from the fact that it is an amazing skill to have—something that few individuals have.

Oh Caesar, those of us who are about to encrypt salute you!

The Caesar Cipher has been around for over 2,000 years, but it still provides us with a great mechanism to illustrate the concepts we need. Julius Caesar used this process to encrypt or encode his messages to his commanders in the field for the same reason the military today does—to keep sensitive information private. Although the cipher is simple in design and implementation, it is still in use today, and in fact is the one that most school children would be familiar with because it has appeared in countless puzzle game books and cereal boxes over the years.

Simply put, the process Caesar used was one that shifted each letter some number of spaces to the left (for example, Y would become B, and R would shift to U). Although the process could use any shift amount, Caesar settled on a shift of three spaces, but he could have used any number, positive or negative, in theory. It was effective at keeping secrets at the time because anyone encountering the message would most likely assume it was in a foreign language—if they could even read at all. Figure 3-1 shows that the Caesar Cipher fits in as the component doing the actual encryption process.

Let's look at some examples. Guess the keyshift I used in each and in which direction I went.

Plaintext	T	R	I	F	O	R	C	E
Ciphertext	X	U	L	I	R	U	F	H

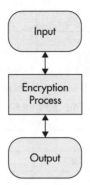

Figure 3-1   The encryption process. The Caesar Cipher would be placed in the middle step.

Got that one? Let's try another one. Remember, though, I may not be using the same key shift for each (wouldn't want you to get too comfortable, young apprentices).

Plaintext	L	A	S	V	E	G	A	S
Ciphertext	K	Z	R	U	D	F	Z	R

Let's do one more, but pay closer attention to what I have done.

Plaintext	G	L	A	D	O	S
Ciphertext	H	N	D	H	T	Y

Is that a tricky one? If it is, go back and look again at each letter individually to see how many spaces to the left I shifted each letter. Does the shift match? Look carefully: This type of trick can be used to make decoding just a little more difficult.

So with this knowledge in hand, let's have you try some of your own. Practice with the Caesar Cipher so you can understand it a little better. Let's try a set of puzzles based on the Caesar Cipher, use a shift of three to the right, and put your answers in the boxes below each letter.

Plaintext	C	A	E	S	A	R
Ciphertext						

Plaintext	Z	E	L	D	A
Ciphertext					

Plaintext	M	U	S	T	A	N	G
Ciphertext							

Now that you have done that, let's go the other way with some ciphertext that has been encrypted using the Caesar Cipher. I want you to reverse the encryption process, assuming that the encryption has been done using the three-spaces-to-the-right method.

Plaintext					
Ciphertext	S	R	N	H	U

Plaintext							
Ciphertext	D	L	U	S	O	D	Q	H

Plaintext							
Ciphertext	V	D	P	X	U	D	L

If you are having problems decrypting the ciphertext in these examples, remember what the Caesar Cipher does: It shifts the characters three spaces to the right to encrypt. This means that to decrypt you need to shift the ciphertext three spaces to the left to reverse the process.

In this next set, I am going to give you some plaintext and a keyshift that I want you to use to create some ciphertext. So put on your crypto hat and let's have some fun. Remember that a keyshift that is preceded with a sign plus is a shift to the right, whereas one preceded with a minus sign is to the left. If you reach the end of the alphabet, continue your count from the beginning of the alphabet.

Plaintext	R	E	D	H	E	A	D
Ciphertext							

Do this first one with a keyshift of +6.

Plaintext	K	A	T	R	I	N	A
Ciphertext							

For this one, I want you to use a keyshift of -3.

Plaintext	Z	E	L	D	A
Ciphertext					

For this one, use a keyshift of +4.

Plaintext	C	H	E	A	T	E	R
Ciphertext							

Use a keyshift of -4.

Now that you have done some encryption firsthand (and I am proud of you; you have taken the first steps on the road to insanity and enlightenment), you now can see how the basic encryption process works. Let's reverse it now and see how you do (I'll be watching).

In this next set of exercises, I want you to take the ciphertext and reverse the message into plaintext, given the key only.

Note

If you see yourself coming up with garbage or nonsensical results when you are attempting to uncover the plaintext, really pay attention to the keyshift value and what it does. Your answer is there.

Plaintext						
Ciphertext	G	E	I	W	E	V

Key shift +4 to encrypt.

Plaintext						
Ciphertext	Y	K	Y	L	B	Y

Key shift -2 to encrypt.

Plaintext				
Ciphertext	P	M	R	O

Key shift +4 to encrypt.

IMHO

If you got garbage when decrypting these messages, you may have missed the detail or clue I left you. I admit I played a little trick, but it was meant to make you think a little more and see if you were paying attention. Remember we're working with ciphertext. So what is ciphertext? Earlier in this text it was defined as a message that is already encrypted. Now look at the keyshift I attached to each table. I said that the keyshift represents how may spaces had been shifted on the original plaintext to encrypt. You are being asked here to *decrypt,* so that means you must use the opposite direction. In other words, plus will become minus, and minus will become plus.

Let's look at one final set of examples. This may be an advanced exercise, but what the heck. I think you may be able to handle this early on and take the title "Junior Codebreaker" and earn yourself a spot at the 2020 code-breaking Olympics (it could happen).

I am going to provide you with a set of encrypted messages using the Caesar Cipher and let you see if you can figure it out. I won't pull any funny business—the messages will all be in English and will use the same keyshift all the way in each example.

- Exercise 1: Figure out the keyshift and the original message:

  VJKU DQQM KU CYGUQOG CPF KU YQTVJ GXGTZ RGPPA

- Exercise 2: Crack the coded message here:

  HQFUATWLRQ LV IWQ

- Exercise 3: This one's the same as the first two, but maybe a little trickier and with some "nuggets" embedded in it that we'll come back later:

  FODSZQUJPO JT FBTZ JT JU OPU

Good luck with these exercises. While completing them, keep with a mind to detail as you learn the process of one of our simpler systems.

Here's what you saw with the Caesar Cipher:

- **Plaintext/cleartext**   Plaintext (also sometimes called cleartext) is the original unadulterated message. It has not been transformed in any way; this is the usable information. Remember, even though Caesar's cipher operates on text, it is but one form of plaintext. Plaintext can literally be anything.

- **Ciphertext**   This is the opposite of plaintext—it is a message or other data that has been transformed into a different format using a mechanism known as an algorithm. It is also something that can be reversed using an algorithm and a key.

- **Algorithms** Probably the trickiest and most mysterious part in the encryption process is the algorithm or cipher. The algorithm or cipher is nothing more than a formula that includes discrete steps that describe how the encryption/decryption process is to be performed in a given instance. For example, let's look at a method used by a process discussed earlier to understand this relationship. In this previous example, each letter in a message is shifted a certain amount of spots to the right, yielding an encrypted message or ciphertext. Conversely, the algorithm specifically states that to decrypt the information, the individual characters must be shifted the exact same amount of steps to the left.

- **Key** Let's move on to an important, and frequently complicated, item: keys. Keys are incredibly significant for us if we are to understand the encryption process fully. In the strictest and most technical sense, a key is a discrete piece of information that is used to determine the result or output of a given cryptographic operation. A key in the cryptographic sense can be thought of in the same way as a key in the physical world: It's a special item used to open or unlock something (in this case, a piece of information). In the encryption world, the key is used to produce a meaningful result. Without it, one would not be possible.

Figure 3-2 shows you again how these components fit together.

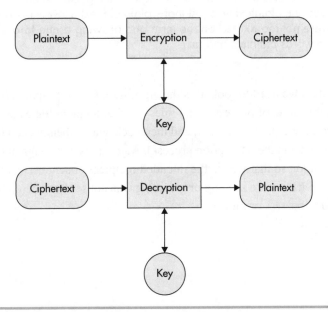

Figure 3-2 The encryption/decryption process and the relationships of the components.

IMHO

Yes, I know I gave these definitions already an earlier chapter, but I'm introducing them again here because I want to use and apply them to the Caesar Cipher to help you understand the process from both a theoretical and practical viewpoint. Why else do you think I had you do those puzzles here?

Dissecting the Caesar Cipher

Let's take a second look at the Caesar Cipher, with the caveat that we are going to apply the terms from earlier to the system now that you have gone through it on your own.

First, let's talk about what the plaintext was in the examples. Plaintext is the words (or in the advanced examples, the phrases) I gave you prior to encryption by the process. In my examples, I used words and simple text, but in the real world this information could be anything—alphanumeric or otherwise.

IMHO

Again, I want you to remember that plaintext is not necessarily *plain,* as the name may imply. Plaintext is just a term that refers to anything that is entering the encryption process—whether it is just text or something else altogether. In our earlier examples and exercises, the plaintext was just that—plain old text. However, I wanted to make sure you were not too fixated on the term and drawing a one-to-one relationship between the words *plaintext* and *text.*

The next item we need to look at is the algorithm. Cryptographic algorithms are nothing more than a set of processes and rules or other methodologies used to transform information from one state to another, and then back again when needed (at least in the case of encryption and the decryption process). Algorithms are designed to protect and/or conceal information so that we (as the intended recipient or sender) can have a level of comfort that what we are sending or receiving was not seen or altered by anyone else not authorized to possess or view it.

In this section, we discuss the Caesar Cipher due to its relative simplicity, which makes it easy to understand at this stage in the game. You will find later on, though, that algorithms can and do get extremely complex, but the concepts we will cover here will give you a strong foundation to build upon when learning about the others later on.

Let's take a look at the Caesar Cipher and dissect it to see what the algorithm looks like. According to historical records (from the Roman historian Suetonius, as a matter of fact), Caesar simply replaced each letter in a message with the letter that is three places further down the alphabet. The process is not that complex, but it did work at that time. We can see how this works by looking at the following table, where the first row represents our regular alphabet and the second row represents Caesar Cipher and how it encrypts the standard alphabet.

A	B	C	D	E	F	G	H	I	J	K	L	M	N	O	P	Q	R	S	T	U	V	W	X	Y	Z
D	E	F	G	H	I	J	K	L	M	N	O	P	Q	R	S	T	U	V	W	X	Y	Z	A	B	C

In the world of cryptography, the original alphabet is commonly known as the plaintext alphabet. The second row is what is known as a ciphertext alphabet, which reflects the new positioning of the characters after a keyshift has been applied. In actuality, this ciphertext alphabet is used to substitute new characters in place of the original plaintext characters. In fact, this type process, as used in the Caesar Cipher, is the reason that the process is sometimes called the Caesar Shift Cipher.

If we wanted to write this process down in some sort of code, we could write it as a formula. Keep in mind that the cipher shifts the letters by three spaces to the right; this makes the process simple to represent as an equation (sorry about the math):

$X+Y=Z$

Where X equals the original location of the letter in plaintext
Where Y equals the number of spaces to move the letter
Where Z equals the new location of the letter in ciphertext

Here's an example that shows what the Caesar Cipher specifically looks like:

X+3=Z

Where X equals the original location of the letter in plaintext
Where 3 equals the number of spaces to move the letter
Where Z equals the new location of the letter in ciphertext

Let's think about this formula a bit in both its original form and in Caesar's form, with three as the number of spaces. You can see the formula is essentially the same, except for this minor replacement. Does this mean that we can use any number in the position of Y? Yes, it does in fact. Let's look at something known as ROT13.

ROT13 is a variation of the letter substitution that we have already been using with one variation where the letters are shifted 13 spaces instead of three. Much like the previous cipher, the encryption is done with a shift of 13, but it is reversed with that same amount in the opposite direction. For example, the phrase

live long and prosper

translates to the following in ROT13:

yvir ybat naq cebfcre

Another example is the following famous phrase:

veni, vidi, vici

Shift the characters 13 spaces and you get the following result:

irav, ivqv, ivpv

Let's have you try some examples of ROT13 to see how it works:

Plaintext	M	O	N	T	R	E	A	L
Ciphertext								

Plaintext		S	W	O	R	D
Ciphertext						

Plaintext		H	A	W	A	I	I
Ciphertext							

Note

You can encrypt or decrypt a message using ROT13 using the same number. You could go 13 forward or 13 back and arrive at the same result. This property is only one of the many reasons that ROT13 is used as an example of a weak cryptographic scheme.

Much like Caesar's Cipher before, ROT13 functions the same way, but with the difference being the number spaces used. Much like the previous cipher, the algorithm provides little-to-no cryptographic security because it is so simple and easy to figure out. In fact, the ROT13 is commonly considered a weak encryption strategy and, as such, is not used alone, but it may be combined with other mechanisms when it is used.

In Actual Practice

As an interesting piece of trivia, ROT13 was used in newsgroups way back when to hide offensive content such as dirty jokes or to hide items such as spoilers for movies or TV shows.

People would post jokes online, something like the following:

Cnffjbeqf ner yvxr haqrejrne. Lbh qba'g funer gurz, lbh qba'g unat gurz ba lbhe zbavgbe be haqre lbhe xrlobneq, lbh qba'g rznvy gurz, be chg gurz ba n jrofvgr, naq lbh zhfg punatr gurz irel bsgra.

This would translate to:

Passwords are like underwear. You don't share them, you don't hang them on your monitor or under your keyboard, you don't email them, or put them on a website, and you must change them very often.

ROT13 was chosen because it's a known system that's easy to work with and is the only system that allows the same value to encrypt as to decrypt a message. Additionally, ROT13 was commonly supported by software applications such as newsreaders at the time.

Another application of ROT13 that may surprise you is that it was actually used in early browsers (specifically Netscape Communicator) back in 1999. The mechanism was used to store email passwords from the browser. Later in 2001, another vendor of e-books was found to be encrypting their documents with ROT13 and using the scheme in production.

One final example comes to us from the Windows XP world, where the scheme is used to encrypt some of the registry keys within Windows itself.

Caesar Cipher and ROT13 look simple, right? Well, let's kick it up a notch and look at a system that's a little more complex: the Vigenère cipher. This cipher builds on the Caesar cipher by using multiple shifted alphabets to encrypt information instead of the single one used in the Caesar cipher. For example, look at the following table:

	A	B	C	D	E	F	G	H	I	J	K	L	M	N	O	P	Q	R	S	T	U	V	W	X	Y	Z
A	A	B	C	D	E	F	G	H	I	J	K	L	M	N	O	P	Q	R	S	T	U	V	W	X	Y	Z
B	B	C	D	E	F	G	H	I	J	K	L	M	N	O	P	Q	R	S	T	U	V	W	X	Y	Z	A
C	C	D	E	F	G	H	I	J	K	L	M	N	O	P	Q	R	S	T	U	V	W	X	Y	Z	A	B
D	D	E	F	G	H	I	J	K	L	M	N	O	P	Q	R	S	T	U	V	W	X	Y	Z	A	B	C
E	E	F	G	H	I	J	K	L	M	N	O	P	Q	R	S	T	U	V	W	X	Y	Z	A	B	C	D
F	F	G	H	I	J	K	L	M	N	O	P	Q	R	S	T	U	V	W	X	Y	Z	A	B	C	D	E
G	G	H	I	J	K	L	M	N	O	P	Q	R	S	T	U	V	W	X	Y	Z	A	B	C	D	E	F
H	H	I	J	K	L	M	N	O	P	Q	R	S	T	U	V	W	X	Y	Z	A	B	C	D	E	F	G
I	I	J	K	L	M	N	O	P	Q	R	S	T	U	V	W	X	Y	Z	A	B	C	D	E	F	G	H
J	J	K	L	M	N	O	P	Q	R	S	T	U	V	W	X	Y	Z	A	B	C	D	E	F	G	H	I
K	K	L	M	N	O	P	Q	R	S	T	U	V	W	X	Y	Z	A	B	C	D	E	F	G	H	I	J
L	L	M	N	O	P	Q	R	S	T	U	V	W	X	Y	Z	A	B	C	D	E	F	G	H	I	J	K
M	M	N	O	P	Q	R	S	T	U	V	W	X	Y	Z	A	B	C	D	E	F	G	H	I	J	K	L
N	N	O	P	Q	R	S	T	U	V	W	X	Y	Z	A	B	C	D	E	F	G	H	I	J	K	L	M
O	O	P	Q	R	S	T	U	V	W	X	Y	Z	A	B	C	D	E	F	G	H	I	J	K	L	M	N
P	P	Q	R	S	T	U	V	W	X	Y	Z	A	B	C	D	E	F	G	H	I	J	K	L	M	N	O
Q	Q	R	S	T	U	V	W	X	Y	Z	A	B	C	D	E	F	G	H	I	J	K	L	M	N	O	P
R	R	S	T	U	V	W	X	Y	Z	A	B	C	D	E	F	G	H	I	J	K	L	M	N	O	P	Q
S	S	T	U	V	W	X	Y	Z	A	B	C	D	E	F	G	H	I	J	K	L	M	N	O	P	Q	R
T	T	U	V	W	X	Y	Z	A	B	C	D	E	F	G	H	I	J	K	L	M	N	O	P	Q	R	S
U	U	V	W	X	Y	Z	A	B	C	D	E	F	G	H	I	J	K	L	M	N	O	P	Q	R	S	T
V	V	W	X	Y	Z	A	B	C	D	E	F	G	H	I	J	K	L	M	N	O	P	Q	R	S	T	U
W	W	X	Y	Z	A	B	C	D	E	F	G	H	I	J	K	L	M	N	O	P	Q	R	S	T	U	V
X	X	Y	Z	A	B	C	D	E	F	G	H	I	J	K	L	M	N	O	P	Q	R	S	T	U	V	W
Y	Y	Z	A	B	C	D	E	F	G	H	I	J	K	L	M	N	O	P	Q	R	S	T	U	V	W	X
Z	Z	A	B	C	D	E	F	G	H	I	J	K	L	M	N	O	P	Q	R	S	T	U	V	W	X	Y

This square is an example of what is known as a tabula recta, Vigenère table, or Vigenère square. As you can see, the table consists of the entire alphabet written out 26 times, with each row shifted to the left, making up each one of the potential Caesar ciphers. Depending on the point on the cryptographic process, a different alphabet is used. The alphabet you would use is based on a repeating keyword you would choose going in. For example, let's use the word "day."

	A	B	C	D	E	F	G	H	I	J	K	L	M	N	O	P	Q	R	S	T	U	V	W	X	Y	Z
D	E	F	G	H	I	J	K	L	M	N	O	P	Q	R	S	T	U	V	W	X	Y	Z	A	B	C	D
A	B	C	D	E	F	G	H	I	J	K	L	M	N	O	P	Q	R	S	T	U	V	W	X	Y	Z	A
Y	Z	A	B	C	D	E	F	G	H	I	J	K	L	M	N	O	P	Q	R	S	T	U	V	W	X	Y

Our plaintext for this exercise will be

JULIUS CAESAR

The resulting ciphertext would be

NVKMVR GBDWBQ

Let's see how I arrived at this as the ciphertext, which is actually very simple. First, look at the plaintext phrase, which is Julius Caesar. Using this phrase, we locate our first letter across the top portion and then line it up with the first letter in the side column. Our second letter we locate in the top row and then line it up with the second letter in the side column. We keep doing this as we rotate through the letters time after time until the phrase is completely encrypted.

IMHO

The Vigenère cipher was so well designed that the mechanism was only broken 200 years later, and by the time of the U.S. Civil War it was considered to be severely compromised and not suitable for important secrets.

In the case of the Confederacy, they made things easier for the Union by using the same code words over and over again.

As you can see, the phrase that's the code is used on the left-hand side and is used as the seed or start for each cipher alphabet. With a little bit of effort, you can create your own Vigenère cipher and encrypt your own messages.

In Actual Practice

The origin of the Vigenère cipher can be traced back all the way to the Italian genius Leon Alberti, who was born in 1404. Later in life Alberti became a polymath, with expertise as a painter, composer, poet, and philosopher. He also was responsible for designing Rome's first Trevi fountain and having written *De Re Aedificatoria,* which is one of the first printed books on the subject of architecture.

Coincidentally, he also is responsible for one of the most significant developments in encryption in about a thousand years, although he failed to develop it to its full extent. This came later at the hands of several famous figures, including Johannes Trithemius, Giovanni Porta, and finally Blaise de Vigenère.

I'll let you play with the Vigenère cipher on your own, but I am confident you will have some fun with this more advanced algorithm or encryption mechanism.

So let's talk about the algorithms in a generic sense now that we have looked at some examples. Algorithms, for serious applications at least, are much more complex and powerful than what is seen here in our two examples. The following is an example of another encryption algorithm known as RSA, which is in a larger family of algorithms known as *asymmetric* or *public key algorithms.* I have provided some extra information, just to show how things look "under the hood." Don't get too caught up in the numbers and other details.

P = 61 ← first prime number (destroy this after computing E and D)
Q = 53 ← second prime number (destroy this after computing E and D)
PQ = 3233 ← modulus (give this to others)
E = 17 ← public exponent (give this to others)
D = 2753 ← private exponent (keep this secret!)

Your public key is (E,PQ).
Your private key is D.

The encryption function is:

$$\text{encrypt}(T) = (T\char94 E) \bmod PQ$$
$$= (T\char94 17) \bmod 323$$

The decryption function is:

$$decrypt(C) = (C^D) \bmod PQ$$
$$= (C^{2753}) \bmod 3233$$

So now that you know what an algorithm does (or at least what you need to know for right now), let's talk about a few things. First, algorithms exist for many applications and at many different strengths, so you will never need to create or otherwise develop your own. In fact, it is highly unlikely you will ever even have the chance to create your own or even want that chance. You will most likely be in charge of selecting the appropriate encryption algorithm or cryptosystem to use in a given application or situation. Here are some factors you may consider:

> **LINGO**
> **Algorithms** are formulas used to describe and define the encryption and decryption process. Many different types exist, with varying levels of complexity and different potential applications as well as accompanying strengths and weaknesses.

- **Ease of use**   The system is relatively easy to use, implement, and understand. You may not be able to understand the underlying mathematics, but you should be able to have a body of reliable knowledge to support the choice.

- **Reliability**   This simply refers to the fact that you have that "warm, fuzzy feeling" that the algorithm will work the same way each and every time it is applied. This means that the designer met their stated goals and that subsequent audits and reviews by the community show that the algorithm actually does work as designed.

- **Security**   Simply put, this means that the system will keep your information safe and sound and hidden from any unauthorized parties. Additionally, it means that authorized parties will indeed be able to recover the information when they seek to do so.

Let's now add something else into the discussion of algorithms—namely, Kerckhoffs' Principle. This principle, which is considered to be a guideline, calls for several steps to be taken when creating or evaluating a new algorithm. As we go through the items that are part of this principle, keep in mind that they are not laws—there are no fines or other penalties for not following them.

Note
Auguste Kerckhoffs was a Dutch linguist and cryptographer who was professor of languages at the École des Hautes Études Commerciales in Paris in the late 19th century.

Kerckhoffs originally put forth six principles as to the proper and careful design of algorithms:

- The system should be, if not theoretically unbreakable, unbreakable in practice.
- The design of a system should not require secrecy, and compromise of the system should not inconvenience the correspondents.
- The key should be memorable without notes and should be easily changeable.
- The cryptograms should be transmittable by telegraph.
- The apparatus or documents should be portable and operable by a single person.
- The system should be easy, neither requiring knowledge of a long list of rules nor involving mental strain.

Although the second point is what is formally known as Kerckhoffs' Principle, we should cover some of the other principles on this list to fill out your knowledge of algorithms:

- **Peer review and collective experience** Algorithms are complicated, potentially mind numbing, and convoluted in design. As such, it is not a bad idea to have some sort of peer review and other experiences brought into play to ensure that the system is as strong as it could be (or, conversely, to find out where the weaknesses are). In fact, if multiple eyeballs and experiences are brought into play, it is more likely that defects in design are going to be picked up.

- **Taking advantage of experience** Kerckhoffs allowed for the designers and reviewers of algorithms to leverage the experience of past developers and others research—the idea being that by having access or using previous knowledge, stronger systems may be possible by avoiding old mistakes and pitfalls.

- **Standards** If you exchange information and ideas, it is much more likely you will leverage standards that make your algorithm more interoperable and understood by others. This also has the benefit of making sure your new algorithm meets established testing standards and reviews. Examples of standards include NIST Computer Security Division, NSA Suite B, OASIS, and ISO.

What Kerckhoffs' principles do not directly cover are the topic of a key. Although the third point does mention that the key should be memorable and changeable, it doesn't mention directly that the strength of the system relies in large part on the secrecy of the key.

Think about this for a moment: Is it practical to change or create an algorithm every time you need to encrypt something? No, absolutely not. Any useful algorithm requires that a new key is able to be selected for each and every use of the system. In order to encrypt/decrypt the plaintext/ciphertext, you need the algorithm and the key used for that particular action. If an encryption algorithm doesn't use a key, then as soon as you know the decryption algorithm, you can decrypt all the things encrypted with the algorithm.

We can think of the problem in a different way: Is it easier to design a lock that can only ever take one design of key, or is it easier to design a lock that can take many different forms of a key? Designing a lock the first way would be incredibly stupid because you would have to design a new lock each and every time you wanted to lock something up, which is not convenient. This is why the key must be able to be changed easily without great effort.

In Actual Practice

Cryptographic wisdom considers an encryption process secure when the only way to recover a plaintext message from ciphertext is to know or discover the key. Furthermore, this rule should still be true even if every other detail about the encryption process is known. In fact, cryptographers become very concerned about the security of an algorithm when more than a key must be kept secret.

The design and use of a key is important, and indeed a large part of the strength of the cryptosystem depends on this item. A lot of misconceptions exist regarding the key within a cryptosystem, so let's try to clear things up in this chapter.

As I said in a previous chapter, a key in a strict technical sense is only a discrete piece of information used to determine the specific settings for a given cryptographic operation. This sounds really technical and confusing, but it doesn't have to be if we look at it in the right way. Let's look at the key using the analogy of a lock, specifically a combination lock just like you would use on a gym locker. When this lock is designed by the manufacturer, it can have any one of a number of different combinations, but each lock will only have one specific combination that can open it. Just because you know the combination for a specific lock does not in any way mean you know the combination of another lock of the same model. In the encryption world, the key is what is used to produce a meaningful result, and without it one would not be possible.

IMHO

One way to think of a key is like the combination for a lock. You may purchase a hundred combination locks of the same model, but they will all typically have different combinations if they are preset by the manufacturer. Although it is theoretically possible that you may acquire locks with the same combination, this is intended to be highly unlikely.

I personally like the lock analogy in relation to keys because it helps when thinking of the overall encryption process later.

In the cryptographic world, a key is not the same in its purpose, though. Although a lock has a key to open it, a key in the cryptographic world dictates how the process will be performed at any one time. The choice of key is built into the algorithm itself, with a well-designed algorithm having a large keyspace (in other words, a large selection of possible keys). Encryption keys are defined by the algorithm in use at a given time. As the design of a lock that dictates all the possibilities for the shape of a physical key, an algorithm defines the range of keys that can be used.

Think of it this way: Suppose you have a combination lock much like the one you would use to lock up a bike or a gym locker. This hypothetical lock needs (in our case at least) to have a combination of eight digits that will be used by an individual to unlock the lock and open their locker or bike. In this case, we can we can write the parameters of the proposed key down in a pseudo formula as such:

Combination Length: Equal to 8
Valid Digit Range: 0 to 9

With this information in hand, we can see that the combination must be eight digits in length and each digit can only be in the range 0 to 9, inclusive. If we look at the numbers and amount of combinations that are valid, we can calculate that there are 100 million possible arrangements of digits given the information we have.

Is 100 million a lot? Well, it is and it isn't. In human terms, the number of keys is a lot, but in the digital world not so much. In fact, many of the stronger algorithms include substantially larger numbers of keys than are possible with our simple example. In cryptography, all the potential key types possible with a particular algorithm are commonly known as the *keyspace*. Algorithms are designed to provide the greatest amount of protection and as such modern algorithms are designed to have a vast amount of potential keys in order to thwart guessing or brute-force attacks. Figure 3-3 shows the how the keyspace fits in to the picture.

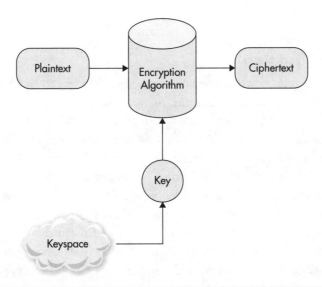

Figure 3-3   Encryption and the involvement of a keyspace

Let's not get too comfortable, though, and think that the number of keys is a potent defense against attack; it is not the only one. Another factor is key length or size. Key length or size means that as a key gets longer, it offers stronger protection against attacks. Key length together with key size forms a stronger solution and defense against many types of key weaknesses, both by design and through outside attack.

> **LINGO**
> **Key length** or **size** refers to how "long" a key resulting from an actual algorithm may be, but there is another term referring to length of which you should be aware. This term is *bit,* as in a key is 40 bits or 1,024 bits.

So do longer keys make a given particular encryption scheme stronger? Well, this can be debated, but the answer is that the length of keys can have a substantial impact on the power and strength of an encryption system. Consider that a cryptosystem developed only 40 years ago with 56-bit keys would now be viewed as much weaker in the face of stronger computing systems. In fact, over the last 30 years as computing power has increased thousands of times, algorithms have had to be developed and strengthened to increase the length of keys and the number of keys available in any given system.

In Actual Practice

As increased computing power showed up on the scene, key lengths had to be increased with more bits being added to the scheme. So how much power does an extra bit add to a scheme? Consider a 56-bit key: Adding a single bit onto this changes it to a 57-bit key, which doubles the strength of the system. adding 10 more bits to make a 66-bit key makes the key 1,024 times stronger than the original 56-bit key.

By the mid-1990s, computing power that had the ability to break many of the shorter keyed cryptosystems became widely available to the public when it had been solely the domain of governments and corporations before. Moving forward 20 years to today's world, we can see that commodity hardware (or hardware that can be purchased off the shelf) is much more accessible and available than it ever has been before. In fact, many of the computers available today to the consumer are able to process at a minimum 50,000 56-bit keys per second.

So how much does key length make a difference? The following table shows the relative strength of keys compared to one another as well as how long it would take to break each one on different hardware. The second table shows the relative value of each key length.

Power	40-bit	56-bit	64-bit	128-bit
Individual	1.4 minutes	73 days	50 years	10^{20} years
Corporate	2 seconds	35 hours	1 year	10^{19} years
Governments	0.2 seconds	3.5 hours	37 days	10^{18} years

Key Length	Value
40	Of no use to companies and governments. Effective at stopping casual attackers.
56	Good for privacy, but vulnerable and has in fact been broken. DES is the best example of a broken 56-bit encryption scheme.
64	Safe, but vulnerable and has been broken.
128	Considered generally unbreakable, but some newer technologies and implementations have been vulnerable.
256	Impossible to break with today's technology.

When looking at these two tables, it would seem that a longer key would automatically equal a greater amount of protection, and in many cases this is true. However, there are trade-offs in performance. A longer key generally equates to a longer encrypt/decrypt time. Additionally, the old axiom that says that "if some is good, more is better" is proven wrong here as well in relation to the length of the key and protection. In fact, the length of a key will only result in a stronger algorithm up to a point, and anything after that will just slowly plateau and result in the aforementioned increased processing time.

It may seem that if a long key is good, a longer key is better, but that is definitely not true and not for the reasons I just gave you. It may seem like keys of 4,096 bits are great (and they are used, by the way), so using something around 10,000 bits or longer is better—and we can create dedicated hardware devices that can process these keys effectively. But is it worth it? What we do not have at this point in time is a reasonable motivation to use such excessively long keys. For example, a 128-bit key is "strong enough" to defeat even the majority of the sophisticated brute-force attacks that have been employed today.

We've Covered

Components of cryptography

- The components of cryptography including the key, algorithm, and plain and ciphertext.
- A key is used to set a particular encryption sequence.
- An algorithm can come in one of many forms.

How the various components fit together

- How a key and algorithm work together with plain or ciphertext to encrypt or decrypt information.
- Plaintext and ciphertext are the products of the decryption and encryption process, respectively.
- Encryption is a complex process.

The role of keys

- A key is used to dictate the specific sequence that will be used to perform a cryptographic operation.
- Keys can be generated at varying lengths.
- Keys can be weak or strong depending on the design of the algorithm.

Algorithms and ciphers

- An algorithm or cipher is used to dictate not only the particular mechanism for how encryption will be performed, but also the types of keys that may be used.
- An algorithm defines a keyspace.
- Algorithms can be based on many different concepts.

Managing keys

- Keys need to be kept secret to ensure security of the system.
- Keys must be changed frequently.
- Longer keys do not translate into stronger security.

CHAPTER 4

Algorithms and Ciphers

We'll Cover

- The purpose of an algorithm

- Symmetric vs. asymmetric cryptography

- Types of algorithms

- One-time pads

In the last few chapters, we have looked at the different components of cryptography as well as some examples and some applications throughout history. What we want to do now is zoom in and focus on the algorithms themselves and how they work as well as the different categories you need to be aware of.

Cryptographic algorithms are sound incredibly complex and may even seem like magic to some, but the reality is that they can be understood at a basic level if you take the time. Algorithms are nothing more than a set of rules, sequences, and processes used to encode and decode messages in a cryptosystem. As you know, they are designed to protect data from prying eyes and make sure it is only accessible by those allowed to view it.

Cryptographic algorithms are used to encrypt data both when it is in "motion" and while it is at "rest," preventing unauthorized parties from using or understanding the data. They do this by using some defined set of rules to transform the information from plaintext to ciphertext (and back, when necessary) upon request of the sending or receiving party. Both encryption and decryption operate based on algorithms.

In this chapter, we focus on several aspects of algorithms, including the two main categories: symmetric and asymmetric. We explore and attempt to demystify these two categories of algorithms as well as compare and contrast the two types. We also explore how the two systems are sometimes used together in hybrid approaches and systems.

You'll also learn that algorithms do a good job at providing security, but they are in no way foolproof. You learn about sub-par algorithms that can and have been cracked or subverted and have yielded sensitive information as a result. We also discuss how testing of algorithms against established standards and peer review make the systems stronger than they might be otherwise.

Your Plan

In this chapter, I want you to focus on the different categories of algorithms (symmetric and asymmetric) and their strengths and weaknesses. This is very important to be able to identify the different categories, what they are good at and what they are not so good at. You should also recognize the different algorithms in each category, the strengths they are available in, and what the implications of the various features of an algorithm are.

When you apply the knowledge in this chapter to areas such as technology, you will recognize what it means to implement DES, 3DES, AES, or ECC (we cover each of these in this chapter).

A High-Level Look at Algorithms

No matter where encryption is implemented—whether it is in a standalone application or built into another piece of software—the process is exactly the same at a high level. All encryption methods (other than hashing, as you will see later) convert plaintext to ciphertext and back via a mathematical formula known as an algorithm. The algorithms use an item known as a key, which is a variable used during the encryption process. It is the key that dictates the "level" of encryption to be performed at that point in time. The tricky parts are the complexity, safety, and security of this key.

As we will investigate in this chapter, there are two very different, but similar, types of encryption: symmetric and asymmetric. Now although it may sound like doublespeak for me to say that they are different but the same, it actually is not. Symmetric inputs a piece of information along with a key to scramble the information into ciphertext. You can then distribute the information to whomever you wish, as long as you provide them the key and the encryption method or algorithm. Simple, right? Well it is, but it isn't (okay, now that is doublespeak... or is it?) because the finer details of each algorithm in the family can be tricky.

Note

Symmetric systems (conventional encryption) are the oldest family of algorithms and methods used by man. Symmetric systems are very simple in design and function, as evidenced by the Caesar cipher (easy) and the Vigenère cipher (not so easy). The symmetric systems are the still used widely today for reasons that you will see later.

Asymmetric (or public-key) methods are more complex and much more secure than their symmetric cousins. Essentially, a public-key system solves many of the downfalls of symmetric systems, but then again it introduces some other problems along the way. You have probably heard of asymmetric systems if you have heard the term *public key* or *private key* because both are integral to the asymmetric system.

Both symmetric and asymmetric systems have their own algorithms used to provide ciphertext. In the symmetric world, data may be broken up into blocks or processed, bit by bit, repeating operations on the data as a stream accordingly. The process involves the use of a key that is encrypted along with the data itself. Asymmetric is a little different in its process, opting to operate on input by running it through a series of mathematical operations before converting everything back into text. Encryption programs can use the same algorithms differently, which is why the recipient needs to use the same application to decode the message that you used to encode it.

A *cryptographic algorithm* or *cipher* is a process designed to convert information in some specific manner. As we explored earlier, a cryptographic algorithm is something that works in combination with a key to convert plaintext or cleartext to ciphertext. The secrecy, security, and safety of the information are dependent on the strength of the algorithm itself and the secrecy of the key.

IMHO

Remember our friend Auguste Kerckhoffs? Just in case, let me restate his principle here again for you because it is important to you to keep in your mind in this chapter. If you recall, the principles Kerckhoffs put forth are used as a set of guidelines in the development of new algorithms or the evaluation of existing ones. Although there are no legal penalties or other issues involved with not following them, they are generally considered to be good advice or guidance. However, do not expect everyone to use Kerckhoffs' advice because organizations such as the National Security Agency (NSA) don't routinely follow these rules.

Kerckhoffs originally put forth six principles as to the proper and careful design of algorithms:

- The system should be, if not theoretically unbreakable, unbreakable in practice.
- The design of a system should not require secrecy, and compromise of the system should not inconvenience the correspondents.

- The key should be memorable without notes and should be easily changeable.
- The cryptograms should be transmittable by telegraph.
- The apparatus or documents should be portable and operable by a single person.
- The system should be easy, neither requiring knowledge of a long list of rules nor involving mental strain.

Although the second point is what is formally known as Kerckhoffs' Principle, we should cover some of the other principles on this list to fill out your knowledge of algorithms:

- **Peer review and collective experience**   Algorithms are complicated, potentially mind numbing, and convoluted in design. As such, it is not a bad idea to have some sort of peer review and other experiences brought into play to ensure that the system is as strong as it could be (or, conversely, to find out where the weaknesses are). In fact, if multiple eyeballs and experiences are brought into play, it is more likely that defects in design are going to be picked up.
- **Taking advantage of experience**   Kerckhoffs allowed for the designers and reviewers of algorithms to leverage the experience of past developers and others research—the idea being that by having access or using previous knowledge, stronger systems may be possible by avoiding old mistakes and pitfalls.
- **Standards**   If you exchange information and ideas, it is much more likely you will leverage standards that make your algorithm more interoperable and understood by others. This also has the benefit of making sure your new algorithm meets established testing standards and reviews. Examples of standards include NIST Computer Security Division, NSA Suite B, OASIS, and ISO.

What Kerckhoffs' principles do not directly cover are the topic of a key. Although the third point does mention that the key should be memorable and changeable, it doesn't mention directly that the strength of the system relies in large part on the secrecy of the key.

In our exploration of algorithms, we are first going to discuss the two main categories used for encryption: symmetric and asymmetric. These two categories are distinctly different in their operation and usage as well as advantages and disadvantages. All the algorithms we will cover in this chapter fit into one of these two categories.

The first algorithm category we discuss happens to be the oldest and most widely used type of system available. In fact, this family of algorithms has been around so long it is sometimes called *classic, traditional,* or *conventional encryption.* The defining characteristic of this type of algorithm is centered on the key, which is used to both encrypt and decrypt. Remember the Caesar cipher? This would be a classic example of a symmetric algorithm.

The second type we talk about is the asymmetric algorithm. The development of this type of algorithm is fairly new because the mathematics and technology needed to carry it out only became available in the 1960s and 1970s. Much like the symmetric systems, asymmetric algorithms have a defining characteristic in their key. However, unlike symmetric systems, asymmetric systems use two keys, where whatever is performed with one key can only be undone with the other.

IMHO

Yes, I am well aware that we could reference a third type of algorithm here, known as a *hashing algorithm* or *message digest function.* We will discuss the intricacies and "magic" of this special type of algorithm in a later chapter, but I wanted to make a reference to it here.

Symmetric Algorithms

Let's get this out of the way upfront before we delve into the finer points later. Symmetric algorithms do some things really well and other things not so well, just like their asymmetric cousin. Modern symmetric algorithms are great at all of the following:

- Preserving confidentiality
- Speed
- Simplicity (relatively speaking, of course)
- Authenticity

So what do symmetric algorithms do poorly? Well I have a list for that too:

- Key management
- Non-repudiation

Your Plan

I will present the details of symmetric algorithms to you and what makes them powerful, unique, and popular as well as the weaknesses that make them a poor choice for some applications. What you should do when reading about this category of algorithm is remember the points that make it special. Think about why you would want to use a symmetric algorithm and why you would not.

So let's first focus on the biggest defining characteristic of symmetric encryption algorithms—the key itself. All algorithms of the symmetric variety use a single key to both encrypt and decrypt, hence the name *symmetric*. This is an easy concept to grasp if you think of a keycard used to open your gym locker (you are going to the gym, aren't you?). The same key used to lock the lock is the same key used to unlock it. A symmetric algorithm works exactly the same way—the same key used to encrypt is the same used to decrypt. Figure 4-1 shows a diagram illustrating the symmetric encryption process.

LINGO
Symmetric systems are sometimes referred to as *secret key cryptography* due to the fact that the key must be kept secret between the sending and receiving parties. In fact, in this type of system the key is sometimes referred to as a *shared secret* for the same reason. We'll talk more about this item later.

Symmetric systems use the same key to encrypt and decrypt information. Once this key is generated according to the rules of the algorithm, it must be distributed to anyone you wish to share encrypted information with.

Figure 4-1   Symmetric algorithm showing the same key encrypting and decrypting

Common Symmetric Algorithms

A myriad of symmetric algorithms are currently available to you; in fact, a Google search will turn up an endless sea of algorithm alphabet soup. I present some of the more common algorithms in the symmetric category for your review; we will talk about some of these throughout our journey:

- **Data Encryption Standard (DES)**   Originally adopted by the U.S. government in 1977, the DES algorithm is still in use today. DES is a 56-bit key algorithm, but the key is too short to be used today for any serious security applications.

- **Triple DES (3DES)**   This algorithm is an extension of the DES algorithm and is, in essence, three times more powerful than the DES algorithm. If you can do the math, you will note that the algorithm uses a 168-bit key.

- **Blowfish**   Blowfish is an algorithm that was designed to be strong, fast, and simple. The algorithm uses a 448-bit key and is designed and optimized for use in today's 32- and 64-bit processors (which its predecessor DES was not). The algorithm was designed by encryption expert Bruce Schneier.

- **International Data Encryption Algorithm (IDEA)**   Designed in Switzerland and made available in 1990, this algorithm is seen in applications such as the Pretty Good Privacy (or PGP) system, which we will discuss much later.

- **MARS**   An AES finalist developed by IBM with key lengths of 128 to 256 bits.

- **RC2**   Originally a trade secret of RSA labs, this algorithm crept into the public space in 1996. The algorithm allows keys between 1 and 2,048 bits. The RC2 key length was traditionally limited to 40 bits in software that was exported to allow for decryption by the U.S. National Security Agency.

- **RC4**   Another algorithm that was originally a trade secret by RSA labs, but was revealed to the public via a newsgroup posting in 1994. The algorithm allows keys between 1 and 2,048 bits.

- **RC5**   Similar to RC2 and RC4, but with a key length that can be defined by the user.

- **RC6**   An AES finalist developed by RSA Labs with key lengths of 128 to 256 bits.

- **Rijndael or Advanced Encryption Standard (AES)**   The successor to DES and chosen by the National Institute of Standards and Technology (NIST) to be the new U.S. encryption standard. The algorithm is very compact and fast, and can use keys that are 128, 192, or 256 bits long.

- **Serpent**   An AES finalist developed by Anderson, Biham, and Knudsen with key lengths of 128 to 256 bits.

- **Twofish**   An AES candidate developed by Bruce Schneier with key lengths of 128 to 256 bits.

Note

RSA is an acronym based on the initials of the last names of the founders of the company: Ron Rivest, Adi Shamir, and Len Adleman. They also have a popular algorithm named after them known as RSA.

Each of these symmetric systems has a complex sequence of operations behind it. The sequence varies, depending on the specific algorithm in use (some of which we will see in a bit when we talk about substitution, transposition, and block and stream ciphers). However, let's first revisit the Caesar cipher and see if we can't look at it in a new way.

IMHO

We can only delve so deep into algorithms before this book becomes a book on mathematics, which it is not. Each algorithm operates differently under the hood, but retains certain characteristics that we are covering here. If you wish to find out how a specific algorithm works, you can find online papers for many of them, such as Twofish, Blowfish, and DES. Although you can start with any of these algorithms, you may want to explore DES first because it is well documented and explained. However, keep in mind that even if the algorithm is well documented, understanding it is still a daunting task for the uninitiated.

As you'll recall, the Caesar cipher is a simplistic cipher that converts plaintext to ciphertext through the use of a keyshift. In the case of the Caesar cipher, the keyshift was three spaces to the right for encryption and three spaces to the left for decryption. Although it was simple and effective at the time, it has since been surpassed or incorporated into other algorithms. The system showed up in other iterations later, such as ROT13, which simply changed the shift to 13 instead of three. No matter how you slice, it the process is still the same—it's just a matter of the shift.

The algorithm is extremely simplistic in design, but for our purposes it is perfect to illustrate how an algorithm works. So let's start our analysis of the cipher by examining the process itself, which is shifting characters three spaces to the right and the same in reverse to decrypt. If we look at ROT13, the shift is 13 instead of three. Therefore, the only difference in these cases is how many characters to shift. We can express this mechanism in the following manner:.

To encrypt the Caesar cipher:

> Plaintext + 3 (right) = ciphertext

To decrypt the Caesar cipher:

> Ciphertext − 3 (left) = plaintext

To encrypt ROT13:

> Plaintext + 13 (right) = ciphertext

To decrypt ROT13:

> Ciphertext − 13 (left) = plaintext

We can simplify the algorithm by making a little adjustment via Algebra class (sorry for bringing up old memories).
To encrypt:

> Plaintext + X (right) = ciphertext

To decrypt:

> Ciphertext − X (left) = plaintext

See what I did there? In the first two examples, where I showed the Caesar and ROT13 ciphers, respectively, I included the keyshift, but in the last example I removed the keyshift and replaced it with a variable. You can simply replace X with any number. (Or can you? We'll see about that in a moment.) Replace X with 3 or 13, and you can describe either one of our ciphers.

If we now look at the Caesar cipher examples of plaintext-to-ciphertext conversion, we should see them in a new light. Here are the examples from the previous chapter:

Plaintext	T	R	I	F	O	R	C	E
Ciphertext	X	U	L	I	R	U	F	H

Plaintext	L	A	S	V	E	G	A	S
Ciphertext	O	D	V	Y	H	J	D	V

Plaintext	G	L	A	D	O	S
Ciphertext	J	O	D	G	R	V

These examples should make even more sense to you now considering the algorithm. (Yes, I know this is very simple and actual algorithms such as DES, 3DES, and AES are much more complex, but this gives us a simple-but-effective example to look at.)

We can write formulas for any of the ciphers we have discussed so far, including the Vigenère cipher, which we could write like this:

Encryption:

$E_{ki}(a): a \rightarrow a + k_i \pmod{26}$

Decryption:

$D_{ki}(a): a \rightarrow a - k_i \pmod{26}$

A little more difficult, huh? Well, it gets much more complex and tricky as we go further. I won't worry about breaking down the Vigenère cipher formula because I am only putting it here for reference to show you that algorithms can quickly get crazy and we could get in way over our heads.

IMHO

Keep in mind that for the most part, you will not ever need to know the mathematics behind an algorithm or cipher—that is rarified air that only a few people need to know about. People who design, analyze, and break cryptosystems absolutely need to know mathematics at this level and typically have letters such as Ph.D. behind their names. If you are intending to design algorithms, you have a lot of work ahead of you. When you look back at my meager and simplistic formula, you will see that there are worlds of difference between the two levels.

So What's the Key?

Let's put the main discussion of algorithms aside for a moment and talk about keys. Keys substantially impact the effectiveness of an algorithm; if the item is compromised or poorly constructed, the whole system can go badly really quick. As we discussed in the previous chapter, keys can be long or short as well as have a myriad of different designs and work that goes into them. We also discussed that there is indeed a trade off between longer keys and shorter keys, with shorter keys potentially offering reduced security and increasingly longer ones offering more security—but only to a point. In this section, we are going to demystify keys a bit more so you understand how length and design have an impact.

Let's first talk about the item that is most discussed and mentioned when describing keys, which is length or bits. In the digital world, a key is stored and represented inside a system as a series of binary digits (or ones and zeros). In the binary world, a digit can only be a one or a zero. So if a key is a single bit in length, there are only two possible keys: 1 or 0. If a key is 2 bits in length, there are now four possible keys, as follows:

00, 01, 10, 11

Therefore, it stands to reason that as we add additional bits, the number of keys continually doubles, as in our example. We don't have to guess at this, though; we can state this relationship as a formula:

Number of keys = 2^x

Here, X is equal to the number of bits, as shown in the following examples:

$256 = 2^8$
$512 = 2^9$

Have I confused you yet? Well, just in case, we can look at the key issue again from a different angle using our old friend the Caesar cipher. Let's examine how many possible keys there are with this system. As you'll recall, the system uses a simple shift, but what does this mean for keys? Let's set some ground rules first to keep everything simple for our exploration. The rules are as follows:

- Use only letters from the English alphabet.

- Majuscule and miniscule letters are the same (in other words, upper and lowercase).

- No special characters are allowed.

- No numbers allowed either (come on, it's letters only).

So with these rules in mind, let's look at the number of keys available with old Julius's system. With the parameters we have set, we have 26 possible keys available because we can move the plaintext letters anywhere from 1 to 26 spaces to generate our ciphertext. Why? Because there's only 26 letters in the alphabet we have chosen. Now keep in mind I could have said 27 keys if I included zero spaces, but I have discarded that as a choice.

IMHO

Also notice that I could have increased the number of keys possible if I said upper- and lowercase letters were different and made some provision to include special characters and numbers.

So, according to our rules we have only 26 possible keys. That's not a lot in our keyspace, and it would make breaking any ciphertext message because as we don't have that many keys to try. In fact, we could probably use common sense in some cases to just guess the key or shift sequence. We obviously want to avoid this ability, which is the Caesar cipher is not be considered strong on its own (same thing with the Vigenère cipher, thanks to modern technology).

In Actual Practice

One of the symmetric algorithms mentioned earlier, known as AES, allows keys up to 256 bits. If you were to use our formula to figure out the number of available keys for 256, you would see that a ton of keys are available in the keyspace. To put this in some perspective, it would be like saying each grain of sand on the beaches of the Hawaiian islands represents a key (definitely a huge number and hard to get our heads around). In terms of computing power, let's say we have a computer that can process a billion, billion keys per second. If we had access to this amount of computing power, it would still take around 3×1,051 years to exhaust the 256-bit keyspace.

Trust me, that's a large number (and a long time to wait).

So let's talk about what we are implying by saying that we could try every key in the keyspace (or what is commonly known as a brute-force attack). Although not always considered a true way of cracking a message, it is nonetheless effective and is a process that will always work. Essentially, *brute forcing* means we try every possible key until we find one that works in our particular case. Keep in mind that brute forcing will always work because we are trying every key until we find the one that works; however, we need to ask ourselves, "Will we find it in enough time for the information to be useful?" Think of it this way, too: If you were a World War II U-boat captain and were relying on breaking a coded message to make a decision, but it would take a 100 years to find the right key, it wouldn't matter, would it?

In Actual Practice

So how long is too long? Well, its all relative to how much power you think an overly curious party will have and how long you think the information needs to be kept secret. If an attacker didn't have the computing horsepower, perhaps a 40- or 56-bit key would be enough. However, if an attacker has more computing power (such as what a government has), then longer keys would be better. Making things even more interesting is *distributed computing,* where large numbers of computers are linked together to accomplish a task, essentially combining their computing power.

Think about this: If you possessed technology that allowed you to search a million keys per second, you could try all 40-bit keys in only 13 days.

Fortunately, based on what we have already explored, we can use longer keys if the algorithm allows it. We also know that every single bit that is added to a key increases the number of keys by doubling them, meaning that it will take even more resources to find the correct one.

If we look at DES, one of our other encryption schemes, we can see what the impact of a shorter key can be. In the case of DES, the key is only 56 bits long, which results in much fewer keys than a 128-bit key or a 256-bit key. In the case of the 56-bit key, that the algorithm was weaker than it needed to be and resulted in the algorithm being replaced later (although not for some time later). You can do the math once again using the formula from earlier to see the difference in the number of keys between 56 and 128 or 256.

IMHO

An interesting footnote to the story of DES is the story of NSA involvement. At the time DES was developed by IBM, the NSA got involved during the incubation of the algorithm and did some tweaking to the system. Several comments or rumors have been made over the years about this involvement, including the implication that the NSA intentionally weakened the algorithm so they could decipher messages enciphered with the system. We are not going to get into tinfoil-hat-wearing rumors here, but I should note that later analysis showed the NSA strengthened the algorithm.

We should also talk about something else relating to keys that's separate from breaking the system (namely, legal requirements). Up until the 1990s, software vendors and others were not allowed to export cryptosystems with keys longer than 40 bits out of the United States, thus severely crippling products for overseas usage. These controls have since been relaxed, but there still exist certain restrictions on the export of cryptosystems.

In Actual Practice

In the United States, exporting cryptosystems with keys over the 40-bit length restriction (when this restriction was still in effect) was treated the same as exporting weapons systems. In fact, exporting systems in violation of this limit could have landed you in extremely hot water with the U.S. State Department.

Don't Forget Your Key

Ever left a key under the doormat at your house? (If you have, please e-mail me your home addresses and stock up on some good snacks.) If you have left a key under your doormat, you have a problem, which is key management related. Think about it: When you put that key under your mat, you are taking a leap of faith that no one will find it because if they do they will be able to gain access to your house. In encryption, we have the same problem, at least with symmetric systems—namely, how do we keep the key out of the wrong hands? Do we send the key along with the encrypted data? Well, that would be the same as locking the front door to your house and then hanging the key on the door handle—not very bright. We have to find a way to get the key to someone while at the same time protecting it from falling into the wrong hands. In a physical example such as this, common sense tells us we could just meet with our authorized partner and give them the key. However, in the nontangible digital world, key management and transfer is a bit more challenging.

Do we have a way to protect our keys? Yes, the common method involves sending the keys through what is known as "out-of-band" methods. Essentially, it means getting the key to someone using an alternate method to the way you send them the data.

LINGO
Out of band means that the key is sent to its intended recipient using an alternate transmission method—for example, sending someone a key via a secure courier while sending the encrypted data over e-mail.

Don't Cross the Streams, You Block... Head

Now we need to talk about how algorithms differ in their design—that's right, it's time to talk about blocks and streams. Both are extremely important to understand and explore, so we shall do so here to round out our discussion.

First, we can play with some blocks (block ciphers, that is) to see what we can find out about this process. Essentially, block ciphers take whatever plaintext is put into them and break it into pieces calls *blocks* (imagine that). The algorithm being used then operates on each of these blocks, one at a time, until all the plaintext is converted. This is sort of like an assembly line, where each piece is worked on in sequence. So how much is put in a block? Well, that depends on the algorithm's own specific design. Some algorithms will put 64 bits of data in a block, whereas others will use larger or smaller sizes (keep in mind the sizes are built into the design and cannot be changed). So what happens if you have a bunch of blocks that are completely full, but you don't have enough data to completely fill the last one? Well, the algorithm will fill the space with padding or extra bits that are discarded later during the decryption process.

LINGO
A **block cipher** is a particular flavor or type of symmetric algorithm that changes plaintext to ciphertext by operating on fixed-length blocks of plaintext. When this process is undertaken, plaintext is converted in blocks into ciphertext of the exact same size. The encryption process takes places using a user-supplied key that is applied to the process. The whole process can be reversed by using the same key and the same algorithm. The block size is defined by the algorithm, but in many cases it is set at 64 bits. However, as newer technology has become available, larger block sizes in the 128-bit range have started to appear.

So what is a block? A block can be described as a box, bucket, or other vessel that holds a certain amount of something (specifically a set of characters or bits, in our case). Most of the time the block size is 64 bits, but this could change depending on the algorithm. If the bits that are put into the algorithm are not equally divisible by the block size of the algorithm, extra characters or bits are added to complete the division with no remainder. Here is an example of how a block cipher would break some plaintext into blocks:

Plaintext	Oops I missed my due date for this chapter again
Modified plaintext	oopsimissedmyduedateforthischapteragain
Plaintext blocks	oops imis sedm ydue date fort hisc hapt erag inxe

Note how two extra characters were added to the end of the message to make a full 4-bit block? This is what padding would look like conceptually, but it is accurate as to how the process works.

Try, just for fun, to break the following messages into equal-sized blocks, as indicated. Remember that each block must be the same size; to make things easier I have defined a block size for each of the following three messages and I want you to come up with the modified plaintext and plaintext blocks.

Convert to Eight-Character Blocks	
Plaintext	If I am late with another chapter my editor is going to beat me
Modified plaintext	
Plaintext blocks	

Convert to Six-Character Blocks	
Plaintext	I always seem to have bad luck with redheads
Modified plaintext	
Plaintext blocks	

Convert to Four-Character Blocks	
Plaintext	Steven, Tony and Jennifer are keeping a secret
Modified plaintext	
Plaintext blocks	

We can also visualize block ciphers by looking at the simple diagram shown in Figure 4-2.

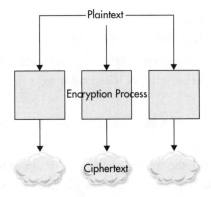

Figure 4-2 The block cipher encryption process showing plaintext getting split into equal-size blocks.

There are different modes of operation (or different ways a block cipher can operate) that make the process as depicted the figure very basic. Although I don't want to get into the specifics here, I do feel that I should at least mention the different modes:

- Iterated block cipher
- Electronic code book
- Cipher block chaining
- Cipher feedback
- Output feedback

Don't worry too much about these different modes at this point, but do know that each one processes the block data and applies the encryption key just a little bit differently. Although each of these modes offers certain advantages (and has disadvantages) over the others, just know that they are all forms of block ciphers and break the input into pieces as they enter the algorithm.

So why do we care about block ciphers anyway? Why am I making you know this stuff? Because block ciphers have some properties worth knowing:

- Block ciphers can require more memory than stream ciphers (more on this in a moment).
- Block ciphers are easier to implement in software and hardware.
- Block ciphers are very susceptible to corruption of data in transit.
- Block ciphers can provide integrity protection in addition to confidentiality.
- Block ciphers are useful when the amount of data is known ahead of time.

Here are some common examples of block ciphers:

- **DES**   DES has a block size of 64 bits and a key size of 56 bits. After DES, 64-bit blocks became common in block cipher designs.
- **3DES**   Triple DES triple-encrypts each block with either two independent keys (a 112-bit key and 80-bit security) or independent keys (a 168-bit key and 112-bit security).
- **IDEA**   IDEA uses 64-bit blocks and a 128-bit key. This algorithm was one of many intended to replace DES.
- **RC5**   Debuting in 1994, this a block cipher was designed by Ronald Rivest. This cipher offers a variable block size (32, 64, or 128 bits) and key size (0 to 2,040 bits).

- **AES**   Originally adopted by the United States in 2001, this algorithm is a block cipher that has a coded block size of 128 bits and key sizes of 128, 192, or 256 bits.

- **Blowfish**   This block cipher debuted in 1993. Blowfish utilizes 64-bit block sizes and has a variable key size that can go from 1 to 448 bits. This algorithm was seen as an alternative to DES and has since been included in many products. Also, Blowfish is one of just a few algorithms released freely into the public domain without patents of any kind.

Note

Many more block ciphers are available than those listed here.

So with block ciphers out of the way, let's now talk about stream ciphers—the other method in which symmetric ciphers can operate. A stream cipher is another flavor of symmetric encryption algorithm. On average, stream ciphers tend to be much faster than block ciphers (but not always—this is a design factor). Whereas block ciphers work on chunks of data, stream ciphers work specifically on each individual bit, converting each from plaintext to ciphertext in turn. With a stream cipher, the encryption of smaller units means that the resulting ciphertext will vary, thus offering less potential to crack a code. Let's take a closer look.

Because stream ciphers encrypt data at the bit level (and we are talking computers now), the data has to first be in binary form. So let's assume our data has already been converted to binary form, which will be represented by the following binary string:

    1001101111010000111001010000110111101

Stream ciphers encrypt their data by utilizing a special construct known as a *keystream generator.* This generator (at least for our purposes) only spits out a stream of 1's and 0's to be used during the encryption process. We can make the idea of keystreams a little simpler by using the following example. For this example, I have chosen the plaintext Samus. The process in this matrix is simple to follow. Here are the steps:

1. Convert plaintext to numbers.

2. Select a keystream. (In this case, I have chosen a word that works for our example, but the keystream generator would put out something random.)

3. Convert the keystream to numbers.

4. Add the plaintext numbers and ciphertext numbers.

5. Convert the numbers to something between 1 to 26 by subtracting 26 from any number over 26. This is done because we can't convert numbers such as 27 and 0 to a real letter in the alphabet, in this example.

6. Convert the ciphertext numbers back to text.

Plaintext	S	A	M	U	S
Plaintext as numbers	19	1	13	21	19
Keystream	T	I	G	E	R
Keystream as numbers	20	9	7	5	18
Ciphertext as numbers	39	10	20	26	37
Ciphertext as numbers 1–26	13	10	20	26	11
Ciphertext as text	M	J	T	Z	K

So how do we use this info? First, we know the computer works in binary, so we would be converting the message to binary. Once we're done with this, we use a process known as *exclusive OR* (or XOR). Let's cut through the funny names and look at an example. An exclusive OR compares two bits. If exactly one of the bits is a 1, then the exclusive OR returns a 1. If both bits are 1 or both bits are 0, then the exclusive OR returns a 0.

Plaintext	1001101111010000111001010001101111101
Keystream	1010101010101010101010101010101010101
Ciphertext	0011000101110100100111110110001010111

Need to reverse the process? Simple: Just get the keystream and XOR it with the ciphertext, like so:

Ciphertext	0011000101110100100111110110001010111
Keystream	1010101010101010101010101010101010101
Plaintext	1001101111010000111001010001101111101

Easy, right? But do you see the problem here? It is easily broken because if we get any two of the items (ciphertext, plaintext, and keystream), we can XOR them together to get the remaining one. Here's an example:

Plaintext	1001101111010000111001010001101111101
Ciphertext	0011000101110100100111110110001010111
Keystream	1010101010101010101010101010101010101

We can tighten up the stream cipher a bit by introducing a key and using it to modify what comes out of the keystream generator. We'll modify the bits a little more, making the stream cipher tougher to obtain. Without getting into the mechanics, just know that the key will be input to the keystream generator, thus altering the output every time new key is used. Think of this as guessing what number will come up in the lottery or when playing keno. The likelihood of a set of numbers appearing twice in a row is statistically slim.

IMHO

Also note that the key we have used here has what is known as a *short period*. Essentially the period is short and repeats every two digits, which are easy to detect. The more secure method of creating a keystream is to have one with a much longer period, where the period does not repeat as often. This is why we would use a different key each time to generate a new keystream because this would randomize the key and change the period.

It is important to remember that you need to try to avoid predictable or discernible patterns wherever and whenever possible to avoid detection and discourage code breaking.

One-Time Pad

One type of stream cipher I should mention here is known as the one-time pad. This system uses a key that is generated, used once, and then discarded. That means it is used to encrypt and decrypt one message before it is disposed of. Yes, the key is XOR'd with the plaintext to create ciphertext exactly like we explored previously.

One-time pads are sometimes used when two parties start in one physical location and exchange the key and then use it once later. The method was used extensively in World War II to exchange secure messages between the ship and the shore. Essentially, the keys were generated at headquarters and then copies were numbered and given to each party. Different parties would encrypt using a specific key and then transmit the message to another party, telling them the number of the key they used. The receiving party would then decrypt the message, at which time the key was destroyed by both parties.

Which Is Better, Getting Hit with a Block or Drowning in a Stream?

So now that you know your options, the question may be going through your head as to which method is better. There really isn't a straightforward answer because it all comes down to what you are looking to do with the algorithm.

Typically, like most things in life, they both have their strong points and weak points. Stream ciphers typically are ideal for situations where the amount of data is unknown. However, there are potential problems with this situation because the keys in stream ciphers are regenerated as each is used up (a new keystream is generated as needed based on data requirements). Because the key has to be regenerated to avoid repeated patterns, as well as for other reasons, performance can be impeded to a degree. Block ciphers, by design, tend to offer a much larger number of keys to use, meaning that it is less likely you would get the same key all that often, if at all.

Block ciphers tend to be slower than stream ciphers, but nonetheless are more commonly used. Some of the more popular members of the symmetric family—DES, 3DES and AES—are block ciphers and present in many modern applications. Because block ciphers are common, they tend to be used in many applications due to the need to have interoperability with other applications that use encryption; hence, its advantageous for vendors (and you) to use this type.

It is best for you to remember, though, that neither one is better than the other. This isn't a popularity contest; rather it's a question of what you will use the algorithm for.

Asymmetric/Public-Key Cryptography

So with symmetric or traditional cryptography out of the way, we now need to talk about asymmetric encryption. As we have just explored, in traditional cryptographic systems the same key is used by the sender and receiver to both encrypt and decrypt. This key is kept secret. It is for this reason that traditional systems are sometimes also known as *secret key systems,* to emphasize this point. You have seen that a huge part of the challenge of these systems is how to get the key from sender to receiver without another party getting a hold of the key. If you happen to be in a different location than your intended recipient, even more challenges become evident because you must now figure out a way to get the key to that other party over potentially insecure systems. This problem of key management has proven to be a huge problem in otherwise decent symmetric systems.

> **LINGO**
> **Key management** refers to the process of safeguarding and distributing keys in a cryptographic system. The term refers to how we keep the keys away from other parties as well as how to get these keys into the hands of authorized parties.

Key management is a huge problem in symmetric systems, but we just didn't discuss how bad it can get. Consider what would happen in a symmetric system if you needed to assign a unique key to every person in a group (let's say of 10 people). Then consider that to decrypt a message from any one person, we would need to have a copy of their key. The actual formula for this situation looks like the following:

N(N–1)/2 = keys
Where N represents the number of parties communicating

Let's use this formula to figure out how many keys we would need for our 10-person group. If we run the number 10 through the formula, we find that it would take 45 keys to be generated. If we bump up the number to 100, we now need to generate 4,950 keys. If we have 5,000 people who need keys in a symmetric system, the number skyrockets to 12,497,500 keys that need to be generated.

Kinda crazy, huh? Seem unmanageable? You can now see how the key problem quickly becomes ridiculous. So we have to have a better way, right?

In order to solve this problem, two scientists by the name of Whitfield Diffie and Martin Hellman formally introduced the concept of public-key cryptography way back in 1976. These systems change the paradigm introduced by symmetric systems by using two keys (or a key pair)

LINGO
Public and **private keys** are keys that are generated when a user or party joins a system that uses an asymmetric algorithm.

instead of the one key used in a symmetric system. The keys in these types of systems are typically referred to as *private* and *public keys.* What is performed with one key is only reversible by the other.

So why call the keys "public" and "private"? Simply put, it is a question of distribution. The public key is published someplace where those who need it can get a hold of it and the private key is held by the person it was originally issued to and kept secret. With this key distribution method, keys do not have to be transmitted to the people who need them; rather they are given out on demand. Of course, we can't leave it at that because the keys must be associated to the people they are assigned to in order to be trusted and authentic. How we do this association is something that comes later in the book, so let's just concentrate on the algorithms at this point.

IMHO
We will be talking about Public Key Infrastructure (PKI) later in this book, which is how the association and authentication take place.

What you should be asking right now is, how does the two-key system work? First of all, the two keys are linked mathematically to one another, which is an important detail. Although in theory it may be possible to derive a private key from the public key, we can conquer this problem by engineering a system in such a way that deriving one key from another is difficult to impossible. This can be done in a number of ways, but one of the more common ways is to rely on a complex mathematical equation that is easy to perform and not on a number. To help us visualize this, consider the problem of multiplying three or four 18-digit prime numbers—easy, right? Now try taking that

> **LINGO**
> **Public-key cryptosystems** are great examples of what is known as a *zero knowledge proof*. This is a fancy way of saying that you have a means of verifying something is true without having direct knowledge. Consider this: You can verify someone has a private key by using the correct public key to reverse whatever they have done with the private key. Because both keys are mathematically related, one key can reverse anything done with the other while at the same time not requiring the private key to be revealed.

final number and telling me which three or four prime numbers I used—not so easy, huh? One of the well-known cryptosystems, called RSA, uses a method similar to this idea.

So this system may seem ideal considering that we no longer have to worry about key distribution. However, we must look at something else related to the keys. Asymmetric systems can easily have longer keys to achieve the same level of security that is provided in a symmetric system. Additionally, because of the way the algorithms work, asymmetric systems can be at least a factor of 1,000 times slower than symmetric systems. It is for this reason specifically that asymmetric is used where small amounts of data are present and not where large or bulk data is expected.

So what are the common asymmetric algorithms?

- **RSA**   One of the more common and best known algorithms. It's one of the few algorithms designed to do both key generation and encryption. Most asymmetric algorithms only perform key generation. The few that do both either are in marginal use or are in disuse altogether.

- **Diffie-Hellman**   An algorithm that performs a form of key management and does not actually perform encryption itself. It allows two parties that have no prior relationship to exchange keys that may be used to encrypt data safely and securely.

- **Elliptical Curve Cryptography (ECC)**   This algorithm functions by computing intersections of curved lines and intersecting lines on a graph. It has the advantage of using little in the way of processing power and other resources on a system. It has seen widespread use in data storage systems and mobile devices.

- **Digital Signature Algorithm (DSA)**   This algorithm is similar to the one used by the Elgamal signature algorithm.

- **Elgamal**   This is an asymmetric key encryption algorithm for public-key cryptography.

The asymmetric cryptosystem is the most widely used system today; the two-key systems have solved the biggest problem with symmetric systems, which is the issue with key management. In this system, each user has two keys: a public key and a private key. The public key is published and available to any party that needs to have access to it for verifying the action performed with the private key.

The biggest advantage of this system can be said to be the fact two parties never have to meet in person or procure some other means to exchange keys. In fact, in this system you don't need to know the other person personally.

However, it is also worth noting the biggest drawback with asymmetric systems is the overwhelming dependence on technology. Without a powerful computer system on hand, it becomes nearly impossible to perform asymmetric encryption in a reasonable amount of time.

We've Covered

The purpose of an algorithm

- An algorithm is used to define the process of encryption and decryption.
- Algorithms dictate how information is transformed.
- Algorithms define the process of encryption and decryption.

Symmetric vs. asymmetric cryptography

- Symmetric systems used the same key to encrypt and decrypt.
- Asymmetric systems used public and private keys.
- Symmetric systems are faster than asymmetric systems.

Types of algorithms

- Algorithms are either symmetric or asymmetric.
- Algorithms are designed to use block or stream methods.
- Algorithms are a formula designed to perform the conversion or transformation of data from one format to another.

One-time pads

- One-time pads use their keys once.
- Keys must never be reused in a one-time pad system.
- One-time pads are considered the only unbreakable encryption mechanism.
- One-time pads are a type of stream cipher.

CHAPTER 5

Hashing and Message Digests

We'll Cover

- Fundamentals of hashing

- Purpose of hashing

- Applications of hashing

- Types of hashing algorithms

- Key concepts in hashing

- Key terms and terminology

In the previous chapter, we discussed algorithms and ciphers. We discussed how asymmetric and symmetric algorithms work, as well as how the components known as ciphers work. However, what we covered in the previous chapter is only one part of the world of cryptography, as you can imagine. In this chapter, we will move into a different area of cryptography known as hashing. Hashing is a unique and intriguing area of cryptography and is decidedly different from encryption algorithms.

We have already spoken about the conversion of plaintext into ciphertext and back again. Hashing works with plaintext and ciphertext as well, but in a different way. Hashes are known in some circles as *message digest functions* or *one-way functions* due to their unique and seemingly peculiar characteristic of being both compressed and difficult to reverse. The benefit of this method for us is that, unlike with the encryption methods from before, we can detect changes of any item that has been hashed. This is due to the hashed value being engineered in such a way that any change, no matter how minor, can be detected by a well-designed algorithm. What you must remember when reading this chapter is that hashing is not intended to create encrypted data. In fact, you must understand that hashing not only validates data, but also authenticates data as well. Remember the *I* in CIA? Hashes are an integral (no pun intended) part of integrity. As a refresher, *integrity* involves the ability to know when your data is modified by unwanted parties.

Note

Hashing should not be confused with the previous forms of encryption we discussed. It definitely shares similarities, but also has many differences. Remember that encryption is designed to scramble data so that it is not readable by anyone who does not have the proper key to reverse the process. Hashing produces a digest of the plaintext information while leaving the plaintext intact and readable. This is a big difference that you will need to remember to properly understand hashing.

Hashing also has seen usage outside of the security industry and is familiar to computer programmers and database administrators. Its ability to uniquely identify data has proven invaluable to speeding up searches in applications and databases. This is a topic we'll dig into further.

This type of function varies in a number of ways from the previous systems we discussed. It doesn't process information the same way or produce a reversible result. Whereas we previously had to have a key, plaintext, and an algorithm to produce output of any size, the same is not true here. Hashing takes any size data and digests it into a compressed format that is unique and is consistently of the same length. Unlike previous encryption, this process is not intended or designed to be reversible.

Note

Hashes can be used to provide a digital thumbprint of a file, meaning that a unique value can identify a file version or state at any point in time. Hash functions are very commonly used to protect passwords as well as determine versions of files, where such a facility is necessary.

You will notice that hashing addresses different problems and situations than what the techniques in the previous chapter did. In the previous chapter, our intention was to encrypt data in such as way that an authorized party who had the proper instructions could reverse the process. In other words, it was intended that we could go from plaintext to ciphertext and from ciphertext back to plaintext with the right key and algorithm on hand. Hashing does not do this, nor was it ever designed to do so. Hashing was not designed to preserve the confidentiality of information, and it does not keep the information secret. So what does it do? It gives us a way to preserve the integrity of data and ensure that what we receive from a sender is what they intended us to have. Hashing is classic integrity at work. It gives us a usable mechanism to undeniably verify the integrity of virtually any data.

Note

Hashing generates hashes, but these hashes can also go by other names, like I sometimes do (for example, I use the name Mark Cosby when I am sneaking into the gym without permission). In the case of hashing, the end product is sometimes called a *message digest* or simply *digest*. Don't let this name change fool you or catch you off guard. It may help to take the word "digest" in its literal sense. In other words, the meaning behind digest is, well, to digest something. When you eat a sandwich it gets digested, right? Well, hashes work in much the same fashion. It takes the original message (sandwich) and digests it into a measurable output (yuck!). You fill in the blank on this analogy, but you get the point. The "digest" is the digested output of the hash function. Oh, and by the way, in our analogy it should be fairly obvious that once a sandwich is digested, there's no way we're getting the sandwich back to its original state!

Additionally, unlike encryption mechanisms we have seen before, hashing a piece of information is not intended to be reversed and in fact is intended to be mathematically infeasible to reverse (if not impossible). What do I mean by mathematically infeasible? To answer that, let's look at a hypothetical situation. Suppose I have selected an 18-digit prime number. Then I select two more, so I now have three total. I take these three numbers and multiply them together and give you a final result. Once I give you the final result, I ask you (who does not have any knowledge of what the original three numbers were) to reverse the process. Who knows, for some uber-smart math whiz out there this may be easy, but for us mere mortals... whew, no way. I'm going back to playing video games or taking on a simple challenge like swimming from Sacramento to Hawaii.

Confused? Don't be. We've gotten this far and we're just getting started, so let's kick it up a notch and talk about hashing.

Your Plan

When reviewing this chapter, consider hashing alongside our earlier encryption discussions. Think about what encryption offers to a company and to an individual. Then compare and contrast what it offers with what hashing offers. When you compare the two and what they offer, you will get a much better understanding of why you would use one over the other. In fact, comparing the two will allow you to better understand why we combine encryption and hashing to form unique solutions such as digital signatures (which is a topic for later). And don't forget, when you are comparing and contrasting these two fundamental processes, remember to keep the CIA triad in mind. Encryption is a confidentiality function, and hashing is an integrity function.

Fundamentals of Hashing

Simply put, hashing is one-way encryption. Sounds odd, doesn't it? We are introducing a form of encryption that creates a scrambled output that cannot be reversed—or at least cannot be reversed easily. In fact, the process of hashing takes plaintext and transforms it into ciphertext, but does this in such a way that it is not intended to be decrypted. The process outputs what is known as a *hash, hash value,* or *message digest.*

So hashing is designed to be a one-way process and, as such, is sometimes known as a *one-way function* and is commonly used to validate the integrity of information. A hash function generates a fixed-length value that is always the same length no matter how large or small the data entering the process or algorithm is. Additionally, the resulting output, as we already discussed, is not intended to be reversible. It should (the fixed-length value, of course) be unique for every different input that enters the process. It is due to this unique property and behavior that hashes are used to detect the changes that may happen in data of any type.

> **LINGO**
> A **hash, hash value,** or **message digest** is a value that is output as a result of plaintext or ciphertext being fed into a hashing algorithm. The value is of a fixed length and will always be of a certain length no matter what is input into the algorithm. Although the data input can and will vary wildly in length, the resulting output has its length fixed by the design of the algorithm itself.

We can look at hashing as a one-way function that is responsible for verifying the integrity of information. In technical terms, it is said that a hashing function is responsible for generating a fixed-length value that is relatively easy to compute in one direction, but nearly impossible to reverse. The output value (or hash) is designed to be difficult to reverse; it is also unique and will indeed be so for any and all information that is fed into the hashing algorithm (yes, they can be the same for two different inputs, but that is story yet to come). We care about hashing because it gives us the ability to easily detect changes in information. Anything that is hashed and then changed, even minutely, will result in an entirely different hash from the original. Hashed values are the result of information being compressed into the fixed-length value. A one-way hash function is also sometimes referred to as a *one-time cipher key* or a *thumbprint*. Figure 5-1 shows a digital certificate with both an MD5 and SHA-1 fingerprint.

> **LINGO**
> "A rose by any other name" as the saying goes. In this case, a **hash** may also be known as a *thumbprint* or *digital thumbprint*. This name may sound like a grand conspiracy to confuse the heck out of you, but it isn't (and in fact it makes sense). Consider the fact that fingerprints are highly unique to the individual, just as hashes are designed to be to the data that generates them. As such, someone along the way said that a thumbprint is a good way to track the state and current version of a file.

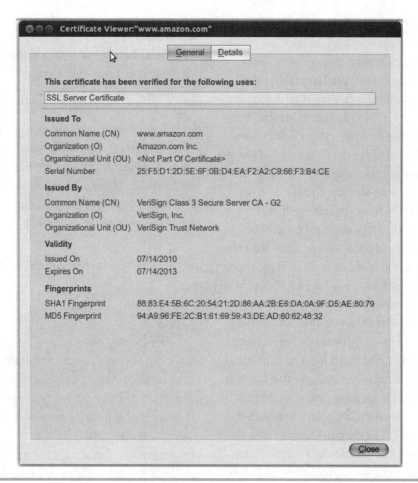

Figure 5-1   Amazon.com's digital certificate with both an SHA-1 and MD5 fingerprint included

The following are some examples of hashing using an algorithm known as MD5. Notice how each hash or digest derived is different given even the slightest change in the input sentence:

- There is a ball in the blue bo | md5sum
  e41a323bdf20eadafd3f0e4f72055d36

- There is a ball in the blue box | md5sum
  7a0da864a41fd0200ae0ae97afd3279d

- There is a ball in the blue box | md5sum
  2db1ff7a70245309e9f2165c6c34999d

- There is a ball in the blue box.. | md5sum
  86c524497a99824897ccf2cd74ede50f

In Actual Practice

Hashes have proven invaluable in many areas, including the verification of updates for software packages. Many software products, such as antivirus applications, use hashing to verify an update. Essentially, the update is created by the manufacturer and then hashed. Both the hash and the update package are placed on a website for download. A visitor can simply download both and rerun the hashing algorithm; if both match, the file is unchanged. However, if they do not match, there is a problem (perhaps corruption or deliberate alteration of the original for reasons unknown).

So what would you use a message digest for? Well, there are a great number of places that the technique is used—some of which will explore here, others will be explored later. Here are few of the places hashing and message digests are used:

- **Digital signatures**   These are an essential part of the creation of digital signatures, as you will see in a later chapter.

- **Digital certificates**   Digital certificates are dependent on the existence of hashing as a core feature. We will explore this subject later in the book.

- **Verifying downloaded software**   Hashing allows you to download a piece of software (such as an ISO file for Linux), device driver, or software update and have confidence that it is in the same state that the author intended it to be in.

Note

Hashes, when used to verify software downloads or files, are frequently known as *checksums*. Look at a Linux download site for Ubuntu or Debian, and you will notice that in many cases, the download has a checksum somewhere next to its description. This allows the party who is downloading the file to run whatever hashing algorithm the creator of the file has used against the file to verify that the download was not corrupted, and to see if they got the correct download.

- **Verifying e-mails**   Hashing can allow for the validation of e-mails and other messages so that you have proof that they came unaltered from the original owner.

- **Storage of passwords**   Many operating systems rely on hashing to verify stored passwords instead of storing the passwords themselves.

- **Verification of communications**   Data that is transmitted over a network can include hashing functions to ensure that it has not been altered either accidentally or maliciously during transit.

- **Forensics**   In the world of forensics, you must be able to prove that the evidence you have collected is authentic and has not changed since it was collected from the crime scene. This can be done through careful hashing of the original files and then presenting the hashes in court or other venues later (obviously there is much more to it than is mentioned here).

- **Intrusion detection**   Systems known as host-based intrusion detection systems (HIDS) use hashing to detect changes in files. In essence, the software will hash files when installed and at different times after that when authorized changes are made to the system (such as software updates or the installation of new software). If a change is made without authorization, the system can detect this by comparing the hashes, thus preventing key files from being altered unknowingly.

- **Searches**   Hashes have played an instrumental role for a long time in database searches, increasing the performance of these applications dramatically. Due to their ability to generate a unique value for each input, hashes are used to speed searches for data inside a database. A computer can simply search through hashes instead of looking for the individual pieces of data themselves.

In Actual Practice

Hashes are not only used in computer applications, but in other places as well that you might not even think of offhand. One example is databases, where the values stored in each record of the database are hashed in some manner. Because each hash is unique and all are of a fixed length, they can be searched very easily and quite rapidly to locate any particular record within the database itself. Another use for this technique is to find duplicate files or datasets. Again, because each hash is unique to the data or information it was generated from, two identical inputs would produce the same output, meaning that a duplicate piece of data has been located.

A Closer Look

Let's take a close look at hashing by way of an example. As I said previously, hashing functions are also known as *message digests.* They are designed to take any input of any length and convert it into a unique fixed-length value. Although the process is not designed to be reversible, it does provide integrity-checking features that we do not have in other forms in quite the same way. Due largely to the way message digests function, an item of plaintext can be hashed, then altered, then hashed again, and two different unique values will be rendered, indicating a change has been made.

To illustrate a hash in action, let's look at some hashes made with what is known as the MD5 hashing algorithm:

```
MD5("Wisdom, Power, Courage") =
4F8F5CB531E3D49A61CF417CD133792CCFA501FD8DA53EE368FED20E5FE0248C

MD5("Courage, Power, Wisdom") =
3CCF8252D8BBB258460D9AA999C06EE38E67CB546CFFCF48E91F700F6FC7C183

MD5("Power, Courage, Wisdom") =
B97DE512E91E3828B40D2B0FDCE9CEB3C4A71F9BEA8D88E75C4FA854DF36725F
```

Note that even though I have hashed the same three words each time, only changing their order, the hashes are still radically different from one another. In fact, with the words being rearranged, you may think that the hashes would be only somewhat different. Essentially, you might expect that the hash is in thirds (one third representing each word) and that these thirds would only be rearranged and the characters they were hashed into would be the same. However, this is not the case either.

Enough talk for right now. Let's create some hashes and see how they change. For this exercise, you will need to download a copy of WinMD5 or an MD5 hash generator for your operating system.

Once you have downloaded and installed the application, perform the following steps:

1. Use a text editor such as Microsoft Word or Notepad and enter in a few lines of text.

2. Save the file.

3. Using the MD5 hash generator, browse to the file and perform a hash against it.

4. Note the hash sequence generated.

5. Using the same text editor, reopen the original text file and change a character or two.

6. Save the file.

7. Once again, using the MD5 hash generator, browse to the file and perform a hash against it.

8. Note the new hash sequence that is generated.

If you perform these steps, you will notice that even with the smallest of changes to the text file you created, the hash changes dramatically.

Figure 5-2 shows a series of hashes that were generated from a JPG file using a Linux application known as GtkHash. Note that my example also shows a hash from MD5 as well as SHA-1 and SHA-256.

IMHO

I would recommend that for further study and experimenting, you try the same steps with other types of files such as images. If you are good with an image editor such as Photoshop, Paint, or GIMP, grab an image, any image, and make a copy of it. Take that copy and make alterations to it, such as resizing it or drawing a line on it, and then save the alterations. Next, use your hashing program to hash both versions and observe that once again the resulting hashes are quite different.

In theory, you could also try the same process on executable files on your computer before and after they are patched to see that they are indeed different, even though they look the same on the outside.

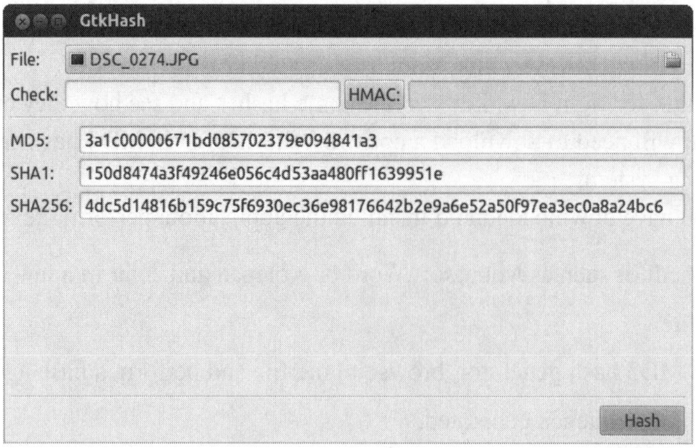

Figure 5-2 Examples of hashes generated from a file

Hashing Algorithms

Let's now take a look at a hashing algorithm itself and how see it functions. First, what types of hashing algorithms are there? Well, there are several, with some seeing more usage than others.

In Actual Practice

MD5 is one of the most widely used hashing algorithms and can in fact be found in use in many applications, including digital signatures. MD5 is also used in network communications as well as forensic investigations.

In fact, MD5 is one of the algorithms commonly used in what are known as *host-based intrusion detection systems,* or *HIDS.* This type of software is designed to do many things, all intended to detect unmonitored or unexpected behavior on a given computer system. One of the functions they typically include is the ability to detect changes in files on a computer that may indicate a file has been altered, or tampered with, in some way. How do they do this? You should know this by now. Hashing files in their original state and then doing the same thing later should show that a file is either the same or has been altered. If the hashes are different, the file has been altered and the question then becomes, how did it get that way? That's a question you have to answer at that point.

Remember earlier when I stated that you could hash executable files? This is exactly the type of thing an HIDS does.

The following is a list of some of the hashing algorithms currently in use:

- **Message Digest 2 (MD2)** A one-way hash function used in the privacy-enhanced mail (PEM) protocols along with MD5.

- **Message Digest 4 (MD4)** A one-way hash function used for PGP and other systems. No longer in use. It has been replaced for all intents and purposes by MD5.

- **Message Digest 5 (MD5)** An improved and redesigned version of MD4, producing a 128-bit hash. MD5 is still extremely popular in many circles, but is being phased out (or at least being considered for phasing out) due to some potential weaknesses that have been of minor concern.

- **Message Digest (MD6)** A hashing algorithm designed by Ron Rivest.

- **HAVAL** A variable-length, one-way hash function and modification of MD5.

- **Whirlpool**   A hashing algorithm designed by the creators of AES.
- **Tiger**   A hash that is optimized for 64-bit processors, but works well on other systems.
- **RIPE-MD**   A hashing algorithm commonly used in Europe.
- **Secure Hash Algorithm-0 (SHA-0)**   Used prior to SHA-1 and has since been replaced by SHA-1.
- **Secure Hash Algorithm-1 (SHA-1)**   One of the other more commonly used hashing algorithms, which is notable because it has been broken.
- **Secure Hash Algorithm-2 (SHA-2)**   Designed to be an upgrade to SHA-1.
- **Skein**   A hash algorithm designed by encryption guru Bruce Schneier.

In Actual Practice

In mid-2012, SHA-1 was involved in a much publicized break-in and theft of passwords with the social networking service LinkedIn. In LinkedIn's case, the use of straight SHA-1 and some other factors allowed for passwords to be compromised and posted online. Reportedly 6.5 million passwords or password hashes were stolen from the site and posted online.

Applications of Hashing

So where is hashing used? Several places actually, all of which rely on the unique features present in the hashing process we have discussed. Here are some places that hashing is used:

- Digital signatures
- File integrity
- Password storage

Let's take a quick glance at the first item on this list—it will be something that we cross paths with later, and I want to make sure you understand its dependence on hashing.

A little more than a decade ago, digital signatures became more common and popular to use in businesses and e-commerce. Many organizations have made the conscious choice to move away from traditionally signed documents and toward their digital counterparts. Due to their verifiability and ease of use, digital signatures have made electronic documentation just as (if not more) trustworthy than its paper counterpart. For example, it is not uncommon for documents such as those used to purchase a home to be signed entirely in digital form, whereas in the past this would have been done with inked documents. Additionally, other documents such as the budget of the United States have been made available by the United States Government Printing Office (GPO). It is also not unheard of for personal documents such as medical records and college transcripts to be digitally signed.

In Actual Practice

During the Clinton administration, in the United States a bill was signed into law that made the use of digital signatures legally binding. This means that a digital signature carries the same weight legally as a traditional pen-and-ink signature in a court of law.

The questions for us to ask ourselves are, where and why do hashing play into this? What is the significance?

The answer here is simple, if we consider why we use a signature in the first place, digital or otherwise. Consider when you sign a document, such as a car lease or a check. When you apply your John Hancock to the "dotted line," what are you actually doing? First, you personally agree to the document by virtue of you applying your signature because your signature is unique to you—it identifies you and shows that you agreed to the document by placing it there. Second, by applying your signature to the document, you are agreeing to the version of the document with which you have been presented. Think about both concepts for a moment: If you need a process that can uniquely verify an identity, and something that confirms your agreement to a specific version of an item, it would seem that hashing is a good candidate. Why is this so? Well, think back to our previous conversation on the fundamentals of hashing. It's an integrity function, and what is represented by your John Hancock? You are creating a physical representation (signature) of your agreement (integrity) with the document being signed.

In practice, digital signatures are used for the following reasons:

- **Authentication**   Although we will not discuss the specifics of how a digital signature is authenticated (this will appear in another chapter), digital signatures are indeed used to verify the authenticity of a message to ensure that it came from a valid source. However, we have discussed pretty much everything you need at this point to figure out how a specific party could be identified.

- **Integrity**   When you receive a message from someone, you presumably want a degree of confidence that what was sent is what is received. You wouldn't want something such as a financial statement sent to you without you knowing whether is correct, would you? Of course you wouldn't. Hashing can and does give digital signatures the means to provide this function. With digital signatures and hashing, any alteration in a message will render the signature (via the hash) invalid and therefore you would not accept the message.

- **Non-repudiation**   Non-repudiation, or more specifically *non-repudiation of origin,* is another important aspect of digital signatures we need. By this property, an entity that has signed some information cannot at a later time deny having signed it. Keeping things simple, conceptually, non-repudiation and integrity are linked because they relate to digital signatures. Integrity gives us, the receiver, confidence in knowing the message received is unaltered. Similarly, non-repudiation forces the sender to back the integrity of their signature by not allowing the sender to deny they sent the message. In other words, they can't say, "It wasn't me."

Digital signatures are a very effective tool for authenticating e-mails and other messages, but they are also used for many other types of transactions, as you will see later. Signing items such as software, device drivers, and many other items is possible and does happen frequently, but that is a discussion for another time.

Note

We will be talking about digital signatures a little later after we discuss Public Key Infrastructure and digital certificates, but I wanted to point out hashing's significance in the process now so you would start thinking about the components early. In fact, hashing plays as significant a role as asymmetric encryption did earlier, which is why I pointed some important details in Chapter 4. If you are an astute observer you may be able to pick up some "nuggets" of information that we will use when discussing digital signatures later.

File integrity is another common application of hashing and is frequently seen in host-based intrusion detection systems (HIDS). Although a discussion of the full range of features available in an HIDS is outside of the scope of this book, we can still discuss the file integrity feature or the protection they provide and how hashing relates.

Note

Host-based intrusion detection systems are a fascinating topic. I would encourage you to explore HIDS at some point, if you are interested.

Picture, if you will, your computer (Mac, Windows, or Linux—it doesn't matter), and then think of what happens when you patch files or what can happen when you browse the Internet. In the former example, you will find that updates change or replace files on your computer—such is their design. In the latter example, files are changed for a number of reasons, but the one we will focus on are those changes that happen because you were exposed to some sort of malware.

Malware is a malicious piece of software that essentially is designed to do harm. Whereas updating your system with the latest patches is usually a desirable action to be taking, getting infected by a piece of malware is not. With some types of this software, it is possible to have an infection without any visible evidence—it

LINGO
Malware is sort of a catch-all term that covers any sort of software that the owner of a computer system didn't specifically ask for and/or does harm when it is present. Some common types of malware include viruses, worms, rootkits, Trojans, spyware, adware, and even the somewhat oddly named greyware. Although a discussion of what makes each one of these types unique is something left for a different time, it is important to note that some of these types of malware (rootkits, for example) can modify files and effectively hide in plain sight. This is the challenge that hashing is able to meet—detecting those items that are hidden or are invisible to normal means.

just stays in the background doing whatever it is designed to do. So how do we detect its presence? One effective way is through the use of hashing.

Remember earlier in this chapter when I had you use MD5 to hash a text file? When you hashed the initial file, then modified it, and then rehashed it, the resulting MD5 hash you received was markedly different from the first on the same (but modified) file. Consider the value of hashing files on a system when they are known to be safe and then rehashing them later. If the hashes match, the file is the same; if they are different, however, the file has changed, and therefore we should ask ourselves how it got that way. This is, in essence, what many intrusion detection systems do—to allow for the detection of changes within files with the intent of picking up unauthorized alterations due to any sort of malware of unknown activity. Also, consider again our earlier MD5 examples. Just one letter off, or an added period at the end of a phrase, and the hash is substantially altered; this is very noticeable even to the naked eye. It is this precise accuracy and extremely sensitive state of integrity that allows hashing to catch even the smallest alterations. Figure 5-3 shows an example of a hash used to verify the state of a file.

L0PHTCRACK

Home page   Learn about L0phtCrack   Download   Purchase   Support

Download

L0phtCrack 6 is available as a 15 day free trial download. To continue using it after the trial period you must <u>purchase</u> a license key.

Click the LC6 icon to download the the L0phtCrack 6 setup program.

Primary Download Site

LC6

lc6setup_v6.0.15.exe (14MB)

MD5 Hash:
284ed52523bade2dff8004a1a8cdd6f9
SHA1 Hash:
281f6ebfc312cae9063b620a210b724fc3e5aa69
(to verify hashes, check out <u>md5deep</u>)

Backup Download Site
lc6setup_v6.0.15.exe (14MB)

Changelog

v6.0.15 - Improved handling of NTLM-only rainbow tables.
v6.0.14 - Added character range option for brute forcing, and fixed 'machine list' loading issue.
v6.0.13 - Improved 'Credentials' dialog, corrections for FreeBSD and Linux importing.
v6.0.12d - Better fix for file loading issue, rainbow table issues, wizard issues, *empty* password issue.
v6.0.12c - Fix for file/save/load issue
v6.0.12b - More fixes for Windows Server 2003 issues. Updates to rainbow table format support.
v6.0.12a - Fix for DEP issue on Windows Server 2003.
v6.0.12 - Rainbow table pathname issue fixed. Memory usage improved, now

Figure 5-3 A download page for a piece of software with both an MD5 and SHA-1 hash, which can be used to verify a file.

IMHO

Hashing is commonly used to detect changes in files and, as such, offers strong detection measures against malware such as rootkits. Due to the way rootkits operate, detection through many normal means can be difficult at best and impossible at worst. However, using methods that include hashing, it is very possible to detect something such as a rootkit that may not be observable using standard means. This allows rootkits to be located and removed (if possible), where the same task would be much harder otherwise.

The last application we should talk about here is the use of hashing in password management—something you probably use all the time, but don't think about.

Remember that hashing algorithms are designed to be "one way," or at least mathematically infeasible to reverse. The hash that we get as output represents a compressed, fixed-length "fingerprint" of the item put into it. Although this property is great for a number of applications, the protection of passwords represents something of extreme value.

Let's first look at a situation where hashing is not used to see what the "grand scheme" of things is like. Think of a situation where you are trying to log in to a computer. You type in your username and password and then click OK or hit ENTER. The system checks to see if the information entered is correct and then grants you access based on who you are. Pretty simple, huh? Let's look at this process in graphical form, as shown in Figure 5-4.

Again, it's a pretty simple process, but let's change the diagram just a bit to reflect how the computer we are working on factors in. The process is shown in Figure 5-5.

If you take a look at Figure 5-5, you can see an additional step labeled "Check against database." Essentially what's happening at this point is that the credentials you are providing as the user (or more specifically, the password) are being compared to what the system has on file. However, consider the problem of storing a password in a database on a system where multiple people have access, physical or otherwise. Potentially another user could access this database and extract your password, or someone with physical access could copy the database and use any one of a number of available methods to crack or extract the password. This presents real problems, but hashing can help us out here. In this situation, the password could be entered when the user initially creates an account, which would then be hashed with the resulting hash being stored in the database along with the associated username. Subsequently, the user would enter their password whenever they logged in, which would then be hashed and compared to what's on file

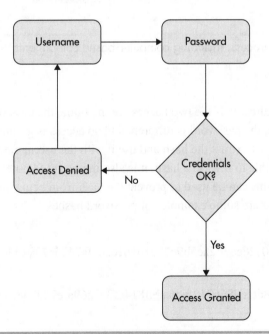

Figure 5-4 Login process as described without hashing

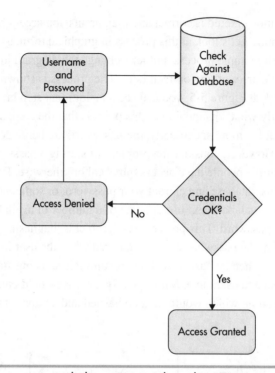

Figure 5-5 The login process, including computer-based components

with the computer already. If the two hashes are the same, the password must be the same; if they are different, the password is different and no access is granted. Now you may ask yourself, Why not just extract the hash and use it with the username? Well, aside from the fact that it is infeasible to reverse a hash, it is also important to note that time-stamping and other mechanisms can be used to prevent the hash from being used by a malicious party. The following are some examples of password hashes:

- chell
  2cf24dba5fb0a30e26e83b2ac5b9e29e1b161e5c1fa7425e7304336293
- glados
  58756879c05c68dfac9866712fad6a93f8146f337a69afe7dd238f3364
- wheatley
  c0e81794384491161f1777c232bc6bd9ec38f616560b120fda8e90f383

IMHO

Remember the algorithms I mentioned earlier that perform hashing? Many of them are supported in modern operating systems for this very purpose. Hash algorithms such as SHA-256, SHA-512, RipeMD, and Whirlpool are cryptographic hash functions that are ideally suited for the purpose we are talking about here.

I should also add that some operating systems will support some or all of the algorithms mentioned here, and yet others even have their own that the system designers themselves came up with. Vendors such as Microsoft, for example, have been known to come up with their own algorithms for various reasons. In the Linux world, it can get even more confusing with different distributions offering a wide range of choices that you may be able to choose from based on your security policy or performance needs.

The overall process you would use to enroll or register for an account (including generation of a hash) would be similar to the following:

1. The user creates an account or has one created for them.

2. The user enters their password, which is then hashed and stored in the database. The plaintext password (in most systems) is never stored to the hard drive; only the hash is stored.

3. When the user attempts to log in, the hash of the password they entered is checked against the hash of their actual password as stored in the system's own database.

4. If the hashes match, the user is granted access. If not, the user is told they entered invalid login credentials.

5. Steps 3 and 4 repeat every time the user attempts to log in to their account.

Note

I have paraphrased the process of creating and logging in to an account here to make things simple for us. This is not meant to be an IT text, per se (although much of what you learn here will translate directly over). I want you to be aware of the process overall and where hashing fits in and why. If you are an IT person, you can easily figure out or research how the process we talk about here is actually implemented on your system of choice.

It is easy, and not too farfetched, to think that all you have to do is run the password through a cryptographic hash function and your users' passwords will be secure. This is far from the truth. There are many ways to recover passwords from plain hashes, some of which take a long time, while others take considerably less. Several easy-to-implement techniques make these "attacks" much less effective. Clearly, simply hashing the password does not meet our needs for security.

IMHO

In the hacking world, a series of attacks known as *offline attacks* are designed to extract hashes from a system database. Tools such as L0phtcrack and LCP are very effective at retrieving these items from a system (many others are readily available and free). This is one of those topics I would recommend that you explore more if you are someone who has an IT background or are looking into doing system audits or security. It can be an eye-opening experience to see how readily available some things can be on a system.

Hashing is great for protecting passwords, which is why it is commonly used. We want to be able to store passwords in a form that's difficult to reverse, but at the same time we need to be able to verify that a user's password is correct quickly and easily.

In the Windows world, a system that uses hashing that you may have heard of before is NTLM, and its predecessor LM. These two protocols have been widely used over the years for various reasons you don't need to worry about right now. They are of interest to us because of weaknesses or flaws in hashing. These two protocols, as you will see a little bit about, both have flaws that could allow someone to guess or retrieve your password.

Additionally, in the Windows world, this information is stored (along with many other things) in the Security Accounts Manager (SAM). This is a big freaking database that stores account information. Due to its importance, the database has had several protective mechanisms implemented into it, including (wait for it) encryption. Figure 5-6 shows a view of the SAM using a piece of software known as L0phtcrack.

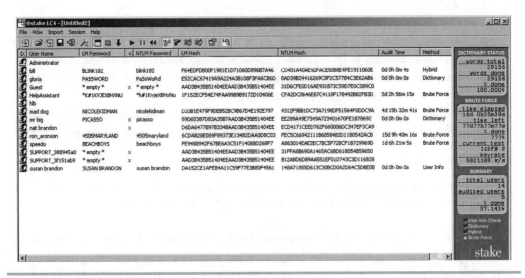

Figure 5-6   A view of L0phtcrack showing LM and NTLM hashes retrieved from the SAM

Breaking Hashes and "Kicking Hash"

Much like any mechanism or method we have spoken of so far, hashing has weaknesses and limitations that you should be aware of. It is ideal that you are aware of how hashes can be defeated and what can be done to strengthen the process. Let's take a look at some of these methods.

Consider that a good hashing algorithm should take into account many or even all of the bits of information from anything that is put into it. This is sort of like saying that when information is put into a hashing algorithm, is every tenth letter collected and then the hash generated from this, or is every single character collected and used as input in the hash? In the latter case, the greater amount of data coming from the source gives a much higher degree of security and uniqueness because all the variations in the input are captured.

A second weakness or potential exploit of weak or poorly designed hash algorithms comes in the form of collisions. Collisions occur when two or more inputs into a hashing algorithm produce the exact same output. If we consider what we have been talking about in this chapter, we can easily see that if something designed to produce a unique value for every input doesn't in fact do this, a real problem exists. Consider the problem from this angle: If two or more inputs produce the same output, how would you know which input was the correct one for that given hash? Well, the answer is, you can't.

So, how many possible combinations of characters exist for a given hashing algorithm? Well, let's take the 128-bit hashing algorithm as an example. The following astonishing fact is due to the astoundingly large number of possible hashes available: A 128-bit hash can have 3.4 × 1,038 possible values, which is 340,282,366,920,938,463,463,374,607,431,768, 211,456 possible hashes that can be uniquely generated.

Of course, if the hash algorithm is well designed and distributes its results uniformly over the output space, finding a collision by random guessing is exceedingly unlikely.

Note

Other hashes have even more bits: The SHA-1 algorithm generates 160 bits, whose output space is four billion times larger than that produced by MD5's 128 bits.

In a previous chapter, we discussed brute-force attacks, which provide one way of attacking a hashing algorithm or hash to determine what character sequence generated it. Although on the surface the brute-force strategy may seem simple, we know it is not, based on our prior discussions in this book. We have all seen the movies where the hero or villain tries numerous combinations of characters and miraculously finds the right one just in the nick of time. The reality is that unless you are from some super-powerful alien race such as the Daleks from *Doctor Who* or are just incredibly lucky, you aren't going to work it out this fast.

Note

Yes, you could get lucky by breaking a hash from a good hashing algorithm using single computer in record time, but this is unlikely. Doing so would be like winning one of those $400 million lottery jackpots... twice. It could happen, but it's unlikely.

With a brute-force attack, you will try every combination of characters up to a length you specify ahead of time. The problem with this attack—or the difference between fiction and reality—is that it is extremely computationally expensive (or in layman's terms, it takes a lot of horsepower and usually a lot of time). The upside, and the reason why a brute-force attack may be tried to break a password (or in this case, recover a hash) is that it will always work. However, remember that the time required to recover a hash could be longer than you have—a lot longer. Passwords or hashes should be long enough that searching through all possible character strings to find one will take too long to be worthwhile or effective.

IMHO

As with everything in the real world, things are "open for negotiation," as I like to say. In the case of brute-force attacks, this is very much true. In the past, recovering the original input for a given hash would have taken quite a while, but that has since changed. In today's world of distributed computing, the time to recover a hash has decreased. Distributed computing is rewriting the rules as we know them. Simply put, distributed computing uses the resources of many computers together in order to solve some problem, such as breaking a hash. The fact is, using one computer to solve a problem will get results, but using multiple computers together can make a seemingly impossible task much easier. In fact, one project currently in play has broken MD5 hashes using distributed computing. The interesting thing is that you can capture an MD5 hash using any means you desire and then input it into the site, which will then return the characters used to generate the hash.

Interestingly enough, this same technology was used some time ago for a project known as SETI@home, or the Search for ExtraTerrestrial Intelligence. The project used distributed computing to process the data collected from radio telescopes from deep space in an effort to locate signals of advanced alien civilizations. Alas, the project did not uncover signs of intelligent life in space (some would argue we haven't found it here yet), but the project did underscore the power of distributed computing and what could be done down the road.

Another, more effective way of recovering hashes is through the use of what is known as a dictionary attack. This type of attack employs a file containing words, phrases, commonly used passwords, and other combinations of characters. When the process is started, the different strings of characters are tried against the target system with the hope that one of them is the correct one and the system accepts the attempt as valid.

Conceptually, the attack would look something like this:

```
Trying P@ssw0rd     : failed
Trying Password     : failed
Trying Pa$$w0rd     : failed
Trying Password1    : failed
Trying P@$$w0rd     : success!
```

This method of attempting to crack passwords is easy to try—many modern password crackers can do this very thing with extreme speed and efficiency. Tools such as L0phtcrack, THC Hydra, and others are very adept at retrieving passwords and preying upon the many weaknesses seen in them.

Of course, there is another problem with hashing and passwords—the real possibility that the mechanism for storing them may not offer great protection in the first place. One example I want to point out is a technology known as LM or LAN Manager protocol, which used something known as LM hashing. In theory, the system sounded secure, but in further analysis it was less than so. Just as a quick note: The LM protocol is a very old legacy technology that is inherently unsecure; however, for our purposes it makes for a great illustration of how a supposed secure function can easily become an exploited vulnerability. First, let's look at the process through which an LM hash is created:

1. The user's ASCII password is converted to uppercase.

2. This password is null-padded to 14 bytes.

3. The "fixed-length" password is split into two 7-byte pieces.

4. These values are used to create two different DES keys (yes, the same DES we talked about earlier), one from each 7-byte half.

5. Each of the two keys is used to DES-encrypt the constant ASCII string "KGS!@#$%", resulting in two 8-byte ciphertext values.

6. These two ciphertext values are concatenated to form a 16-byte value, which is the LM hash.

To show what some LM hashes look like when extracted from a Windows SAM, take a look at Figure 5-7.

LM Hash	NTLM Hash	Audit Time	Method
F64EDFDB00F1981E1D71060D896B7A46	CD401A40AE92FACE50B8E4FE1911060E	0d 0h 0m 4s	Hybrid
E52CAC67419A9A224A3B108F3FA6CB6D	0AD39B24416269C8F2C57784C3E62AB6	0d 0h 0m 0s	Dictionary
AAD3B435B51404EEAAD3B435B51404EE	31D6CFE0D16AE931B73C59D7E0C089C0		
1F152ECF54E74FAA9989B9172D10406E	CFA2DC0646E87C4110F178492B82FB3D	5d 2h 56m 15s	Brute Force
D33B1E479F9DEB52BC9B67D4E192E797	4312F9BB1DC73A7198DF51564F0DDC9A	4d 15h 32m 41s	Brute Force
59D65387D83A35B7AAD3B435B51404EE	EE289A49E7349A723401670FE1B78692	0d 0h 0m 0s	Dictionary
D6DA6477B97B334BAAD3B435B51404EE	ECD4171CEED762F660006DC347EF3CA9		
6CDAB28E089F89373E13482DAA0D8C03	FEC5C66942111B6058482D1180542ACB	15d 9h 40m 16s	Brute Force
FE9488942F67BE6A3C51F14088D268F7	A863014EAE2EC7BC5F728CF1B7299690	1d 6h 21m 5s	Brute Force
AAD3B435B51404EEAAD3B435B51404EE	31FFA8B690A1465AC6BD618054B59650		
AAD3B435B51404EEAAD3B435B51404EE	B12ABD6D89AA551EF01D743C3D116828		
DA152CE1AFE84A11C59F77E3B80F4561	148A71855D613C30BCD0A2D64C5DBE0B	0d 0h 0m 0s	User Info

Figure 5-7 Values extracted from a Windows SAM. Note the column Audit Time, which shows the method used to retrieve the values.

On the surface, it may sound like the protocol is pretty secure, or at least reasonable so, but let's examine this a little closer. In fact, we can go point by point and see where the weaknesses in the system are and why they are there:

- **Not a one-way function**   The hash is created from the two pieces, as described in step 3. From what we know so far about encryption, the more bits that are added to something, the more time in tends to take to break. In fact, the process to break typically takes exponential amounts of power. Because of the fact that each hash is so short, it means that an average desktop system in today's world could break the hash in less than half a day in many cases.

- **Upper vs. lowercase**   In addition to the hashing length reducing the time it would take to crack a hash using average computer power, the conversion from any case to uppercase is another factor. Because the letters are all converted to uppercase, the number of potential possibilities underneath the hash is reduced to half. This happens in step 1.

- **Use of DES**   To be fair, at the time LM was conceived as a protocol, DES was still considered to be somewhat strong (although showing its age). Now with current technology, or even that released since the mid-1900s, DES can be broken. In fact, the shorter key lengths and weaknesses in DES make it a poor choice for many applications, including what we are discussing here.

- **Passing the salt**   Something we will talk about in a moment, known as *salt* or *salting,* is not used in the LM process and therefore makes the protocol vulnerable to some offline attacks, such as rainbow tables. In LM's case, some salt would be good (unlike what it does for your blood pressure).

- **Afraid of change**   LM hashes only change when a user initiates a change of their password and not until that time. This also exposes vulnerabilities that could be exploited by an attacker.

So why do I point all this out about LM? It's to show you that even if a particular cryptographic protocol may appear to be decent or strong, it may indeed not be. Implementing a cryptographic protocol or system is something that takes careful consideration and planning. Many of the mistakes or weaknesses in LM could have been avoided with a little more thought given to the system. You should never look at a cryptographic protocol or algorithm as being secure just because it appears so on the surface. Consider how things are implemented and how they fit together.

Want to try generating some LM (as well as other hashes) yourself, just to see what some hashes look like? Take a look at a piece of software for the Windows operating system known as Cain and Abel, as shown in Figure 5-8.

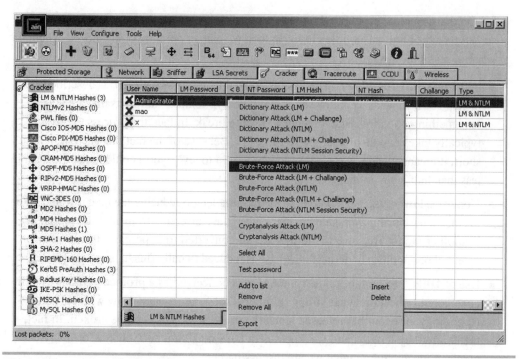

Figure 5-8 Cain and Abel software interface

With Cain, it is possible for you to use the built-in hash calculator to generate LM and other hashes. In fact, you can use the built-in hash calculator to generate LM hashes and see how they stand up against other hashing algorithms. I suggest that if you are going to do this you use phrases that are 14 characters or more. If you try this out, increase your phrase by a single character or two each time and rehash them and watch how all the hashes change—that is, except for the LM hash at a certain point. This little exercise (if you choose to do it) will show you a good reason for the disuse of LM hashing in today's environments.

A word of caution to you before you try this exercise, specifically before you download the Cain and Abel software: Be careful. I would only download the software from www.oxid.it and nowhere else. It is not uncommon for this type of software to be used for both benevolent and malicious purposes. It has been known to be infected in some cases, so consider yourself warned and only download from the location presented here. Additionally, you should refrain from installing this software on a client in your office network! "Legitimate" software tools such as this can throw up some major red flags if found on your internal network.

IMHO

For the record, LM is not widely used anymore, at least not as much as it used to be. Many modern operating systems have the use of LM disabled by default because of the weaknesses discussed here. The problem is that in cases where a company has older applications or an older operating system, backward compatibility is an issue and as such the scheme may have to be reenabled to make things work together properly.

If you are one of these cases and now know the risks, you should research mechanisms to protect yourself or see if an upgrade is possible to remove the weak system.

Lookup Tables

If you want to go a different route than brute forcing things, you can always try an offline attack in the form of a lookup table. This is an interesting way to find out what a hash actually represents in plaintext form, which can crack what is behind multiple hashes very quickly. In a nutshell, the attack essentially pre-computes hashes and stores them in a database known as a password dictionary. Once this is done, it is possible for a lookup table to process hundreds of hash lookups per second, even when they contain many billions of hashes.

This attack quickly allows an attacker to apply a dictionary or brute-force attack to many hashes at the same time, without having to pre-compute a lookup table.

To carry out this attack, follow these steps:

1. A lookup table is created, which maps each password hash from the compromised user account database to a list of users who had that hash.

2. The attacker then hashes each password guess and uses the lookup table to get a list of users whose password was the attacker's guess.

Note

The effectiveness of this attack is magnified dramatically when many users use the same password, which is far from being a rare occurrence.

Rainbow Tables

One last way of defeating hashes involves the use of rainbow tables. The process is simple and can be effectively used to recover password hashes. Tables are made up of hashes that are generated from certain lengths of inputs (for example, the different combinations of characters using six to ten characters). What happens if you were going to carry out this attack is that you would generate all the different hashes and store them on the hard drive. The idea being that you could easily search the hard drive for the matching hash and accompanying plaintext for a specific hash that you may have obtained.

Adding a Pinch of Salt

Some of these attacks only work because hashes are hashed the same way each and every time. If two or more users have the same password, the password hash will match. We can thwart these attacks by adding some entropy or randomness to each hash, thereby making hashes for even the same password different.

So how does this work? By adding some salt to each hash (in other words, appending or prepending a random string to each plaintext input before the actual hashing takes place). So how does the system know the hash is correct for a given password or input? The salt itself is typically stored alongside the file or password or is combined with the hash.

Keep in mind that the salt does not need to be and is not required to be kept secret. Randomizing hashes makes the process of using rainbow tables or lookup tables problematic because the hashes generated ahead of time will only give results that do not include the salt.

We've Covered

Fundamentals of hashing

- Hashing is known as one-way encryption.
- Hashing produces a message digest or hash.
- Hashing produces a fixed-length output no matter the length or size of the input.

Purpose of hashing

- Hashing is designed to verify the integrity of a message.
- Hashing can assist a receiving party detect changes in a document or other piece of information that may otherwise remain unknown.
- Hashing is not a way to preserve the confidentiality of a message.

Applications of hashing

- Hashing is used in digital signatures.
- Hashing is used to verify the status of certain files, such as key system files or other data.
- Hashing is used to verify items, such as the status of antivirus updates or other types of files.

Types of hashing algorithms

- Hashing algorithms are known to the public and can be scrutinized.
- Hashing algorithms are used to determine how the creation and evolution of a hash will be done.
- Algorithms that are in use today include SHA, MD5, and others.

Key concepts in hashing

- Hashing algorithms will always generate the same length message digest for every input.
- Hash algorithms are embedded in many software applications.
- Hashing is designed to create powerful non-reversible digests.

Key terms and terminology

- Hashes are the output of a hashing algorithm.
- Hashes are sometimes also known as message digests.
- Collisions refer to two or more different inputs that generate the same output.
- High numbers of collisions indicate a weak or poorly written algorithm.

CHAPTER 6

Cryptanalysis and Code Breaking

We'll Cover

- What is cryptanalysis?

- A look at Enigma

- What is code breaking?

- Methods to code break

- How to break a coded message

- What makes code breaking easier?

- Examples of code breaking

As you have seen so far, encryption is concerned with concealing secrets, but when a secret is hidden, someone will try to find out that secret. *Code breaking* is the art of accessing information that someone else doesn't want you to have. We've all seen the spy movies, read Cold War novels, or maybe even dreamed of breaking secret codes like James Bond (I dream of this all the time; who hasn't?), where that secret message is uncovered through some clever technique or blind luck.

Code breaking may seem to be easy based on what the movies and popular culture shows us, but in reality it usually is much more involved. Code breaking, commonly called *cryptanalysis,* is the body of knowledge relating to studying cryptosystems, as well as taking encrypted data and decrypting it without a key. The process of breaking codes may be as simple as being lucky or exploiting a weakness in a cryptosystem. Although accessing a piece of information without authorization may seem malicious or underhanded (and indeed it may be), it is also used to gain access to information that may be used to defeat an enemy such as a terrorist group. Cryptanalysis is also commonly employed by the authors of a particular system with the intention of uncovering and addressing any weakness in the system before a malicious party is able to do so.

In this chapter, you will see how cryptanalysis and the sweet art of code breaking have evolved alongside cryptography—with cryptanalysts breaking existing ciphers and systems, then the cryptographers developing new and more powerful ones designed to thwart and confound them. You will see that code breaking and code making are in fact two pieces to the same puzzle, with each complementing and making the other one possible.

Now, Mr. Bond, I don't expect you to talk, I expect you to code break....

Setting Things Straight

There are two major categories of cryptographic systems: ciphers and codes. Nearly all military systems fall into one or the other of these categories, and some in both. Cipher systems are those in which the encryption is carried out on single characters or groups of characters without regard to their meaning (Cipher is a cool hacker name, too, in case you need one). Codes, on the other hand, are more concerned with meanings than characters. The basic unit of encryption in a code system is a word or phrase. When a message is encrypted by a code system, code groups primarily replace words and phrases. Code groups may also replace single characters where necessary, but the substitution for complete words is the key distinction that separates a code from a cipher. Because of this, the cryptanalytic approaches to codes and ciphers are quite different from each other.

An example of a code appears first in our discussion of the Japanese codes of World War II. Codes such as the famed JN-25 system were broken and proved instrumental in the winning of the war by Allied Forces. Some background of the Japanese system is worthwhile exploring, even if we only dip our "toes" in a little bit.

IMHO

In this text I will look at both code and ciphers, so keep this simple description in mind when going through my examples: A *code* focuses on the word or phrase level rather than actual characters, whereas ciphers convert characters to other characters.

A great example of this concept is my example from World War II, where the Imperial Japanese Navy referred to Midway Island as AF instead of stating the name of the island itself.

A Look at Cryptanalysis and Code Breaking

Code breaking has probably been around as long as people have tried to keep secrets by putting them into code in the first place. The science, much like cryptography itself, has undoubtedly been responsible for changing the course of history, laying bare the thoughts and ideas that some would otherwise preferred to be kept secret. People such as Mary, Queen of Scots, learned the hard way that writing secret messages in code doesn't mean that they will stay that way—which, in her case, resulted in the untimely loss of her own head to the executioner's blade (keep this in mind if you make any mistakes on the puzzles in this chapter).

Some time later, the American colonies also got involved in the code-breaking game, but without the centralized mechanism present in Europe. In fact, in the colonies, encryption was carried out through the dedicated work of clergymen and other religious types who possessed knowledge of languages and other information. Significantly, the colonies had a major code-breaking coup early in the war when a coded message from Dr. Benjamin Church was intercepted. The message was suspected of being a message intended to aid the British, but without it being deciphered this could not be confirmed. The message later showed evidence of a crime and resulted in Dr. Church's exile from America.

IMHO

If you are so inclined, there are many fascinating examples of code breaking from both the U.S. Revolutionary War and the U.S. Civil War that I simply cannot cover here. Looking at the various examples of breaking codes during this time period will not only shed light on numerous historical events that you most likely were unaware of, but will also reintroduce you to many famous figures, including General George Washington and the traitor Benedict Arnold.

In a little over a half century, ciphers (or polyalphabetic ciphers) that were considered strong (such as the Vigenère cipher) were subject to be broken somewhat routinely. In a previous chapter we took a look at this cipher and saw just how it works. Although such a cipher originally seemed to be unbreakable (and indeed it was considered to be so for around 200 years) time caught up with it and it was broken (routinely, in fact). As you learned earlier, the Confederacy made the job even easier for the Union by reusing codes, especially three phrases: "Manchester Bluff," "Complete Victory," and "Come Retribution." It was suggested by future U.S. president and Civil War general Ulysses S. Grant that the routine breaking of the Vigenère cipher shortened and influenced the war itself. Of course, I would also like to point out that everything old is new again, and although the polyalphabetic cipher in the form of Vigenère was broken, the concept is still sound and was even reused (albeit with more complexity) by the Germans in their Enigma machine.

In Actual Practice

Cryptanalysis, as you know, is the practice of changing ciphertext into plaintext, and back, without the knowledge of the underlying cipher or key. This art has a long history, with one of the earliest practitioners being the Arab cultures of the Middle East. Specifically the Arabic author al-Qalqashandi wrote down a technique for code breaking that is still in use today. This method, now commonly known as "Frequency Analysis," is still very much in use and is something we will look at later on.

Organizations known as "Black Chambers" were set up all over Europe and spread to the New World, all dedicated to breaking codes. The Black Chambers commonly included skilled linguists, mathematicians, and other such talented individuals who would focus their talents on obtaining the secrets hidden of foreign and domestic targets. The practice of using Black Chambers was widespread (and still is) and probably influenced or changed several major and minor events in history.

One example of how history was influenced by cryptanalysis is the infamous Zimmermann note. As you may remember, from 1914 to 1917 all of Europe was in the midst of what is now known as World War I. During the opening years of the war the European powers were the main combatants in the conflict. During this same time the United States remained neutral, or as neutral as was possible. Although the U.S. attempted to keep neutral and even reelected President Wilson on the promise that the U.S. would stay out of the war, events would dictate otherwise.

In 1917, British blockades had proved effective in frustrating the German war effort. In response, the Germans restarted unrestricted submarine warfare against British shipping, breaking prior treaty obligations. In response, the U.S. severed diplomatic relations with Germany, which set up a series of events where code breaking would enter the scene.

In 1917, the British intercepted a message from German Foreign Minister Arthur Zimmermann to the German Minister in Mexico. The message, now known as the "Zimmermann note" or "Zimmermann Telegram," offered Mexico territory in the U.S. if they joined the German cause by engaging the U.S. in military action. When this message was decoded and made public in the U.S., public opinion was galvanized and on April 6, 1917 the United States declared war on Germany and its allies.

Many historians have cited the interception and breaking of this single message as changing the course of the war and history.

In Actual Practice

What you may not know is that the United States had its own Black Chamber that was founded in 1919 and closed down in 1929 when funding was cut. The U.S.'s Black Chamber had many successes, including giving the U.S. a decided advantage in dealing with the Japanese during the Washington Naval Conference, which was credited with preserving peace during the 1920s. The American delegation was able to use their efforts to discover exactly what the Japanese expected out of the conference and, in their view, the worst possible outcome they were willing to accept. With this

(continued)

information in hand, negotiators were able to push the Empire into a situation more favorable to the Americans and less favorable to the Japanese.

Coincidentally, the Washington Naval Conference has also been described as only delaying or enabling the rise of the Empire of Japan and their building of a more powerful naval surface fleet leading up to World War II.

So what did the Zimmermann note look like? Well, let's take a look at it. Figure 6-1 shows a sample from the original coded message, and Figure 6-2 shows the decoded message.

We will examine some of the methods used to break this code later in this chapter. Do take note, though, that Figure 6-1 uses sequences of numbers to represent the message. We will talk about this again in a bit and see what is actually happening.

IMHO

I would love to take a moment and give credit where credit is due by pointing out the efforts of Room 40. This organization was in existence from 1914 to 1919, but in its short lifetime it made a tremendous impact on the course of history, in my opinion. Its code-breaking efforts led to the tracking of German naval movements in the North Sea and affected the outcomes of a handful of engagements, including the Battle of Jutland (which was the only major full-scale naval battle of World War I). It has been suggested that the biggest event Room 40 was involved in was the Zimmermann note, as mentioned here.

A somewhat understated or too rarely talked about action that occurred during the war in the Pacific is that of the Navajo code talkers. The code talkers were a group of Native Americans who used at least two things to their advantage to prevent the Japanese from understanding American military secrets. First, the group used code words to identify important assets, such as birds for aircraft and fish for ships. Second, the Navajo language was understood by so few that the possibility someone other than a Navajo would understand it was small. This system turned out to be extremely successful. In fact, after the war it was revealed that the Japanese had broken several U.S. codes, but had no success in breaking communications based on the Navajo language.

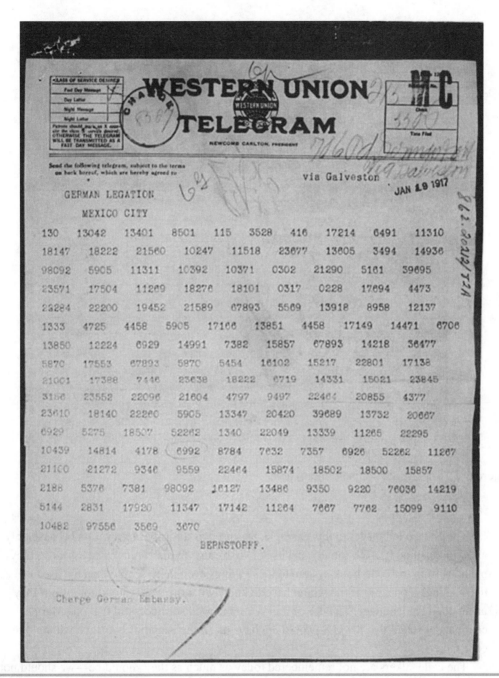

Figure 6-1   The original Zimmermann note (or Telegram)

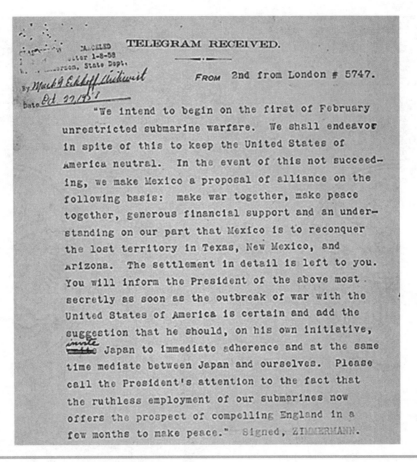

Figure 6-2 The decoded Zimmermann note

The Navajo language, in this example, was used as a form of encryption because only a few understood it. Additionally, the use of "fish" and "birds" to describe assets employs methods from the code-book system to make things even more secure than the use of the language alone. Someone would have to know what the words stood for even if they understood the language. The use of this system proved so successful that one Marine commander stated that the U.S. would not have taken the island of Iwo Jima without the code talkers.

The code talkers are not remembered today as much as they should be—we should not forget their contribution.

IMHO

One lesser-known fact about the use of languages during the war is that the Navajo language was not the only one that was used to carry secrets. The Basque language was also used for the same purpose. Because few speak the Basque language (compared to other languages), native speakers could be used in areas where there was little possibility of others being present, thereby preserving the secrets.

If we fast-forward a few years, we can see some of the same code breaking taking place between the Axis and Allies. After having their codes and secrets broken and laid bare in the first World War, the Germans developed new methods, including the legendary Enigma machine. However, the successor to Room 40 known as Bletchley Park stood ready to take up the challenge to break the codes and secrets of the Third Reich. In fact, the folks at Bletchley Park would play as big a role if not bigger than Room 40.

In Actual Practice

Code breaking during the war was such an important tool or weapon that some sad and tragic sacrifices had to be made, such as with the town of Coventry. On the nights of November 14th and 15th in 1940, Winston Churchill and the Prime Minister made the choice to leave the town to the mercy of the German Luftwaffe.

It all started with the interception of a message that had the name of the town of Coventry in the "clear," when it was normally coded. Faced with evacuating the city and risking that Germany would discover that the Allies had broken the code or leaving the town to its fate and not evacuating, the latter option was chosen. When the options were presented, the Prime Minister told Churchill to leave Coventry to burn and the people to their fate.

The aftermath of the attack was heartbreaking and tragic, to say the least. The German raid led to massive firebombing and considerable damage to the city, even destroying historic landmarks city and leaving only a few remnants. Additionally, over 4,000 houses were destroyed or heavily damaged, along with three-quarters of the industrial base. The human toll was extremely painful, with over 800 confirmed dead and thousands injured and/or homeless. The raid led the Germans to coin the term "Coventrate" to describe the tactics used and developed for the raid.

This one event is still the source of debate by scholars over whether the actions taken were right or wrong.

The code-breaking efforts at the Park were later given the name Ultra and rapidly became the standard for Allied cryptanalysis efforts with other nations using names such as Magic.

IMHO

I don't think that we can really appreciate how significant the operation of Ultra actually was from our standpoint all these years later, so maybe seeing the opinions of several prominent figures at the time would help. Here are some examples of the opinions of the impact of Ultra:

- "It was thanks to Ultra that we won the war." —Winston Churchill
- "Ultra was decisive to Allied victory." —Dwight D Eisenhower
- "Ultra shortened the war by two to four years.... With an absence of Ultra, the outcome of the war is uncertain." —Sir Harry Hinsley

I just wanted to point out how some of the famous people at the time viewed the significance of the code-breaking efforts and the program in general.

The story of the breaking of the Enigma machine and its code starts in Poland in the years leading up to 1933. Due to strong links between the Polish and German manufacturing industries, the Polish Cipher Bureau was able to completely reconstruct an Enigma machine. After this, the Polish were able to decrypt messages sent by the German military from 1933 to 1938. In 1939, this information was provided to the British code breakers at Bletchley Park for them to further break the code.

So how much did the code-breaking effort contribute to the Allied cause? Here are some examples:

- Ultra uncovered evidence that the Luftwaffe was developing new radio-based guidance systems for their bombing raids on Britain.

- The RAF received information on Luftwaffe bomber and fighter aircraft during the Battle of Britain, allowing advance warning to be sent out to intercepting squadrons.

- Advance warning was received of Operation Sea Lion, which was the planned invasion of Britain by the Nazis. Also uncovered was the plan's cancellation.

- Enabled the victory of the British Army over the Italian Army in Libya in 1941.

- Aided the Royal Navy victory in the Battle of Cape Matapan in 1941.

- Revealed that the Nazis planned to invade the USSR, but information was not acted upon by Stalin.

- Stopped Nazi General Rommel from reaching Cairo.

- Helped sink many tons of ships that were supplying the Nazi effort in North Africa.

- Confirmed that Britain's Security Service (MI5) had captured all German agents in Britain.

- Allowed the monitoring of German developments at Peenemünde and the creation of the V-1 and V-2 missiles and rockets.

- Aided in the success of the Battle of North Cape, which led to the sinking of the German battleship Scharnhorst.

- Revealed that the Germans did not believe the Normandy or D-Day invasion in general was real.

This is only a short list; a tremendous amount of events were influenced or averted due to Ultra and its efforts.

In Actual Practice

A little bit of arrogance is irritating, a lot can be dangerous, and the Germans may have learned this the hard way. The Germans were convinced that Enigma was unbreakable and, as such, made some mistakes that we will talk about later on in this chapter. The reality is that the experts at Bletchley Park had started to successfully read Enigma messages starting in 1940 during the Norwegian campaign, and then later on they hit "pay dirt" during the invasion of Greece in 1941. Later on still, the Allies gained the upper hand in North Africa against Rommel's Afrika Korps (German military force in North Africa from 1941 to 1943).

Of course, the British weren't the only ones to have code-breaking efforts in place—all sides recognized the value of cryptanalysis and the crucial role it could play. Germany had its own code-breaking organization in the form of B-Dienst (or Beobachtungsdienst), which had itself broken the British Navy code in 1935, which led to the ability to track Allied convoys very early. The U.S. switched codes later in the war, around 1942, but by the time this had been done the Kriegsmarine (the German Navy during WWII) had already conducted a U-boat campaign off the East coast of the United States. The Germans had other successes with Danish and Soviet codes, but due to the infrastructure in place during the Nazi era, their code-breaking efforts were not as effective as Allied efforts.

IMHO

I would like to point out that the Kriegsmarine's efforts along the coast of the United States, together with other campaigns in the Atlantic, resulted in major losses for the Allies. From January to August 1942, the German Navy sunk a quarter of all Allied shipping lost during the whole war. Just think what the impact could have been if the Allied powers had a stronger code or if Germany had not broken the code in the first place.

To put real numbers on this campaign, keep in mind that over 600 Allied ships were sunk at the cost of just over 20 U-boats. A 30-to-1 ratio is impressive by any standards. This also was over 3.1 million tons of shipping, which is a massive amount in losses.

I also would also like to point out that the majority of information about this campaign on Allied shipping by the German Navy was kept secret in order to maintain a high sense of morale in the U.S. In fact, the famous saying "Loose lips sink ships," which first appeared in 1942, was partially about keeping the American public unaware of what was happening.

We'll take a look at how Enigma was broken in just a bit, because I want to introduce you to the U.S. code-breaking effort again. The U.S. code-breaking effort was based partially at Pearl Harbor and Stateside. Prior to the events of December 7, 1941 the United States had been regularly decrypting Japanese codes. In fact, the United States had decoded the Japanese declaration of war several hours before the Japanese embassy had even decoded it themselves. At the time preceding the attack, the United States was already actively reading the Japanese diplomatic codes and was aware that an attack was imminent with the next 24 hours or less. Furthermore, the messages that were intercepted and decoded indicated that the attack would most likely be on American naval interests somewhere.

The code the United States broke was known as JN-25, which was used by the Imperial Japanese Navy. The code was so named because it was the 25th separate code identified by the U.S. The code evolved several times after its introduction in 1939 and was updated just prior to the Japanese strike on Pearl Harbor. The version that was introduced on December 4, 1941 was the version that was completely broken by the U.S. code breakers and led to the events later on in 1942. This code allowed the U.S. to get forewarning of the upcoming attack on Midway Island.

A little background on the JN-25 code: the Japanese Imperial Navy came up with the secure code with the intention of passing command and control information to their fleet. The Japanese developed a very strong code that relied on secure and complex algorithms. The code was frequently updated by the Japanese, which amounted to almost an entirely new system each time. This obviously was a code that, when discovered by the Allies, had to be used to protect something extremely sensitive.

The Allies launched a coordinated effort to break the code and reveal its secrets. After the events of December 7, 1941, radio communications between members of the Japanese navy increased as their aggression increased across the Pacific and Asia. With this increased radio traffic, the Allies were able to collect transmissions that made analysis much easier and the eventual breaking of the code possible.

IMHO

One figure who proved instrumental in the breaking of the code was Eric Nave. Nave was a member of the Australian Navy from 1917 to 1949 and was a brilliant code breaker and cryptanalyst. Due to Nave and his team's efforts, the U.S. was warned that the Japanese had shifted interest from New Guinea to the Midway Island chain in the wake of the famed Doolittle Raid bombing of Japan (which you may have seen in movies such as *Thirty Seconds Over Tokyo,* with Jimmy Stewart). His team also was responsible for warning General Douglas MacArthur that Milne Bay was being targeted for invasion by Japanese forces a month before the planned attack. The Battle of Milne Bay was significant because it was the first time Japanese forces had been defeated in a land engagement (by U.S. and Australian forces). Finally, and incredibly intriguing, was the fact that the group warned the U.S. Navy on December 2nd that the U.S. would be at war with Japan within seven days.

Another interesting footnote to Captain Nave's story is that he was known as being brilliant but hard to work with due to his attitude. In fact, his attitude at one point led the U.S. Army to comment that if the Australians didn't want him, they would be glad to take him off their hands. Of course, this never happened, but it is a rather humorous note.

During the Second World War, the Japanese made rather extensive use of codebooks. The code that was to become known as JN-25 was the most famous example, with it being the first broken in the late 1930s by both U.S. and U.K. experts. Essentially, the system used a process where a word in a plaintext message was looked up in a book and essentially replaced using a predefined process that would yield a number as the end result. The recipient of the message would then reverse this process using a similar codebook to reveal the original message.

Interestingly enough, the Japanese may have also been thinking some of the things that were being said about their language. The Japanese language is extremely or even entirely different from other languages, so much so that at the time it was thought to be almost unlearnable by some. It was partially due to this reason alone that the Japanese did not place as much emphasis on codes and ciphers as their counterparts.

Admiral Chester Nimitz had at his disposal a team at Pearl Harbor that had broken the JN-25 code. In early 1942, the U.S. intercepted numerous messages that stated the Japanese would move against a target only known by the code "AF." Because this codename was unknown, the U.S. had to figure out what it was to avoid another surprise attack that it could ill afford. To reveal what the location was, a trick was used to supplement the cryptanalysis being performed. The base sent a special transmission out that stated water was running low at the base over a method the Japanese were known to be monitoring. The Japanese intercepted this message as expected and shortly thereafter started to transmit messages to their forces stating that "AF was short on water." This, coupled with the fact that the Japanese were slow in getting their secret codebooks' updates, meant that the U.S. also had time to decode other messages almost right up to the time of the attack.

The result of the battle was decisive due in no short measure to the misuse of encryption and the careful application of cryptanalysis. The broken code had allowed the U.S. Navy to know the size of the force, its strength, and the general direction of the attacking force. Admiral Nimitz was even able to use the broken messages to understand the tactics that would be employed against him. Using his own force, carefully deployed to work against the Japanese weakness, the Americans were able to win the Battle of Midway.

So enough of the history lessons, let's do some code breaking ourselves.

Note

You may be asking yourself if there is such a thing as an unbreakable code. Well, there are some, such as the one-time pad and some others. However, to make these unbreakable, an exceptional amount of care must be taken in design and practice. In many cases, these types of extremes are not necessary and would be too much overhead for a given application.

How it Works, Breaking the Codes

Let's first do some code breaking by looking at the Enigma system a little more closely to see how it works as well as the how and why it was broken.

The Enigma system, which we already looked at in a previous chapter, is a symmetric cipher that uses substitution as its method of enciphering. The system used a series of rotors that determined how encryption would be performed during that particular instance. For any particular usage of the system, the mapping of plaintext to ciphertext is determined by the position of the rotors.

IMHO

For the record, I am simplifying the Enigma machine greatly to make your understanding easier. If you wish to explore the system more in depth, I would definitely encourage you to do so. There exists a wealth of information that dissects this system in far more depth than we can explore in this text.

Interestingly enough, if you really find yourself itching for more information and experience with the Enigma, you can get some hands-on experience with the machine itself. A recent search of eBay uncovered at least half a dozen of the systems for sale for under $1000 (USD), but these are replicas. Several original versions have come on the market over recent years, with each fetching a price upwards of $16,000 (USD) due to being a genuine article from the Second World War.

So let's now take a look at the Enigma system in a little more depth to see how it works. Figure 6-3 shows a block diagram of the early Enigma design, which I will describe the operation of here.

This figure shows the more well-known three-rotor system that was in use prior to 1942. After 1942, a four-rotor model was introduced that was used by the Kriegsmarine (German Navy) to communicate with U-boats and other shipping. You can extrapolate how the newer models functioned by looking at the diagram I have made for you here; I won't discuss the new model too much, though, because it is unnecessary for our efforts

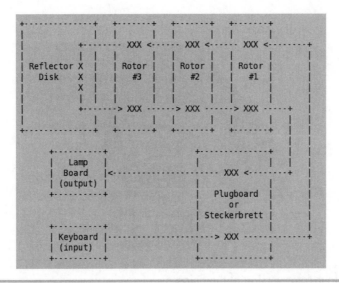

Figure 6-3   Block diagram of the early Enigma design

here. The extra rotor was introduced at the behest of the German Navy because they suspected that their system had been broken by the Allies and pushed for the improvement as a result of their suspicions. Figure 6-4 shows the four rotor model of this version of the Enigma.

IMHO

How good were the code breakers in World War II? Well, to put it simply, the new Enigma system was introduced in 1942, around February, and was broken in December 1942 by Allied code breakers at Bletchley Park. Their efforts were so successful in breaking this system as well as others that the code breakers and the Allied forces had to be careful how they reacted to the information they uncovered. Too blatant a response to the information revealed would have tipped off the Axis powers that their secret codes had been broken, resulting in an inevitable change to a new system.

It is also worth noting that the rotors used in the Enigma were just that: rotors used in a machine. At various times during the war, the Germans issued machines that had anywhere from three to eight rotors issued with them, which at any point the operator of the system could choose to place into the system (that is, an operator could choose three out of five available rotors to place into a system). Figure 6-5 shows a close-up of one of these rotors.

Figure 6-4   The four-rotor version of the Enigma

Figure 6-5   A single version of a rotor used in the Enigma system

In Actual Practice

Yes, there was at least one other known model of Enigma, known as the Enigma II, used briefly in the early 1930s. This model boasted eight rotors and was used mostly for very high-level military communications and had its existence first revealed by the Polish Cipher Bureau. The system was only used briefly before it was pulled out of service due to its tendency to jam and the fact that it was shown to be unreliable at best.

So first things first: How does Enigma function? To answer that, let's first take a look at the rotors themselves and how they were used. The rotors in the system were the foundation upon which the whole process relied. Each rotor was about four inches in diameter and had brass pins arranged in a circle on either side. The pins represented the letters of the alphabet (which I will make easier by saying that we only have 26 instead of the 30 characters in the German language). The pins were wired from side to side in a complex internal wiring arrangement, which formed a simple substitution cipher. Each rotor was identified by a specific number, and a specific rotor (for example, Rotor 3) would be wired the same as every other Rotor 3 issued. Figure 6-6 shows an exploded view of a rotor with sample wiring.

Basically, to keep this simple, the rotors changed position whenever a key was pushed or new character was input. Rotor 1 would advance one position every time a key was

Figure 6-6 Wiring of a rotor that would be used with an Enigma machine

pushed until it reached its rollover position, at which point Rotor 2 would rotate one position. When it reached its rollover position, Rotor 3 would rotate one position. Each change would produce an entirely new substitution or translation of input to output. Figure 6-7 shows a schematic of the Enigma rotor design (but only the outside).

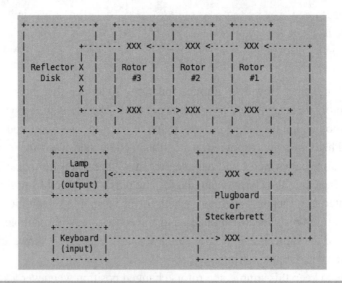

Figure 6-7 The Enigma wiring schematic

IMHO

If you have been paying really close attention to two of our old friends—namely, the Caesar cipher and the Vigenère cipher—you may recognize what is going on here. If the rotor positions stayed the same throughout the encryption process, the system becomes a simple substitution cipher just like the Caesar cipher, which is easily breakable. However, by having the rotors rotate in the manner described here, the system goes from being a simple substitution cipher to a much more complex polyalphabetic cipher like the Vigenère cipher, making the code-breaking process much more formidable.

Also notice in my diagram the presence of something labeled "Reflector Disk." This was designed to connect the outputs of the last rotor, effectively redirecting current through the rotors back via an entirely different route. The benefit here of the reflector is that encryption and decryption would be performed the same way. However, it also introduced a curious little detail that we will see was exploited by the Allies—namely, that no letter could ever encrypt entirely to itself, which was a huge mistake by the system's designers.

Another detail in my diagram is the plugboard, which is simply a set of cables that could be changed depending on the way a cable was plugged into it. If it helps you, think of the old-style telephone switchboards that you may have seen in old movies, where operators manually switched cables to connect phone callers to one another. When configured, it would control how letters were converted during the encryption process. If a cable were configured to connect S and J, it would mean that every S would convert to J, and vice versa. If no cables were configured at all, letters would not be converted aside from the conversion done with the rotors. Although simple in concept and realization, this addition substantially improved encryption over the rotors alone. Figure 6-8 shows a view of an Enigma machine with the plugboard visible.

At this point, the operator would type out the message and the result (or letter that each character encrypted to) would light up on a lampboard (just a bunch of letters that light up). These characters would be transcribed and then sent to the recipient, along with the combination and rotor settings used.

Figure 6-8 An Enigma machine (note the plugboard upfront)

In Actual Practice

To put a different spin on things (or add something else, if I may), every time a key was pushed, the corresponding encrypted letter would appear on the lampboard, but not the same one each time. For example, if the letter S was pushed repeatedly, the letters returned may be something like T, F, O, C, K..., but never S. In fact, the encrypted character would change, but the exact letter being pushed would never appear because the system would not allow a character to encrypt to itself.

In actual practice, on the three-rotor system at least, the same sequence of letters would only repeat after nearly 17,000 keypresses. To prevent the Allies from seeing this repeat, messages were limited in size to prevent the sequence from being detected and thus assisting code breaking.

One more interesting note is that the simple fact that a letter would not encrypt to itself gave away information that assisted in code-breaking efforts.

Want to get an idea of what the Allies were up against when code breaking this system? With the machine in a basic setup, there were at least 60 different ways to put the rotors in the system, with 17,576 settings for each wheel setup. With these numbers plus some other factors, it was possible to have over 150 million million million (yes, you read that right, my friend) possible keys. This alone is daunting, to say the least. Consider the seriousness of figuring out the correct key out of this many possible combinations.

To manage this incredible number of combinations across the vast number of military operations, the Germans issued daily or more frequent instructions of what an operator of the system was to change. These variables included:

- The wheel order or the choice and position of the three wheels to be used
- The ring setting of the left, middle, and right wheels
- The plug configuration

The cipher clerk would set up his machine accordingly. Until the end of April 1940, he then continued as follows:

- He turned his three wheels to a position chosen at random (the "indicator setting").
- He twice keyed his own randomly selected choice of text setting (or "message setting").
- This came out as the "indicator."
- He set his wheels at BGZ and keyed the cleartext of the message, thus obtaining the enciphered text, letter by letter.

Once the signal had been transmitted with the given settings, the message would be received by a cipher clerk who would then decipher the message using the same instructions that would have already been provided.

So with all this complexity, how was Enigma broken? Well, a few things contributed to it:

- The wiring was rarely changed, even during the war itself. This meant that the very mechanism that enciphered letters was greatly reduced, which was something that was easily tackled by Allied code-breaking systems.
- The messages that were transmitted generally included the same opening and closing, such as "TO GENERAL..." or "HAIL THE FUHRER," which made it easier to break the codes.
- Letters never encrypted to themselves; in other words, S would never encrypt to S. This fact, coupled with the habit of using standard phrases at the start of each communication, allowed cryptanalysts to establish informed "guesses."

Note

Don't start doing cartwheels yet, because even with the smartest of minds, Enigma's 150,000,000,000,000,000,000 combinations were practically unbreakable. Without mechanical methods, it would not have been possible to break the codes manually.

As I described to you in a previous chapter, the Poles were the first to crack the Enigma in 1932. They were able to use a combination of statistical analysis coupled with information gained from other sources, such as a German spy and an intercepted system. This helped tremendously later on.

The Germans got to be more clever during the war by closely controlling how the system was configured, which made early cracking attempts easy. Later on, in the years leading up to the war, the Germans become more sophisticated with how they controlled the settings of the system, but they still had flaws that allowed outside parties to obtain the key for a specific day. With the new system of managing settings, it became impossible to use the existing methods in a timely enough manner to recover the keys by an outside party. This drove the need for a better mechanism to crack the Enigma by the Allies.

Two Polish mathematicians developed one of the first systems used specifically to recover keys from a cryptographic system, which was known as the Bombe. The machine was able to recover the key settings in less than two hours, much faster than doing it by hand or the old-fashioned way, don't you think?

Although I won't get into the specifics of the Bombe mechanism, because it is much more technical than we need to get into, I do want to give you a picture of what the machine looked like. Figure 6-9 shows an example of the Bombe.

Figure 6-9 The Bombe system

With the story of Enigma being covered, let's now take a look at code breaking ourselves, starting with some of the systems we talked about before. Ready to code break? Well, put on your thinking cap and get a pencil and a cup of coffee, because here's where the fun starts. For additional atmosphere, I suggest you get a copy of the old *Mission: Impossible* theme song while you're cracking codes—it makes the process much more cool.

The Basics

So how do we break codes? The code breakers during the war broke this complex system by using logic, mathematics, and common sense. Do you have what it takes? Let's see.

First, let's revisit the two ciphers from earlier:

- **Transposition cipher**   With this cipher, the plaintext's letters are rearranged into a different configuration; for example, this sentence could be arranged into a box format, with each line containing 10 characters. Although the same message is still present, the order of the letters has been changed in some manner.

- **Substitution cipher**   This cipher replaces the characters in the original message with new characters. Although the original plaintext has not been changed and the message is still present, the original characters are not. The best examples we have seen of this are the Caesar cipher and the Vigenère cipher, which replace letters with other characters (or in the case of the Pigpen cipher, with symbols).

When we break systems, we need to keep in mind a few things we have gone over earlier as well as some new terms and concepts to make code breaking easier for us to perform. In many cases, a few things prove true that we can use to assist us by applying some measure of logic to the situation. Let's take a look at some basic principles that can help us out:

- *Look for keywords with repeating letters or keywords that are too short.* Think of the Vigenère cipher, as an example. This cipher uses a keyword to encrypt the plaintext. If the keyword is too short or if letters repeat, patterns will emerge. In both cases, the usage of such keywords should be avoided. If we can detect these patterns, however, they can prove to be valuable in breaking the message.

- *Know patterns in words or predictable patterns that are present in a language.* In the English language, a single-letter word is almost always the letter *A* or *I,* which gives us a clue. Also, two-letter words typically have one vowel and one consonant in them, with little deviation from this rule. Additionally, if we see a three-letter word, it is almost invariable the word *and* or *the.* Also, some letter combinations are always (or very nearly always) found together (for example, the letter *q* is always followed by the letter *u).*

- *Know that in every language, certain letters appear more often than others.* For example, in the English language, the letters *R, S, T, L, N,* and *E* appear much more often than other letters. Think about it: How many times do you see these letters picked on *Wheel of Fortune?*

IMHO

It is worth noting that your own brain will work against you at times. The human brain has a tendency to fill in gaps in words, making them sometimes read as something else in your mind. For example, consider the following text:

Aoccdrnig to rscheearch at Cmabrigde uinervtisy, it deosn't mttaer waht oredr the ltteers in a wrod are, the olny iprmoetnt tihng is taht the frist and lsat ltteres are at the rghit pclae. The rset can be a tatol mses and you can sitll raed it wouthit a porbelm. Tihs is bcuseae we do not raed ervey lteter by it slef but the wrod as a wlohe.

You can read all or most of this text without even thinking about it because your brain expects certain letters to be present and visualizes them in their proper place. However, this can also work against you when you read a coded message. Remember: attention to detail.

Enough talking. Let's try some examples of code breaking and see how you do. As before, I will provide some examples and then give you some exercises to practice your new-found code-breaking skills.

First, here are some rules and guidelines so you don't get too sidetracked in your code breaking:

- No letter in these puzzles is the same as its plaintext counterpart. For example, the letter *S* will not encrypt (or decrypt) to the letter *S*.

- All plaintext is in English; no other languages are used.

- Look for single-letter words. In the English language, these two words have to be I or A (and very rarely O). If you can find one of these single-letter words, you may actually be able to solve other words in the puzzle easier if they use the same letter.

- Look for vowels, if possible. Because these five letters alone constitute 40 percent of the English language, locating and translating them can go a long way toward cracking a message.

- Vowels are normally present in every word.

- Vowels may rarely appear three in a row, but almost never four in a row.

- Double-vowels are typically *ee* or *oo* but rarely *aa, ii,* or *uu.*

- The most common vowel is *e* and the least common is *u*.
- The word "the" tends to be the most common three-letter word.
- Watch for apostrophes. The letter after an apostrophe is usually *t* or *s*, and more rarely *m* or *d*. Two letters after an apostrophe are usually *re* or *ve* if the letters are different, or *ll* if it's a double-letter.
- Use clues from punctuation. A conjunction such as "but" or "and" often follow a comma.
- Look for pairs of two-letter words, one beginning and the other ending with the same letter. That letter has a good chance of being *n, o, s, l,* or *t,* and the second letter of the word that starts with the shared letter is likely to be *f, n, o, r, s,* or *t.*

Got it? I know it's a lot, so let's start by converting some quotes to encrypted messages. Then I will turn you loose to do some on your own. Sound good? Let's get started then.

For each of the following three puzzles, I want you to use the keyshift as specified under each puzzle. This should be easy because it is a revisit of the Caesar cipher.

Plaintext	A		S	T	I	T	C	H		I	N		T	I	M	E
Ciphertext																

Plaintext	S	A	V	E	S		N	I	N	E
Ciphertext										

Puzzle 1 Instructions: Use a keyshift of 3.

Plaintext	Y	O	U		C	A	N	N	O	T		O	P	E	N		A
Ciphertext																	

Plaintext	B	O	O	K		W	I	T	H	O	U	T		L	E	A	R	N	I	N	G
Ciphertext																					

Plaintext	S	O	M	E	T	H	I	N	G
Ciphertext									

Puzzle 2 Instructions: Use a keyshift of 6.

Plaintext	T	O		B	E		O	R		N	O	T		T	O		B	E
Ciphertext																		

Puzzle 3 Instructions: Use a keyshift of 4.

Now that you have had time to practice your encryption skills and see how patterns may emerge, let's actually break some phrases that have been encrypted. I know you are up to the challenge, so don't give up on these puzzles and remember the advice I gave you previously.

I will give you the ciphertext, and you just need to look for the patterns to emerge and use some logic and reasoning. You will need to use your skills to guess a keyshift and break the puzzle. I have also given you a clue that requires you to do some research, but will give you a push in the right direction.

Plaintext																	
Ciphertext	W	R		E	H		R	U		Q	R	W		W	R		E	H

Puzzle 4: Hint: "Theater in the Round"

Plaintext																		
Ciphertext	Z	N	K	Y	K		G	X	K		Z	N	K		Z	O	S	K	Y		Z	N	G	Z

Plaintext												
Ciphertext	Z	X	E		S	K	T	'	Y		Y	U	A	R	Y

Puzzle 5: Hint: "The Rights of Man"

Plaintext																	
Ciphertext	O		Z	N	O	T	Q		Z	N	K	X	K	L	U	X	K		O		G	S

Puzzle 6: Hint: Rene Descartes

Plaintext																	
Ciphertext	G		C	O	F	G	X	J		O	Y		T	K	B	K	X		R	G	Z	K	,

Plaintext																
Ciphertext	L	X	U	J	U		H	G	M	M	O	T	Y	.	T	U	X		O	Y		N	K

Plaintext																						
Ciphertext	V	X	K	I	O	Y	K	R	E		C	N	K	T		N	K		S	K	G	T	Y

Ciphertext	Z	U	.

Puzzle 7: Hint: Gandalf

Let's move on to something a little more advanced and see if you can break the code of some secret messages that use a different type of substitution cipher. I want you to look at the following message and see if you can figure out its contents. Note that this new puzzle looks different, but it uses the same concept you just used. It is because of this similarity that I am not going to show you how to solve this type of puzzle, but I know you can do it.

Plaintext																			
Ciphertext	3	1	14		25	15	21		11	5	5	16		1		19	5	3	18	5	20

Puzzle 8: Numeric substitution cipher

Did you figure it out? Well, if you have a good eye and reasoned it out, you saw that all I did was substitute the actual letter with that letter's position in the alphabet (that is, A=1 and Z=26).

Try this cipher yourself by converting the following plaintext to ciphertext using the same method.

Plaintext																				
Ciphertext	1	12	23	1	25	19		18	5	1	4	25		1	12	23	1	25	19		20	8	5	18	5

Puzzle 9: Converting ciphertext to plaintext

Plaintext														
Ciphertext	4	21	20	25		19	5	18	22	9	3	5		8	15	14	15	18

Puzzle 10: Converting ciphertext to plaintext

Had fun with those? Let's make the code-breaking game a little harder by revisiting the Caesar cipher, but with a new twist added for kicks. At this point, you know the cipher and how it works, but now let me introduce code words to the mix to make things more interesting.

In this next set of puzzles, I will use a code word to generate the pseudo-alphabet that we used to encrypt our plaintext in previous examples. I will first show you how the process works and then give you some puzzles to try this new code breaking out.

To use this new process, we must first pick out a code word. For this example, I will choose the word "Mustang" as my code. I use this code word to create my pseudo-alphabet, like so:

m	u	s	t	a	n	g	b	c	d	e	f	h	i	j	k	l	o	p	q	r	v	w	x	y	z

Notice what I have done here? I have used the keyword at the front of the alphabet and then I have written the remaining letters in order. Once I have this done, I can now encrypt the message using this alphabet, as follows (I have put the pseudo-alphabet with the regular alphabet underneath to show how the letters would encrypt):

m	u	s	t	a	n	g	b	c	d	e	f	h	i	j	k	l	o	p	q	r	v	w	x	y	z
a	b	c	d	e	f	g	h	i	j	k	l	m	n	o	p	q	r	s	t	u	v	w	x	y	z

Now let's encrypt a message using this new alphabet. In this case, I'll use the message "The cake is a lie."

Plaintext	T	h	e		c	a	k	e		i	s		a		l	i	e
Ciphertext	d	m	k		i	e	p	k		n	c		e		q	n	k

See how the process works? Now let's have you try the same thing with some new puzzles. I'll make things easier on you by giving you the code word.

Plaintext																			
Ciphertext	a	c	q		e	r	w		b	h	c	g		v	k	l	u		q	r	y

Puzzle 11: Code word "crazy"

Plaintext																
Ciphertext	q	c	t		i	r	h	h	l	l	k		d	p		o	t	e

Puzzle 12: Code word "rivet"

Plaintext	a	l	l		i	s		q	u	i	e	t		n	o	w	
Ciphertext	j	g	g		d	r		n	u	d	p	s		i	l	w	

Puzzle 12: Code word "jackpot"

Note

Notice something unique and problematic with this cipher? It is not uncommon for some letters to actually encrypt to themselves, especially the ones at the end of the alphabet. You may have noticed during your puzzle solving that this did in fact occur in some of the examples. It is because of this property that you want to make sure you choose your code words carefully.

One last topic we will look at in this chapter is codes and codebooks. I mentioned these earlier in reference to the Zimmermann note and the JN-25 code. Let's now look at codes and codebooks and see how we may break them.

To help you understand codes and codebooks, let's use two examples you are familiar with: Braille and Morse code. Braille, as you may know, is a system of conveying messages to the blind via a series of raised dots in various patterns. A blind person or anyone familiar with the system can move their fingers over the dots and by feeling the patterns can interpret the meaning. The patterns of dots and what they mean have already been defined and are documented; this documentation would be akin to creating a codebook of sorts. The code would be the actual dots that render the message onto the page. In the case of Morse code, the series of dots and dashes have been standardized to represent certain letters, because everyone uses the same standardized set of patterns, the transmitted sets of dots and dashes can be understood by all parties. If you haven't seen Morse code before, let's take a look at it. We'll examine a message and then encode it into the dots and dashes that are used in the system. The message to be encoded is:

Writing in code is awesome

If we translate this into Morse code, the message turns into this:

.-- .-. .. - .. -. --.   .. -.   -.-. --- -.. .   .. .- .-- . ... --- -- .

Anyone who knows the code can translate these symbols back into the original message due to everyone having access to the same codebook, which spells out what each symbol means.

Although both Morse code and Braille show us how code systems work, they do not provide us any secrecy because what the systems mean is well known. Governments and other parties typically have a need to keep secrets, and this can be done with codes as well. Essentially what we would do to accomplish this is to create a codebook that describes how to translate a message into code. Once this codebook is created, it would be safely and securely distributed to those we wish to communicate with, and no one else.

To illustrate this, let's create our own codebook:

Code	Word	Code	Word	Code	Word	Code	Word
1287	the	2013	strike	1947	ready	1111	boat
1372	as	1939	operation	6582	enemy	9631	dawn
7834	night	8337	sky	5002	will	2468	noon
9136	attack	1703	beach	4821	it	8008	for
1972	at	4317	troops	2205	from	7227	be
2005	for	3052	begins	1993	water	6973	retreat
2102	light	1705	armed	3887	and	8913	advance

In our codebook (which is small), we have a bunch of numbers and the words they correspond to. Note that the numbers have no particular order to them, which reduces the chance of someone detecting a pattern. With our codebook in hand, let's code a message. Here's what the message will be:

The operation begins at dawn be ready

In code, this message would now be:

1287 1939 3052 1972 9631 7227 1947

Now that you know how it is done, can you decode this message using the same codebook?

1972 9631 1287 4317 5002 7227 1705 3887 1947
2005 9136 3887 5002 8913 8008 1287 2013

Okay, try one more, but this time let me make it more like the Zimmermann note from earlier. Instead of writing the codes as one long line, I am going to format them as a box. Can you figure it out? The victory of our forces depends on you.

7227 1947 8008 6582
1939 1972 7834 2205
1287 1703 3887 2205
1287 8337 6582 5002
8913 3887 9136 2205
1287 8337 1972 9631

See, not too hard at all. Let's analyze this example now with an eye toward the code-breaking tips from earlier. If you look at this last puzzle in code, you can see that several numbers or codes repeat at least twice, and some even more. If we have some knowledge of the underlying message, such as the language (which in this case is English), we can attempt to try some common letters or words to see if they fit and make sense. If the same codebook is used for too long, these codes that appear frequently could potentially reveal to a third party what is being transmitted. This is one of the reasons why codebooks are typically changed regularly in addition to other methods for avoiding patterns and detection, such as adding in some other form of encryption on top of the message before it is coded.

Another potential method of breaking these types of codes would be inference. Let's say that we have the same message as before, but when we intercepted it on the radio it got garbled a bit and we lost certain parts. Now the message looks like this:

```
7227 1947 8008 6582
1939 1972 7834 xxxx
1287 1703 3887 2205
1287 xxxx 6582 5002
xxxx 3887 9136 2205
1287 8337 xxxx 9631
```

Ignore the previous message, which is where this message was derived from, and now use the codebook generated earlier to solve it. Could you safely assume what the missing characters or words are? Depending on your skills, luck, and knowledge of the situation, you may be able to do so.

Note

Another way of figuring out codes and what they mean is to have some knowledge of what the involved parties are doing and then doing something that makes them have to retransmit the message. For example, in our message the enemy is going to attack us at dawn, but what if we didn't know where? Well, we could move our forces to a new location or spread them out and watch what codes change when the enemy transmits updated information to its own forces. Presumably the new codes would include our new location, so we could get clues to where the enemy was and what they were up to.

Code breaking may seem to be easy based on what the movies and popular culture show us, but in reality it usually is much more involved, as you have now seen and experienced. We have done some code breaking in this chapter and explored just the "tip of the iceberg" of this body of knowledge. We analyzed some systems and even saw how the famous Enigma system worked and was broken.

You also now know that the process is as much about skills as it is luck and poor design. Although accessing a piece of information without authorization may seem malicious or underhanded (and indeed it may be), it may also be used to defeat an enemy such as a terrorist group.

We've Covered

What is cryptanalysis?

- Cryptanalysis is the analysis of codes and ciphers.
- Cryptanalysis is sometimes referred to as code breaking.

A look at Enigma

- Enigma was a series of cryptographic systems used during World War II.
- Enigma was used to encode messages during wartime.

What is code breaking?

- Code breaking is the art of cracking cryptosystems without the key or other knowledge.
- Code breaking is intended to defeat cryptosystems.

Methods to code break

- Frequency analysis relies on patterns to reveal the inner workings of a system.
- There are several methods to code break systems.

How to break a coded message

- A message can be broken by uncovering the key.
- A message can be broken by analyzing the ciphertext.

What makes code breaking easier?

- Reuse of a key can make breaking a message simpler.
- A poorly designed algorithm can make code breaking quicker.

Examples of code breaking

- Code breaking has been assisted through poor design and key generation.
- Code breaking of Enigma was started by the Polish.

CHAPTER 7

Public Key Infrastructure

We'll Cover

- What is Public Key Infrastructure (PKI)?

- Components of PKI

- Fundamentals of PKI

- Applications of PKI

- Process of PKI

We have covered a lot so far in this book, and in this chapter we will cover something known as PKI, or Public Key Infrastructure. PKI is an important component of today's world and in fact can be said to be the "glue" that holds together and enables many of the services we may take for granted.

Without PKI, many of the processes and technologies we enjoy would not even be possible, or at least not be possible in their current form. So what technologies depend on PKI? Well, the answer is *many,* so many in fact that we couldn't possibly list them all here, but the short list includes:

- E-commerce applications, such as those used by Amazon.com

- Financial applications, such as those for logging in to your bank account online to manage your account details or to pay a bill

- Webmail systems, which use protected communications to safeguard your credentials, including username and password, as well as your e-mail messages

- Common Access Card (CAC) systems, which are used to safely and securely log in to computer systems and networks such as those used by the U.S. Government

Essentially all these systems require a secure means of transferring information, and PKI facilitates that transfer for us and makes these and other systems possible.

Your Plan

By the end of this chapter, you should be considering and envisioning the ways that PKI may be of help in your organization or in the projects you may have. If you work in an environment where a PKI system is already present, think about why your company may be using the system and what this means to you.

So What Is PKI?

A PKI system can be a lot of different things, but the most prominent and obvious is a system that provides safe and secure communication over an insecure medium. The system also allows for the validation of credentials, known as digital certificates, that themselves are the cornerstone of the system.

PKI is by far the most common implementation of several of the cryptographic systems we have discussed in this book. As has been mentioned, PKI facilitates the mechanism through which two parties can confidently communicate over an insecure medium. So how does it do this? This is both an easy question and a complex one, as you'll see as we break into the actual technical details of the system. First, let's start with the basics.

> **LINGO**
> **PKI** or **Public Key Infrastructure** is combination of software, hardware, and policies used to secure communications. The system itself is platform agnostic (in other words, it doesn't depend on a specific technology or environment; rather, it depends on the mechanisms to maintain a standard).

Let's assume a situation where two parties need to communicate: We'll call them Farore and Nayru. The problem is that neither of these two actually know the other directly, nor do they have any sort of prior relationship. So how do these two parties establish a secure channel for exchanging information if no prior relationship exists? Well, it just so happens that both these parties trust a third party, who we will say is named Din. Because both parties trust Din, they can inquire as to the trustworthiness of the other through Din. In other words, Farore can ask Din whether Nayru is okay, and Nayru can ask Din whether Farore is okay. It is through this use of a trusted third party that two parties with no prior relationship can work together.

> **Tip**
> If it helps, think of the trusted third party as the person your best friend introduces you to. You may not know the person, but because your friend trusts them and you trust your friend, you trust this person as well. Simple analogy, but it does work for us at the most basic level.

PKI is vitally important to us mainly due to the complexities and realities of cyberspace and the Internet that make a trust relationship trickier to establish; in other words, one cannot just walk into a location and verify that it is trustworthy. In fact, the vendor you may be dealing with in today's world online may be on the other side of the planet. In these situations, it is more than possible there may not even be a physical location at all to trust. PKI was made to address these concerns and bring trust, integrity, and security to electronic transactions. The PKI framework exists to manage, create, store, and distribute keys and digital certificates safely and securely. The components of this framework include the following:

- **Certificate authority (CA)**   The entity responsible for enrollment, creation, management, validation, and revocation of digital certificates.

- **Registration authority (RA)**   The entity responsible for accepting information about a party wishing to obtain a certificate. Note that RAs do not issue certificates or manage certificates in any way.

- **Certificate revocation list (CRL)**   A location where certificates that have been revoked prior to their assigned expiration are published.

- **Digital certificate**   A piece of information (much like a driver's license in the real world) that is used to positively prove the identity of a person, party, computer, or service.

- **Certificate distribution system**   A combination of software, hardware, services, and procedures used to distribute certificates.

Note
Don't sweat the details yet, because each of these items will be discussed in this chapter and put into context within the system so as to give you the best view of what the system looks like.

Before we go too far, let's look at each of the components involved in PKI just so we can make sure we are on the same page and have all the information we need to put everything together. Here are the components from previous chapters we need to make this work:

- Symmetric encryption
- Asymmetric encryption or public/private key cryptography
- Hashing

Let's take another look at each briefly.

Symmetric Encryption
As we explored a few chapters ago, symmetric encryption is a form of encryption that uses a single key to perform both encryption and decryption.

In this form of encryption, unencrypted data known as *cleartext* or *plaintext* is fed into the encryption process, where it is transformed into ciphertext. The plaintext is fed into the encryption algorithm along with a specific key chosen from the keyspace at random that is used to come up with the specific settings for a given encryption process. The process cannot be reversed from ciphertext to plaintext if one does not posses the correct key, which is the intended effect.

As you saw earlier, one of the defining characteristics of the encryption process is the fact that the same key is used to encrypt and decrypt. This immediately tells us that the key must be safely and securely distributed to all parties without comprising the secrecy of the key itself. Therefore, a mechanism must be in place to distribute these keys, and this is a role that PKI can fulfill. With PKI, if implemented correctly, the keys can be distributed safely without the worry of a third party getting their hands on them.

> **LINGO**
> Remember, a **key** is used to determine that specific settings for a specific encryption session. Although many potential keys are available in the keyspace, only the one used to encrypt in the symmetric encryption process can be used to decrypt. Always remember that keys represent a significant and substantial factor in determining the effectiveness of a given encryption session.

Here's a list of some of the more common symmetric systems:

- **3DES**   An extended, more secure version of DES that performs DES three times
- **Advanced Encryption Standard (AES)**   A replacement for DES that is more resistant to attack
- **Blowfish**   A highly efficient block cipher that can have a key length up to 448 bits
- **International Data Encryption Algorithm (IDEA)**   Uses 64-bit input and output data blocks and features a 128-bit key
- **RC4**   A stream cipher designed by Ron Rivest that is used by WEP
- **RC5**   A fast block cipher designed by Ron Rivest that can use a large key size
- **RC6**   A cipher derived from RC5

> **Note**
> We discussed a lot of different algorithms in the chapter on symmetric algorithms. The ones listed here are just meant to refresh your memory on the different ones that can be used along with a PKI system. I have chosen the most commonly used ones, just to keep things simple. In fact, as you learned earlier, at this level the different algorithms all essentially look the same on the outside; it is just a case of being implemented differently on the inside.

Asymmetric Encryption

One of the biggest players in PKI is the asymmetric encryption system. In fact, as you'll recall, the algorithms in this class are also called *public/private key* encryption systems. This is a description that will come into play in this chapter and will undoubtedly make much more sense to you after all is said and done.

Asymmetric systems are sometimes called *public key cryptosystems,* which is in fact the name they are commonly known by. In this type of system, whatever is done with one key can only be reversed with the corresponding key, and nothing else. This key pair is generated with one key being held in secret and the other one distributed publicly. In fact, by their very design, these systems are set up so everyone and anyone has access to the public key whenever they want. However, by the same token, the private key is only accessible or available to a small number of individuals—or even just one individual. Whoever has access to the public key can encrypt or decrypt data, but can never do so at the same time to the same chunk of information.

Tip

You need to keep in mind that in practice the only real difference between a public key and a private key is access (or who possesses it at any time). You learned before that when a key pair is generated, either key, by definition, can be given to an individual for their exclusive use. Once this is done, this key becomes that person's private key and needs to be secured. This means that, on the other hand, the other key is put in a commonly available and publicly accessible area where it is now labeled the public key.

With asymmetric systems, much like with symmetric, a number of algorithms are available. Some of the more common ones are listed here for reference:

- **Diffie-Hellman**   Developed in 1976, this process is used to establish and exchange keys over an insecure medium

- **Elgamal**   Functions by calculating discrete logarithms instead of the factoring of large numbers

- **Elliptic curve cryptography**   Commonly implemented on mobile devices or devices with lesser processor power or battery power

- **RSA**   Widely used in various applications and processes such as e-commerce and comparable applications

We care about asymmetric encryption in this chapter because it gives us something we need for PKI: an answer to the problem of key distribution. Whereas symmetric encryption uses the same key to encrypt and decrypt, asymmetric uses two related but different keys that can reverse whatever operation the other performs. Unlike symmetric systems, the unique design of asymmetric systems does not compromise the secrecy of the other key in any way whatsoever. We can safely distribute the public key and can pretty much not worry about compromising security in any way. This public key can be used by anyone needing to send a message to the owner of the public key. Because the public key only encrypts and cannot decrypt anything it has performed the operation on, there is no fear of unauthorized disclosure.

Hashing

The conversion of plaintext to ciphertext is not the only function that cryptography performs, and the science of hashing proves that. *Hashing* is strictly a one-way function that is designed to do what the other forms of cryptography cannot, which is to verify the integrity of information. As you may recall, a hashing function is designed to derive a fixed-length value from a piece of information. This fixed-length value is relatively easy to calculate in one direction, but is not easy to do in the other.

Tip

Think of the one-way function as something that is easy to do one way and not the other. Consider, if you will, three large numbers, any three. Using a calculator, it is relatively easy to multiply these numbers together to get a final result, but taking the final number and trying to figure out the original three numbers is quite hard.

This process allows for the unique and powerful ability to verify information and to detect but not prevent changes. In fact, any change will result in a value that is radically different from the one before the change is done.

Note

It is important for you to realize that the process of hashing does not provide data confidentiality; it provides the ability to ensure integrity only. Hashes are used to create and verify the unique digital fingerprint for a file. Due to the design and functioning of a hash, a change can be readily detected, but its exact location within the file is quite difficult to ascertain. Because the process provides the ability to detect changes, it is commonly used to detect alterations in data and files due to any sort of expected or unexpected behavior.

Hash functions create a fixed-length value that is generated by computing the hash from the plaintext that is put into the process. Once the hash is generated from this process, it becomes essentially impossible to reverse to get the original plaintext that generated it—although some would say it is "mathematically infeasible."

In our system of PKI, you should remember that hashes provide the ability to verify the integrity of transmitted messages. A sender could easily create a message hash and send it on its way, giving the receiver the instructions as to how to repeat the process. In fact, we will use this exact same process later on when we discuss digital signatures and how PKI figures in.

Some of the most common hashing algorithms include the following:

- **Message Digest 2 (MD2)**   A one-way hash function used in the Privacy Enhanced Mail (PEM) protocols, along with MD5.
- **Message Digest 4 (MD4)**   Provides a 128-bit hash of the input message.
- **Message Digest 5 (MD5)**   An improved and redesigned version of MD4 that produces a 128-bit hash.

Note

MD5 figures prominently into digital certificates, as you will see in a moment.

- **HAVAL**   A variable-length, one-way hash function and modification of MD5.
- **Secure Hash Algorithm-0 (SHA-0)**   Provides a 160-bit fingerprint. SHA-0 is no longer considered secure and is vulnerable to attacks.
- **Secure Hash Algorithm-1 (SHA-1)**   Processes messages up to 512-bit blocks and adds padding, if needed, to get the data to add up to the right number of bits.

Digital Certificates

As you'll recall when we spoke about asymmetric encryption and symmetric encryption, one of the many issues at play is key distribution. And one of the problems that goes along with this is how to identify the user or holder of a key. This is one task that PKI is intended to handle. The core item that assists in identifying the holder of a particular key is the digital certificate. Figure 7-1 shows the SSL process with attention paid to certificates.

In all types of transactions, certificates provide several services:

- **Identity**   The binding of a public key to a party such as an individual, organization, or any other entity that needs to prove its identity.
- **Authority**   A list of the actions the holder of the certificate is allowed to exercise, much like a driver's license authorizes an individual to operate certain vehicles.
- **Secure confidential information**   Used to keep information private and safe from unauthorized access

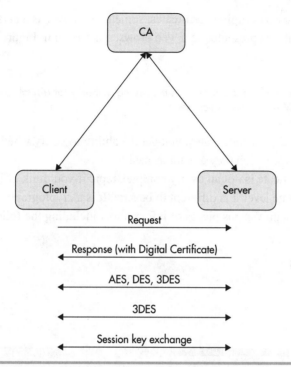

Figure 7-1   The SSL process

Tip

Digital certificates are used for many purposes within many systems, such as SSL and digital signatures. Many of the mechanisms you rely on to safely and securely communicate would not even be possible without the use of digital certificates.

Consider the issues in the systems we have discussed so far if a key is distributed to a given party. If the key is presented by one party to another, the receiving party must take it on absolute trust and faith that the presenter is who they say they are. The recipient, as of yet, has no way of positively identifying whether the owner is who they say they are— which can be a problem. Additionally, the presenting party is also making a claim that they are authorized to use the key for what they are actually attempting to use it for. Let's look at this problem from another perspective to make things a little clearer. Consider a situation where I, your humble guide, present a credential (such as a driver's license) to you. You have to take it on faith that the credential is valid and not the fake one I used in college (long story). So that you don't have to do this, I present you with an official document that you can verify by checking with a third party you trust (which would be the

DMV—or in the case of digital certificates, something known as a *certification authority*). A digital certificate, as presented to a web browser, is shown in Figure 7-2.

Note

You can consider certification authorities as the issuing authority for digital certificates, kind of like the DMV is for driver's licenses.

In the case of digital certificates, you get the ability to verify whether the holder is doing something for which they are authorized.

A digital certificate is not an overly complex topic if you think of it as a driver's license, but on some level it is different to be sure. It is a cryptographically sealed object that is populated with various pieces of information, including the following:

- Version

- Serial Number

- Algorithm ID

- Issuer

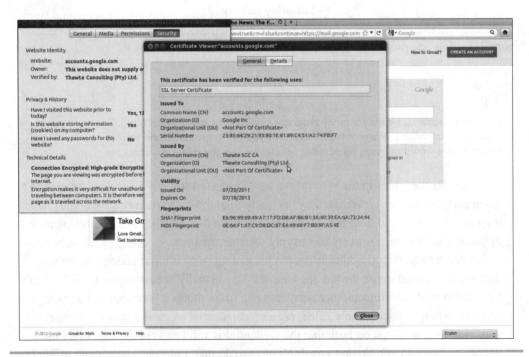

Figure 7-2 A digital certificate as presented to the Firefox web browser

- Validity
- Not Before
- Not After
- Subject
- Subject Public Key Info
- Public Key Algorithm
- Subject Public Key

Note that the digital certificate includes the public key, which is bound to the credential so that the key can be associated with a specific owner. Additionally, it is worth noting that the certificate also includes information stating who issued the credential to the specific holder.

As a matter of normal practice, a certificate typically has a public key bound to it, along with the authority who issued the certificate (and is asserting the individual is who they say they are), a serial number, any supporting policies describing how the certificate was issued, and information on how the certificate may actually be used. Although other information may be included as part of the certificate, only certain basic information is required.

IMHO

Digital certificates are like driver's licenses in the sense that they are issued to people and identify the privileges allowed as well as the period of time for which they are valid. However, a digital certificate can also be issued to a device or even a piece of software, depending on the context. This is where the analogy breaks down for us. After all, as we all know, a driver's license can be issued to a person, but not to a car.

A certificate is not a complex concept. In technical terms, it is a cryptographically sealed object that includes a party's identity and public key. The certificate is populated with various pieces of information and a public key. It is then signed by generating a hash value and encrypting it with the issuer's

LINGO

What is a **cryptographically sealed object**? In essence, it is an object that cannot be changed without the change being noticed. How can this be done? Through the use of our good friend hashing, of course.

private key. At this point, if the certificate is altered (for example, if a party tries to replace the public key), the hash value becomes invalid, the certificate becomes invalid, and the client should see a warning indicating as much. If a client possesses the issuer's public key and trusts the issuer of the key, then the client will assume the public key in the certificate checks out. For an attacker to compromise the system, they would have to have access to either the private key of the server or the private key of the issuer to successfully impersonate one of these parties.

A digital certificate allow us to associate the previously mentioned public key with a particular service, such as a web server for use in e-commerce, which can then be authenticated. If someone was to claim they are the person who is the true owner of the key and certificate, they would not be able to do so as the holder of the private key.

LINGO
When you encounter certificates in the real world, you will undoubtedly hear the term **X.509**. This term refers to a standard that is used to format certificates and thus ensure compatibility between applications and parties. Consider the following situation to understand this better: What would happen if every state in the United States made up entirely different rules as to what to include on a driver's license, with each one being radically different? It would be mayhem. As it stands now, each state has slightly different formatting, but they are all close enough that they can be understood by different parties, sight unseen.

Authenticating the Certificate

A digital certificate can and does complement or replace other forms of authentication. A user who presents the credential must have a method in place that allows for the credential to be validated (such is the role of the CA, which we will discuss in a moment). When you present a certificate to another party, the credential is validated and allows that party to have their identity confirmed as part of the transaction. Once a series of steps is undertaken, secure communication or the validation of items such as the digital signature can take place.

Enter the PKI System

As you would expect, certificates cannot and do not exist on their own and in fact have a home out there in cyberspace, known as a certification authority (CA). A certification authority is nothing more than a repository that controls, creates, and revokes certificates, along with the associated public keys. As you will see, a CA can be controlled by a company for its internal use or by a public entity for use by anyone who wishes to purchase a credential from the controlling party.

So let's take it from the top and start with a discussion of each of the components themselves, starting with the certification authority.

So What Is a Certification Authority?

So what is a CA and what does it do for us? A CA forms the bedrock, if you will, of the whole PKI system and makes it work the way we need it to. A CA is nothing more than a trusted third party responsible for issuing, managing, identifying, and revoking certificates as necessary, as well as enrolling parties for their own certificates. The CA vouches for the identity of the holder of any given certificate. A CA is sort of like a friend who introduces you to a friend of theirs; you may not know this other person, but because your trusted friend does, you trust the other person by extension. A CA acts as this trusted friend and can vouch for the identities of the parties who have been issued certificates by the CA. In the real world, a CA can and does issue credentials to numerous entities, including banks, webmail, VPNs, and smart cards. The CA gathers information and then validates and issues a credential to the requesting party if everything checks out.

> **LINGO**
> A **trusted third-party** is nothing more than someone you (or your computer) trusts. The idea is that a group of parties who don't know each other can each trust a public entity such as the CA. Even though the parties don't know each other, they can trust one another as long as the CA can vouch for them.

Since we are talking trust here and we have to consider that anyone can claim to be someone else, a CA must have processes in place to prevent a person from claiming they are someone else. The CA will require information to be provided that proves identity. Items such as name, address, and phone, physical data such as faxed records, and other records and personal interviews might also be required, as policy dictates. Once this information is obtained and validated, the CA will issue the certificate or validate an existing certificate.

In Actual Practice

In the real world, a certificate can be issued by many commercial certification authorities even if actual documentation has not been provided. In these cases, the certificate that the CA issues is said to be "unverified" until the holder provides supporting documentation of their claimed identity to the CA. Either certificate, verified or unverified, can be used to perform the same actions; it is just up to the party who is presented the certificate to decide whether they wish to accept the credential or not (if it is unverified).

Only a small number of CAs (relatively speaking, of course) can issue certificates. In the real world, a CA will accept a request for a digital certificate or a validation thereof. When the CA accepts a request for a digital certificate, the applicant will undergo some sort of check—background or otherwise—to verify that they are who they say they are or claim to be. A publicly owned CA such as Thawte or VeriSign typically will perform this background check by asking the requester to provide documentation such as a driver's license, passport, or other form of ID.

When a CA issues a certificate, several actions take place that we know about:

1. The request is received.

2. Background information is requested by the CA and then validated.

3. The information provided by the requester is applied to the certificate.

4. The CA hashes the certificate.

5. The issuing CA signs the certificate with their private key.

6. The requester is informed that their certificate is ready for pickup.

7. The requester installs the certificate on their computer or device.

Note

So how does the application or person requesting validation of a certificate know the CA itself is legitimate? That is a question we will address (and answer) later in this chapter, so stay tuned.

In practice, a CA is able to (and typically does) perform a number of different roles in addition to the validation process outlined here. The actions a CA is called upon to perform include the following:

- **Generation of the key pair or the public and private key pair**   When a CA goes through the process of creating a certificate, a key pair that is made up of a public and private key is generated. The public key will be made available to the public at large, whereas the private key will be given to the party requesting the digital certificate itself.

Tip

As you may recall, the public and private keys are mathematically related and what is performed by either key can only be undone by the other. Typically, the only fact that separates one key from the other is who has access to it. If everyone has access to the key, it is public. If only one person or a few people have access to the key, it is private.

- **Generation of certificates**   The CA will generate digital certificates for any authorized party when requested. This certificate will be generated after validation of the identity of the requesting party.

- **Publishing of the public key**   The public key is placed upon and bound to each digital certificate as both are generated. Anyone who trusts the CA or requests the public key will, in practice, get the key for their use.

- **Validation of certificates**   When a certificate is presented by one party to another, it must be validated. Because both parties involved typically do not know one another, they must rely on a third-party who is trusted. This is the role of the CA.

- **Revocation of certificates**   If a certificate is no longer needed or trusted, it can be revoked before it expires. This is much like what happens if a driver's license is revoked prior to its normal expiration date.

When a CA is called upon to validate a certificate, what is really happening? When a CA is asked to perform a validation, it is actually confirming that a specific public key bound to a certificate does indeed belong to the entity named in the credential. During normal operation, a CA will verify a presenter's credentials to allow two parties who previously were foreign to each other to have confidence that they are who they claim to be and that the public key is actually theirs.

But are all certification authorities the same? Absolutely not. There are several different types of CA, and each is a little different from the others, as you will see. A CA has the primary responsibility to create key pairs and to bind these key pairs to a user's identity and certificate. Once this has been done, validation of the key to a user can take place, as needed or requested. The CA in any form is intended to be a trusted entity in much the same way as the DMV is trusted with driver's licenses and the FAA is trusted with pilot's licenses. CAs include the following types:

- **Root CA**   This is the CA that initiates all trust paths. The root CA is the top of the food chain or the point at the top of a pyramid from where trusts emanate. As the entity at the top of the pyramid, the root CA must be secured and protected, because if its trust is called into question, all other systems will become invalid.

- **Trusted root CA**   A trusted root CA (or trusted root certificate) is a certificate from a CA that is added to an application such as a browser by the software vendor. It signifies that the application vendor has a high level of trust in the CA.

In Actual Practice

If you have ever looked into your favorite browser (such as Internet Explorer or Firefox), you will notice that each has some certificates pre-installed by the software vendor. These certificates make it so we automatically trust certain public CA providers automatically. It's kind of like a guest list that we can check people against to make sure we can trust them.

- **Peer CA**   A peer CA has a self-signed certificate that is distributed to its certificate holders and is used by them to initiate certification paths.

- **Subordinate CA**   A subordinate CA is a certification authority in a hierarchical domain that does not begin trust paths. Trust initiates from some root CA. In some deployments, this is referred to as a "child CA."

- **Registration authority (RA)**   An RA is an entity positioned between the client and the CA and is used to support or offload work from a CA. Although the RA cannot generate a certificate, it can accept requests, verify a person's identity, and pass along the information to the CA that will perform the actual certificate generation. RAs are usually located at the same location as the subscribers for which they perform authentication.

LINGO
One notable difference between **registration authorities (RAs)** and certification authority (CAs) is the fact that RAs typically do not possess a database or generate certificates or keys. As a result of this difference, they do not have the same security requirements as CAs. In most cases, an RA will have lesser security than a CA.

Building a PKI Structure

Now that you understand what a CA is and what a digital certificate is, we can now go about the business of building a PKI system. Before we start building a PKI system, let's first make clear that the term does not refer to a single technology, but rather, a group of technologies and concepts that work together as a unit to accomplish the tasks mentioned earlier. PKI is designed to validate, issue, and manage certificates on a large scale. The system is simply a security architecture we use to provide an increased level of confidence for exchanging information over an insecure medium.

Note

PKI should never be thought of as a technology that is the exclusive domain of one software or hardware vendor because it is independent of any of them. In fact, although it may be easy for you to think of PKI as a Microsoft, Linux, Unix, or other technology, it is actually all of these and none of these. The system is indeed a standard used by all vendors and applications.

Any systems that interact with this structure must be PKI aware, but that is a common feature in today's environment. For us, a PKI-aware application is any application that knows how to interact with a PKI system or can be enabled to do so. Fortunately, we do not have to worry about an application having the ability to do this; most applications, such as web browsers, e-mail applications, and operating systems, already have this capability. All of these applications offer us the ability to interact with the system described in this chapter and do so transparently.

When working with PKI, you must understand that tying the whole system together is trust. Trust is absolutely important because without it the system falls apart pretty quickly. In fact, it could be said that without trust, the system is less than worthless to us. For example, if your friend from before introduced you to someone who is their friend, but you didn't completely trust your friend, then you wouldn't trust their friend either. The problem presented here would also be the equivalent to the real-world scenario of having a fake or questionable ID: If the ID doesn't ring true to the party to which it is presented, the credential is essentially worthless.

With this in mind, let's look at some different PKI systems. The first type of PKI system is simple in design and implementation. The design incorporates one root CA with two subordinate CA systems. This is ideal for large- and medium-sized organizations that may handle a lot of certificate management requests and issues. All the CA systems can do the same thing in this environment, but typically only the subordinates will issue the bulk of the certificates, with the root not doing as much. In fact, in this setup, the root would more than likely only be issuing certificates to the subordinate to, in essence, license them to issue credentials. Figure 7-3 shows this simple PKI system.

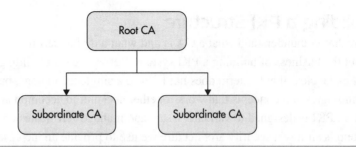

Figure 7-3   A simple PKI structure with a root and two subordinates

Another different type of structure would include an RA, or registration authority. Note that the two look very similar in design, with the RA typically limited to registering potential applicants before sending the request on to the parent CA. Figure 7-4 shows a PKI system that includes an RA as part of its makeup. In this environment, the RA may very well be set up to take some of the load off of the CA, or at least to offload some of the traffic to the RA and leave the other management tasks to the CA.

Finally, in high-security environments, there may exist a situation where the root CA is taken offline; in these cases, it is called an *offline root*. An offline root is created in order to issue certificates to those CA systems underneath it. An offline root does not typically (and shouldn't) do any sort of work on a day-to-day basis. Figure 7-5 shows a PKI system with an offline root.

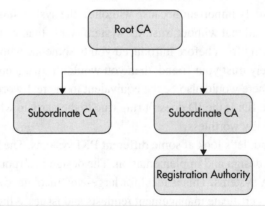

Figure 7-4   PKI system showing an included RA as part of its makeup

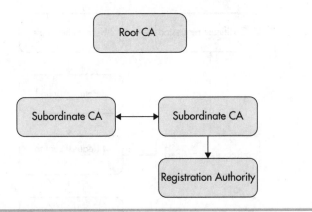

Figure 7-5   PKI system with an offline root

IMHO

In my opinion, an offline root is ideal for environments that have a large and important PKI structure. Because compromising the root would be catastrophic, it makes sense to keep it offline and out of harm's way. Although such a setup does make some tasks a little harder, in many cases the inconvenience is outweighed by the security benefits. Having said that, you may be in an organization where such an inconvenience is too much.

After PKI Has Been Set Up

Once the PKI system has been set up, it is now time to start issuing certificates. The process of issuing certificates is simple, but very methodical and procedural, as you will see. The process can be viewed in Figure 7-6.

Note

In Figure 7-6, take note of step 3. In this step, a requesting party may have been identified or authenticated, but they still may not be allowed to have a certificate for the type of action they are requesting (or maybe not at all). The owner of the CA would include rules that dictate who can have what type of certificate based on their needs at that time.

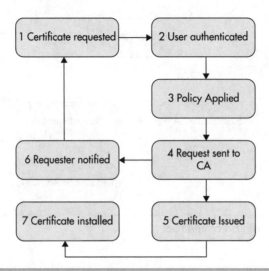

Figure 7-6 The certificate request process with a CA

Let's examine each of the steps in Figure 7-6 a little closer:

1. **Certificate requested**. This means that some party has requested a certificate and, as such, has made one to the CA or to an RA.

2. **User authenticated**. A user needs to be authenticated to positively identify who they claim themselves to be. In some cases, this may already be done, such as with Microsoft's Active Directory and Certificate Services, where the user has already logged in to the network and identified themselves. In other cases, the user may need to provide info that identifies them. The CA may even go the additional step of requesting personal documentation, as needed.

3. **Policy applied**. In this step, the requesting party is checked to see if they are cleared to obtain the certificate they are requesting. This may mean that they are allowed to have only certain types of certificates.

4. **Request sent to CA**. In this step, the CA receives the information and, in turn, creates the public/private key pair, creates the digital certificate, and then cryptographically seals the certificate after placing the user's public key upon it.

5. **Certificate issued**. In this step, the certificate is actually issued and is ready to be used.

6. **Requesting party notified**. In this step, the requesting party is told that their newly minted certificate and private key are ready to be picked up.

7. **Certificate installed**. Finally, the certificate is installed on the device or system that the user originally intended it for.

Note

Steps 2 through 5 may indeed be on the same system, such as is the case with Microsoft Certificate Services and certain systems on Linux and Unix.

So now that the user is in possession of the certificate and is using it, everything is fine until the certificate expires, right? Wrong. In actuality, you can have your certificate pulled or revoked at any time for a number of reasons, with the major reason being that you cannot be trusted anymore. Going back to our driver's license analogy for a moment, consider if you had a license issued that said you could only drive cars, but you somehow decided to go out for a spin on your friend's motorcycle? If you got pulled over, there would be some explaining to do to the officer. Clearly, he could look at your license and see what you are authorized for and even call it in for verification. When you eventually have to appear before a judge, she may decide that you are not responsible enough and cannot be trusted. Therefore, your license is revoked. This is the way it is for certificates generally. If you cannot be trusted or if you no longer need your certificate, it is generally revoked.

IMHO

Yes, I know certificates can be revoked for other reasons, including situations where someone leaves the company or changes jobs and doesn't need one anymore. It is also possible that they simply shouldn't have gotten one in the first place, so it is pulled.

One of the most important roles of a CA is that of revocation of certificates. As I told you previously, a certificate can be revoked for any number of reasons, including misuse, mistrust, and no longer being needed. The CA is responsible for performing this action as well as informing others of the revocation. In the world of PKI, a certificate revocation list (CRL) is used to verify the current status of a certificate. The CA publishes this list at regular intervals, and is responsible for updating it with the most current information as to who has a legit certificate and who does not. The CA must keep the CRL up to date and available to clients of the system who need to check the status of certificates.

When a certificate is revoked and placed on a CRL, it will appear in one of two states:

- **Revoked**   Certificates that have been placed on the CRL as revoked include any that need to be pulled out of circulation permanently, and it is assumed that they will never be needed again. Of course, this should be done cautiously, because anyone who has their certificate revoked will need to get a new one. A good example of this situation would be where you lose your smartcard or laptop that holds your private key; your certificate would be revoked and placed as revoked on the CRL so that it is never used again.

- **Hold or Suspended**   Different than revoking is the status of Hold or Suspended, which is intended to be reversible if needed. However, when a certificate is put on hold or is suspended, it acts exactly like a revoked certificate, meaning that it will not be valid for use in any situation. Citing the example for a revoked certificate, if the individual who lost their private key suddenly found it and it was determined that it wasn't compromised, it could be taken off suspension.

IMHO

If you ever have to manage a PKI system, you may want to consider the benefits of suspending a certificate over revoking it outright. Essentially, you should consider suspending first and then, if a specific interval lapses and no determination can be made as to whether or not there is a compromise, the certificate should be revoked.

When either of these actions takes place, it means the key may no longer be used and a new one must be issued if a revocation is performed.

A CRL is generated, updated, and published on a schedule defined by the CA owner. In addition to being updated on a schedule, it may be manually updated as needed if a particularly hot issue arises—for example, if someone leaves the company on bad terms and no one's sure whether they have a copy of the key. In fact, thankfully for us, CRLs are updated usually once a day to make sure the latest information is always available to the clients. After this time period expires, the CRL is invalidated and a new one is published in its place. During a CRL's validity period, it may be contacted by any PKI-enabled application that needs to verify a certificate prior to acceptance. When placed on the CRL, the key's serial number will be listed for some number of update periods until the normal expiration of the certificate is reached.

PKI in Action

So now that you understand PKI and its cast of characters, let's look at some applications of this technology and see how all the cryptographic factors fit in. We'll first examine the process of Secure Sockets Layer (SSL).

SSL is a technology that powers many online transactions and makes them safe and secure for the exchange of information. Webmail, purchasing, banking, health care, and other applications use this technology to make sure your personal information cannot be pilfered by the "bad guys."

SSL is a simple technology and, as such, can be broken down into a few short steps:

Tip
Don't worry if the steps seem confusing at this point. I will diagram them out for you afterward. This is just to get you acquainted with the process before I dump some graphics on you.

1. **Request**   The client requests a session with the server.

2. **Response**   The server responds by sending its digital certificate and public key to the client.

3. **Negotiation**   The server and client then negotiate an encryption level.

4. **Encryption**   Once they agree on an encryption level, the client generates a session key, encrypts it, and sends it with the public key from the server.

5. **Communication**   The session key then becomes the key used in the conversation.

Figure 7-7 illustrates the interaction between the client and server in a CA system. Note the lines of trust, where each party trusts the other indirectly through the CA.

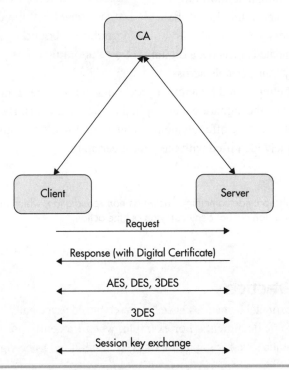

Figure 7-7   The certificate exchange and establishment of an SSL session

Tip

Note that SSL is normally used in e-commerce situations, but the same process takes places when SSL is used for webmail, e-mail, or financial transactions. In fact, the e-mail client I use, Mozilla Thunderbird on Linux, uses SSL because I have configured it to use SSL to secure the communication channel.

Digital Signatures

One of the more popular mechanisms that rely on PKI, and the cryptographic mechanisms that underlie the system, is digital signatures. A digital signature is something that you may have used yourself when you signed a loan application for your new house, signed paperwork online, or sent a signed e-mail. Simply put, a digital signature is something that allows for the authentication and validation of the legitimacy of a message.

When implemented correctly, a digital signature is easily transportable across systems, cannot be replicated by another party, and can be time stamped (meaning that you can verify when the signature was applied to the document). By providing these features, a digital signature offer elements in the digital world that allow you as a creator of one to be uniquely identified with the utmost certainty.

> **LINGO**
> **Digital signatures** are used to verify the authenticity of messages as well as to provide a means through which they can be validated as being original. Think of digital signatures as performing the same function as a traditional pen-and-paper signature. Traditional signatures, when applied to a paper document, assert that you, as the signer, agree to the contents of a document. At the same time, the uniqueness of the signature is bound to you (forgeries not withstanding).

Tip

Digital signatures also provide something known as *non-repudiation,* which means that the originator of an action cannot deny carrying out the action.

In Actual Practice

For over a decade, digital signatures have been recognized as a legally binding method of signing electronic documents. For example, when I recently purchased a home, all of the documents, save for the initial ones, were required to be signed digitally.

(continued)

In essence, what I had to go through signing these documents was a simpler and more secure way of stating I agreed to the terms of the sale and loan than in years past.

So what makes a digital signature so important for us and how is one created? Let's take a look a closer look at the mechanism that creates a digital signature.

First, what is contained in a digital signature? Simply put, a hash, an encrypted bundle, and something that identifies the signer. A digital certificate contains the digital signature of the certificate-issuing authority so that anyone can verify that the certificate is real.

Digital signatures make use of several of the different types of encryption we have used before in order to render their capabilities—namely, asymmetric or public and private key encryption and hashing. By combining these cryptographic functions, we can provide authentication of a message or digital item. Let's look at each component:

- **Public/private key encryption**   Although it is true that you can encrypt with a private key and then decrypt whatever you have encrypted by accessing the public key on the corresponding digital certificate for the encrypting party, this does not provide all of what we need. However, because a public key is possessed by a specific party, only it can (and does) play an important part in digital signatures.

- **Digital certificates**   A digital certificate is absolutely an essential component of a digital signature. Remember early when I said that a public key is bound to a digital certificate? This fact pays off its reward here. The digital certificate tells whomever retrieves the public key that it belongs to a specific party and, by extension, it is the companion of the private key (recall what you learned in an earlier chapter about asymmetric encryption).

- **Hashing**   This is the mechanism that lets us know whether or not an item has been altered. Earlier I said that a traditional signature, when applied, indicates that the signer agrees to the terms of the document as presented. Hashing does the same thing in the digital world with signatures. The hash states that the signer agrees to the current state of the document.

Let's put these items together, along with a CA and trust, and see how the signature is created. Let's say we have two parties by the names of Link and Zelda. Link will be the sender of the message, and Zelda will be the receiver. With that being said, let's take a look at the process:

1. Link creates a message.

2. Link then hashes the message using an algorithm, such as MD5 or SHA.

3. Link then encrypts the hash with his private key.

4. Link then binds the encrypted bundle and the plaintext message together.

5. Link then sends the combination to Zelda.

6. Zelda sees that the message came from Link.

7. Seeing who the sender is, Zelda retrieves Link's public key from the CA they both trust.

8. Zelda then decrypts the hash. If it is decrypted successfully, the identity of the sender is validated.

9. After the hash is decrypted, Zelda then reruns the MD5 algorithm against the plaintext message and compares the new hash with the one she received from Link.

10. If the two hashes match, the message has not been altered since Link signed it.

In Actual Practice

The same process described here is used in e-mail systems all over the world, where enabled. It is very common to see digital signatures in use in government offices, the military, and other places where the verification of a message both in origin and content is required.

We've Covered

What is Public Key Infrastructure (PKI)?

● PKI is a key management system.

● PKI is used to issue and manage certificates.

● Digital certificates are credentials used to identify an entity.

Components of PKI

- PKI is a combination of hardware, software and policies.
- PKI-aware applications can interact with a PKI system.

Fundamentals of PKI

- PKI is software independent.
- PKI is used in many applications.

Applications of PKI

- PKI is used to verify digital signatures.
- PKI is used with smartcards and SSL.

Process of PKI

- PKI sets certificate usage policies.
- PKI is platform independent.
- PKI is a system used to validate certificates.

CHAPTER 8

Steganography

We'll Cover

- Why steganography?

- History of steganography

- Applications of steganography

- Steganography fundamentals

Now with many of the basics of cryptography out of the way, it is time to discuss the "black sheep" of the family—steganography. Typically when cryptography is discussed, the topic of steganography is an area that doesn't seem to get much attention. This is unfortunate, because in many ways it is the most fascinating and intriguing area to study. By the same token, the science is one of the least understood methods of concealing information, losing out to the methods discussed in previous chapters.

Steganography is by no means a new technology and is in fact an old process that has taken many forms, both digital and physical. As of late, the process has received some attention due to its alleged usage by terrorist groups and by some malware writers.

Now, although the process discussed here in this chapter is not as commonly used as its attractive cousin, cryptography, it is still an incredibly and surprisingly effective way to hide information. Unlike its cousin, the steganography process is used to communicate in such a way as to keep a third party from observing the hidden information while at the same time being unaware of its very existence. The process is so effective, in fact, that some experts have suggested its use as a method to avoid detection and persecution by repressive regimes.

One example of steganography involves old works of art that contain hidden messages and symbolism that the artist considered subversive and wished to convey without worrying about authorities noticing. Whether there's any truth to the fact that many of these art pieces contain messages is still a matter of debate today, but this practice would be an early example of steganography.

In this chapter, the art and science of steganography will be discussed along with how it can be applied separate from and together with traditional methods of information concealment.

Steganography Overview

As stated, steganography is not well explored or discussed outside of the cryptography field, but it is one of the more exciting and fascinating areas to explore. Simply put, steganography is designed to provide the ability to hide information in what amounts to plain sight, in such a way that the result is not obvious to even the most savvy observer. At this point, it may sound like the process is not that much different from the previously discussed methods, but it is indeed different. In fact, to understand the difference between steganography and standard cryptography, a simply compare-and-contrast exercise can be done.

In Actual Practice

The word *steganography* comes from the ancient Greeks and means "covered writing." In writings left by the Greek Herodotus, two examples have been given: One is of Demaratus, a spy in the Persian court who sent warning of a forthcoming invasion by Xerxes by writing a message on a wooden pallet and then covering it in wax. The same individual also used the same method to successfully carry the same message upon a "blank" tablet to Sparta. A second example provided by Herodotus comes courtesy of Histiaeus, who shaved the head of his most trusted slave and tattooed a message on his head. After the slave's hair grew in, he was dispatched with the "hidden message." Both examples show us that the technique has been around for a while.

When cryptography is used, as explained up to this point, the main disadvantage is that encrypted information is quite obviously something that the sender wishes to conceal or at the very least keep away from prying eyes. No matter how strong the encryption algorithm actually used, the message or data being transmitted will by its very nature attract and arouse suspicion, and therefore will allow a curious party to dedicate resources to cracking the code. Additionally, cryptography in its traditional form may endanger the sending and receiving parties if the use of such processes is illegal or ill advised.

The advantage of steganography, over cryptography alone, is that the messages do not attract attention to themselves. With this process, messages are not clearly discernible as having anything to hide; in fact, the messages will not even be obvious to those who are not looking for them. So, as opposed to standard encryption, steganography will easily avoid detection in most cases and at the same time protect any parties who may be handling the information from being implicated.

To look at things another way, let's see how steganography and cryptography work at a lower level. Encryption is a process where a piece of information known as plaintext is put through the "meat grinder" and transformed into something known as ciphertext, at which point it is fully encrypted. Although the process of encryption is robust and offers strong protection against breaches of confidentiality, if something is scrambled it will definitely attract attention because it "stands out" from the crowd. This unwanted attention means that someone who may be interested can easily focus their code-breaking efforts on the specific information without having to sort through a mountain of potential "maybes." Of course, with encryption, the idea is that even with the information in hand, without the key you cannot easily get to the "juicy" information that is being hidden. Compare this with the process of steganography, where information is hidden as a payload within something else, such as a video file, image file, or anything else. The idea is that someone who is looking will still not actually "see" what may be right in front of them because it will look perfectly harmless. For example, a JPEG image could be used as a carrier that transports information in such a way that a curious onlooker will only see an image and not what is hidden inside.

Steganography: A Brief History

Before getting too far into the details of the art of steganography, let's first take a look back at how it has been used over the years to hide information and messages of all types. Much like encryption and cryptography in general, steganography has a long and storied history that stretches back to before the digital age.

Getting in the "wayback" machine, we can see that the first widely accepted use of the process comes from the ancient Greeks. Specifically, the example we'll be looking at takes place in the year 440 BC and involves a man by the name of Demaratus, who needed a way to inform his fellow Greeks of an impending attack by the Persian king Xerxes. In order to get this message to his countrymen and allow them to prepare, Demaratus wrote a message on wooden tablets, then covered the surfaces with beeswax. To anyone seeing the tablets, they were simply a couple of blank writing surfaces, but to those who knew what to look for, removing the wax would reveal the message.

Note
Steganography goes back a very long way, with examples going back even before the "widely accepted" and documented examples noted in this text. In fact, some of the earliest examples could be said to be cave paintings, pictures, and other similar types of glyphs that would only have significant meaning to those who knew what to look for.

Some other notable examples of steganography before the modern age include the following:

- **Tattoos**   Ancient Greece has several stories about generals and other military types transmitting messages using tattoos. Using this method entailed the shaving of the courier's head and then the "application" of the message to the scalp, after which the hair was allowed to grow back. In one notable tale, news of an impending invasion (yes, it was the Persians again) was carried to Athens on the scalp of a slave. Although this method is novel and it did work, it has several obvious issues, including the size of the message and the time it would take for the hair to grow back enough to cover the message from view.

- **Eggs**   Yes, you read that right, eggs. So how could eggs be used to transmit messages? Noted Italian polymath Giovanni Battista developed a formula for invisible ink that that could be used to write a message on the surface of a boiled egg. For the message to be read, the egg had to be peeled, and in some cases dyed as well, to see the message as intended.

Note

This technique was also reportedly used in medieval Japan as a way to transport messages between the various Daimyo (feudal lords). The technique was effective for a couple of reasons that made the message nearly undetectable. First, the method of writing the message using invisible ink was a powerful means of hiding the text. Second, the boiled egg was typically accompanied by many other eggs, which allowed it to blend into the "crowd" while it was being transported.

- **Invisible ink**   Many children know of this technique from their science experiments with lemon juice and a heat source, but the idea of invisible ink goes back a long way. Examples of the art stretch from modern day science classes back to the first century AD when a method for using milk from a specific plant was documented by Pliny the Elder (gotta love that name) in his text *Natural History*.

  Here's another interesting fact: During the Revolutionary War, both sides made extensive use of invisible ink. Major John Andre (later hanged for his part in the Benedict Arnold betrayal) had his agents place a letter in the corner of their correspondence to inform the recipient as to how the hidden secret message could be revealed.

  Invisible ink may seem like child's play and the stuff of classroom science nowadays, but this is far from the case. In fact, the technique is still very much in use today, or at least hinted at in some cases.

- In 1999, the U.S. Central Intelligence Agency moved to suppress an old 1940s-era paper on the usage and development of invisible ink. The CIA's reasoning? That invisible ink was still vital to the U.S.'s national security interests and making such information public could impact national security adversely. The report was later declassified in 2011, seventy years after it was first authored.

- In his 1997 book, ex-MI-6 agent Richard Tomlinson revealed that the British Intelligence Agency used rollerball pens that were able to produce secret invisible writing to pass messages during missions undetected.

- Most ominously, in 2008 a citizen of the U.K. was alleged to be keeping a list of high ranking Al-Qaeda operatives in a special contact book written in invisible ink.

- **Microdots** To anyone who has seen old World War II spy movies, the idea of microdots is not a new one. Microdots were frequently small artifacts, less than the size the period at the end of this sentence, that were adhered to a piece of paper such as a newspaper. Because the dots were designed to be detectable under certain lighting conditions, the secret was usually free from detection.

- **Letters** During World War II, Velvalee Dickinson transmitted information to her Japanese conspirators via addresses in neutral South America. She was a dealer in dolls, and her letters discussed the quantity and type of doll to ship, which in actuality were the names of ships, and the description of the doll described the condition of each ship.

- **Photos** One of my personal favorites (although I'm not a fan of the POW angle) comes from the crew members of the USS Pueblo, who were photographed in propaganda photos by their North Korean captors. In order to convey that they were propaganda photos, which the North Koreans said showed that the crew was being treated well, the U.S. crew can be seen flipping the "Aloha high sign," which is another term for giving the finger. Because the North Koreans were unaware of this international sign of diplomacy, the message got out and told the U.S. that things were not as they seemed. A picture of the crew giving the sign is shown in Figure 8-1.

Note

The USS Pueblo is still being held by North Korea to this day. The ship is actually in Pyongyang and is a popular tourist attraction. The ship is still listed as active in the list of ships of the U.S. Navy and in fact is the only ship of the U.S. Navy currently being held by a foreign power.

In the modern age of photographic, invisible inks, similar techniques are still in use to varying degrees, but for the most part examples of steganography have gone digital. Modern computers offer the power to hide information in new and unique ways that are out of reach of traditional means. Some of the newer schemes developed since the early

Figure 8-1   USS Pueblo crew. Note the position of the finger of the crewmen in front.

1980s include all of the following methods (some of which we will explore later in this chapter):

- Packaging messages within the insignificant portions of images, videos, music, or other files.

- Packaging messages or other files within the body of previously encrypted data. Typically this process entails the sender encrypting data and replacing a portion of the contents of another encrypted file. The idea here is that the data is still hiding within another file and is packaged in such a way to make it appear as part of the larger whole.

- Mimicking the contents of characteristics of other files with the idea of blending in with the "crowd." The idea here is much like dressing down in public so as to not stand out from others in the area.

- Embedding files within an executable file of some sort. Because most executable files contain "slack" or empty space due to technology restrictions, there is space to hide another payload within. You can think of a file as a piece of Swiss cheese with holes inside. Stuff something in the holes and the cheese still looks the same from the outside.

- Content-aware steganography hides information in the semantics a human user assigns to a datagram. Think of it this way: You could draw a diagram on a whiteboard using a certain color marker. To anyone else looking at this diagram, it would be simply that, a diagram. To those in the know, using the color red instead of black would indicate a message of some type, kind of like a catcher signaling a pitcher with a hand signal.

- **Printed documents** The result of the digital steganography process can be output in any number of forms, including printed documents. In the context of printed materials, a payload or message can be encrypted using any of the means available to create a ciphertext. A carrier is then created to act as a "covertext," which is then modified to contain the ciphertext created earlier, with the combined result being an entirely new entity known as *stegotext*. A number of examples of this type of technique exist, including methods such as

> **LINGO**
> **Covertext** is the formal name for a file or other carrier that acts as the means of delivering a hidden message or payload. In practice, a covertext can be anything that the sender wishes it to be, but typically the covertext is selected due to the fact that it does not attract too much attention itself or looks harmless or uninteresting. Within the covertext, the ciphertext that makes up the payload is hidden and transported from point A to point B.

  altering the letter size, spacing, typeface, or other characteristics of a covertext, which will then allow them to be modified to carry the desired payload. Only a recipient who knows the technique used can recover the message and then decrypt it, whereas all others will see just the covertext because it is designed not to attract attention.

- **Audio files** In this type of technique, an audio file is used to carry the payload and act as a convincing cover to outsiders. The audio file could be literally anything, from music to a speech or other piece of audio. Audio files act particularly well as cover files because they have varying levels of quality and the files have a tremendous amount of redundancy.

- **Text** Text has also worked particularly well in the digital age, with everything from long documents to e-mail messages. In fact, some applications are used to encode messages inside of an e-mail, making the original cover message look the same as it always has while at the same time carrying a hidden message. It is worth noting that this type of steganography is essentially only possible with modern computing power because it takes careful manipulation of the carrier to effectively hide the payload. Some applications even generate what appear to be spam messages from a payload, making the message uninteresting to anyone except those who know it has something valuable inside.

This list of examples in the physical and digital worlds shows that the technique of steganography has a long history and permeates our lives much more than we realize. The examples show us that the ability to hide information can be performed not just by encrypting information, which would attract attention, but in such a way as to hide information securely and in plain sight. This art has not been lost in the modern world, as the technique has been used in new and intriguing ways that may not be as obvious or in ways that are disconcerting.

In modern printers—specifically laser printers from major vendors—the process is used to hide information that is undetectable to the human eye. The information that is added to the print jobs comes in the form of tiny dots or imprints on documents that are themselves designed to be undetectable. These dots are intended to provide time and date stamp information, as well as other information such as the device serial number, which allows the printer that generated the document to be identified. The information is reportedly added to documents to be able to identify those who counterfeit money more easily and thwart this type of crime.

Most disconcerting about the technique in modern times is the alleged use of the process by terrorist groups such as Al-Qaeda, considering the fact that messages could be transmitted covertly.

In Actual Practice

Stories alleging that Al-Qaeda was using steganography techniques to transmit information covertly first surfaced in February 2001 in the pages of the U.S. newspaper *USA Today.* Later in the year, reports surfaced in another U.S. newspaper, *The New York Times,* that suggested the terrorist group had used such methods to transport information regarding the events of Sept 11th. Evidence seemed to suggest that the terrorist group had used images of a pornographic nature—images posted on eBay and in other locations.

Even more concerning is that one online text used by terrorists, known as the "Technical Mujahid, a Training Manual for Jihadis," actually contains a section titled "Covert Communications and Hiding Secrets Inside Images." This section actually describes how steganography can be used to pass information covertly between cells.

Later reports from the CIA seem to back up this claim, without actually confirming it. Other sources seem to suggest that the idea of terrorists using the technique is

(continued)

tenuous at best. Yet other sources flatly deny that any use of the technique can be said to be employed by any terrorist group.

The somewhat chilling reality for all of us is that terrorist groups and other sources of organized crime and terror are likely using this tool. Although the methods these groups use are as varied as their sick and twisted goals and objectives, it is almost certain they know about this technique and are putting it to use. I mention this only because it is highly unlikely a book like this one would give any of these organizations a new idea to use for their purposes.

I guess I should also mention that, to some, the idea that terrorist organizations use this technique for their purpose is in doubt. Although I will not get into a "he said, she said" discussion in this text, the point still stands that the technique could be very dangerous in the wrong hands.

In other areas, agencies such as the Federal Bureau of Investigation (FBI) have made it known that foreign intelligence services, such as those in Russia and China, have their own customized applications for embedding ciphertext within several given types of covertexts. The process is thought to be used by foreign governments to pass sensitive or confidential information to agents or moles that are not covered by normal diplomatic protocols.

Outside of the criminal world as well as corporate and government environments, are there other uses for steganography that are currently in play? The answer is yes. In the modern world, the technique is used to watermark everything from images to audio files. The movie industry in the United States is known for embedding information, not visible to the naked eye, within movies of the digital type as a means to enforce copyrights and to track down illegal copies and their origin. Other uses include professional photographers who use the technique to preserve their copyrights on images they use in their portfolios, thus providing a simple means of proving ownership of content.

In Actual Practice

One of the best examples of steganography may be in your wallet in the form of U.S. currency. Although not a new development by any means, the newest paper currency incorporates anti-counterfeiting features that are hidden and sprinkled throughout the bill.

(continued)

Traditionally, U.S. currency has had a number of features that deter counterfeiters from producing perfect or near-perfect copies. For example, special paper known as linen rag paper is used. It has a distinctive, pliable feel and has tiny red and blue fibers embedded in it. Also, it is only produced by a special vendor using a secret process. Additionally, inks are manufactured using special and secret formulas specified by the Bureau of Engraving and Printing that also help prevent counterfeiting.

However, as technology has allowed better and more convincing replicas to be produced, additional security features have been introduced to thwart them. Two of these advanced anti-counterfeiting features are security threads and microprinting. These were introduced into bills produced after 1990, and later several additional features were incorporated to strengthen security. In newer bills (those produced since 2004), additional features were introduced to the bills:

- **Color** Since 2004, the coloring of the ink used in the bills has been somewhat unique. First, many subtle background colors were introduced; these colors differ per denomination. For example, on the $20 bill, the background colors are green, peach, and blue. Additionally, "TWENTY USA" is printed in blue in the background to the right of the presidential portrait. On the obverse of the bill, small numbers printed in yellow appear in the background calling out the denomination of the given bill.

- **Portrait** On newer bills, the portrait is larger and the border and surrounding fine lines have been removed, which were present in previous versions. The portrait itself has been moved up and the shoulders of the subject have been extended into the borders. The portrait is off-center to provide more room for the watermark and security thread.

- **Watermark** A watermark, created during the paper-making process, depicts the same historical figure as the portrait. It is visible from both sides when held up to a light. This portrait is not visible using normal means, and most people may not even notice, but it is there.

- **Security thread** An embedded polymer strip with a silver tint is positioned in a unique spot for each denomination. This provides additional safeguards against counterfeiting. In fact, the thread itself is only visible when held up to a bright light. What's more, the thread contains microprinting in the form of the letters USA, along with the denomination of the bill and a flag. Additionally, when the thread is viewed under ultraviolet light, the thread glows a distinctive color for each denomination it is embedded in.

(continued)

- **Color-shifting ink**   One of the less noticed but interesting features of the bill is the ink itself. The ink used to print the numeral in the lower-right corner on the front of the bill looks copper when viewed straight on, but green when viewed at an angle.

- **Microprinting**   Lastly, the incorporation of printing that can only be read when magnified is a powerful security feature. Under normal circumstances the printing appears as a line, but when magnified, it appears as writing that spells out the denomination of the bill. As a security feature, the printing cannot be copied or scanned because it will blur when such a copy attempt is made, making counterfeiting near impossible using most means. The printing itself appears around the borders of the first three letters of the ribbon to the right of the portrait and in the border below the Treasurer's signature.

So Why Steganography?

Let's visit this question again before we discuss the technical aspects of the steganography process. Understanding the why will provide tremendous advantages when we look at the technology itself in more detail.

For many individuals who encounter the technique for the first time, their question is, why use this process in favor of (or in addition to) standard encryption techniques? This quickly becomes the million dollar question, and may be the one you have right now.

In fact, a lot of individuals seem to think that the technique is only good for those wishing to hide information that may be harmful or malicious, but this is neither true nor accurate. Keep in mind that just like anything else, this process can be used for legal or illegal purposes, depending on who is using it and for what reason. Legitimate applications of this process include the enforcement of intellectual properties (such as copyrights) by applying watermarks to an image, as was discussed earlier. On the other hand, some of the more nefarious reasons include hiding information for illegal reasons. Although we could never successfully confirm how widespread the use of this technique is in illegal circles, it probably is safe to say it is in use by criminals, terrorists, and other scumbags for all kinds of mischief. Those of us on the "light side of the Force" can use company security policies and good ethics to prevent the misuse of this technology, but those on the "dark side" don't have such obstacles.

So why do we need to hide information of any type? Why not just use cryptography? Whereas encrypted information attracts unwanted attention, steganography provides an effective means of deflecting attention from our secret. However, that's not the only reason why you would use the technology. The first and biggest reason today for the process is in enforcing intellectual property rights. This use has been driven by the explosion of file sharing sites and the pirated content that is sometimes found on them. Through the use of watermarks, the owner or holder of a copyright can be determined. In fact, these watermarks are typically embedded throughout the content, such as with a movie or audio file, in order to provide an effective means of tracking ownership. These watermarks may contain information about the author or owner or possibly will contain serial numbers or even a copyright notice. The information provides the means to track the content as well as a means of prosecuting violators.

Another reason hidden information is used is to avoid observation by unintended parties. This is where someone will carefully select a carrier to transport their payload. Their goal is not just to scramble the message, as with cryptography, but to keep the very existence of a message secret to those who are not in the know.

Malicious parties can use steganography in ways that can effectively evade many detection techniques or make it very work intensive to actually uncover the payload. This is just what a malicious party wants—the ability to conceal their message in such a way as to not draw unwanted attention. In the case of traditional encryption, attention is drawn simply by the fact it is encoded—the scrambled letters don't look right, which is suspicious in itself. In the case of steganography, an image, video, text message, or other item can still look perfectly okay, while at the same time carrying something within that defies detection.

How Does Steganography Work?

Of course, steganography works by hiding in plain sight—that's the easy description. But how does it work "under the hood"? Several factors are in play with this technique that must be covered.

First, the technique works by employing by what is known as a *covert channel,* which is a fancy way of describing a process of transferring information using a mechanism in a way different from what it was designed for. Our good friend steganography fits this description perfectly because the technique, no matter how it is employed, works by using something in a way other than what it was designed for. For example, an image file is not meant to carry a payload other than what's used to describe the image itself—meaning pixels and image size. However, this same image can be made to carry the information used to describe the image plus additional information that makes up the payload. In this case, hiding information inside an image file can easily evade normal detection methods because these same mechanisms would not be designed to analyze an image in such a way. Also, keep in mind that if something is used in a nonstandard way, such as what is being described here, defensive mechanisms may not be capable or designed to look for it. If defensive and detection mechanisms cannot detect hidden information, this can easily result in a dangerous payload or hidden message passing in and out of the very heart of a secured or hardened system, evading detection until it is too late.

Second, the process depends on a message or payload to be carried. In practice, the payload can be anything, but it should be something that will not unduly increase the size of the carrier. The payload probably will most commonly be a text message or similar piece of content; however, it is not limited to this format by any means. In fact, videos, files, and many other types of data are suitable to be transported safe and sound within a carrier.

Lastly, the process will usually involve a stego-key or password that is used to protect the data. Although not necessary, this extra key will need to be entered in the event that the data is extracted from the carrier. If the data happens to be detected by a third party, the key will still need to be cracked or recovered before they can get at the data.

With these factors in mind, the process of steganography can be simply written as a pseudo-formula:

$$\text{Covertext} + \text{Payload} + \text{Stego-key} = \text{Stego-medium}$$

LINGO
Steganography can also be referred to as a **covert channel**. So what is a covert channel? Well let's take a look. It is important to realize early on that the process of moving or transmitting hidden content is as important as how the content is hidden. For example, if a number of images are processed using one of the techniques discussed in this chapter and then transmitted across a network, the increase in traffic itself may reveal that something is not as it seems. It is imperative that any transmission method not attract undue attention and in fact blend in with the "chatter" around it. If this is carefully considered, stealth can be achieved and a covert channel is created that bypasses monitoring software.

Also remember that a covert channel is only of use if the party who is the intended recipient of the information is actually aware of the hidden item. That is why ahead of time the sender and receiver of such data will need to agree on how the information will be sent and how third parties will be kept out of the know.

However, let's first look at the set of factors that depends on the medium being employed to transfer or carry the data (in other words, what is being used as the covertext). Let's look at the different mediums that can be used and how they are manipulated to carry a payload.

First, we'll discuss substitution. In the digital world, files tend to contain some extra information that is not used, not needed, or at the very least not that important in the overall scheme of things.

To illustrate this process, consider an image in the JPEG format. This type of file is common in today's world because it is generated by everything from digital cameras to scanners and photo-editing software. The format has become so popular because it is highly versatile and supports the full range of colors the human eye can see (16.7 million colors). Consider a photo taken with a digital camera, such as one of a sunset or a landscape. Any such photo will contain a tremendous amount of color and detail and, depending on the camera, a varying amount of what is known as "white noise."

So just what exactly is this white noise, and what does it mean for us? To put it simply, white noise is background or randomized information contained in any piece of data; you can think of it as the imperceptible or unused information within an image. We can use this randomized information to hide our "secrets" by altering the information in ways that cannot be easily noticed. In any given image, consider the fact that each pixel is made up of a combination of numbers (or *channels* for you image geeks) that are used to specify the color to be displayed. This mixture of channels—or Red, Green and Blue (RGB) channels—for the pixel dictates the resulting color onscreen. In an RGB value, any given channel can contain a value anywhere from 0 (no color) to 255 (full color). In the context of the digital world, each of these values is stored in a sequence of 8 bits, with the most significant bit (MSB) being 128 and the least significant bit (LSB) being 1. Each pixel in an image commonly has three numbers associated with it, and these values often range from 0 to 255. Each number or channel is stored as 8 bits (zeros and ones), with 128 being the most significant bit with the bit on the far right being the Least Significant Bit.

Let's take a look at a standard pixel:

- **Original pixel value:** 255, 255, 255 (White)
- **Same pixel value in binary:** 11111111, 11111111, 11111111

Now let's alter this pixel to store data:

- **New pixel value:** 25r, 25g, 25b (White)
- **Same pixel value in binary:** 111111rr, 111111gg, 111111bb

In the second example, the LSBs are marked *r, g,* or *b* to draw attention to them, but they would be a number in the real world. In practice, the LSB of each of these channels would be changed across several pixels to store the codes associated with letters.

In the case of a payload such as a text message, storage is easy because most letters only need 8 bits and there is more than enough space for us to describe a letter in each pixel. Keep in mind that while we are altering the four LSBs of each pixel to describe a letter of text, the intensity of the color of the pixel will change. Such a change would be imperceptible to human eyes and therefore most likely will avoid further scrutiny.

Once you understand how a pixel can be altered to store information—text or otherwise—the next big stumbling block is scale. In other words, the bigger the image or covertext, the greater the amount of data that may be stored within it.

LINGO

LSB or **least significant bit** refers to the bits or digits at the furthest point right of a number and then moving left. For example, in the number 1972, 2 would be the LSB, with 7 being the next LSB. On the other hand, the MSB (or most significant bit) would be 1, with 9 being the next in line.

LSBs are useful in storing data for our purposes here because a change in them is considered very small. For example, changing 1972 to 1974 is only a small change, but on the other hand, changing the 1 to a 3 is a difference of 2,000, so obviously this is very significant. In the case of pixels, changing the LSB means that a color may go from pure white to slightly off-white—something that the human eye is unable to detect on such a small scale.

For argument's sake, let's consider a file that is of the type JPEG and is 1024 × 768, not an unusual size by any measure. Using simple math, it is easy to determine that an image of this size contains around 800,000 pixels, which means there's a lot of place to store information. Going up a size to 1200 × 1600 results in even more places to store information, to the tune of a million pixels. In either case, these pixels can each be altered to carry a message or payload of considerable size. In fact, a million pixels could easily be altered to store the contents of a good-sized novel, with room to spare.

Adding to the ability for a file to store data is the fact that when we create a file of any type, more than likely there's some extraneous information in the file that's not needed or is not that important. These areas could be file descriptors, unused attribute information, or other data that probably wouldn't be noticed if it is altered. These components of the file can be altered or outright replaced with the information that is to be hidden, without significantly changing the file or even damaging it. Again, this method allows a person to hide information in the file and make sure no other human can detect the change in the file without the use of technology or other means.

One of the popular tools for hiding information within an image file is Invisible Secrets, which can encrypt and then embed files of many types within an image selected by the user. Using this product, I embedded the contents of this chapter, originally in Word format, into a JPEG file to demonstrate a little more clearly how the process works.

Figure 8-2 shows the original document prior to any modifications being performed. Note that the image is an average image file with a resolution of 1024 × 768 and a file size of 327KB. I mention the properties of this image so we can perform a before-and-after comparison of the two images in order to observe the changes, if any at all. I purposely chose this image because it is nothing special (unless you like Cessna Citations, which I do), and is not something that would draw attention if placed on a website.

Now that we have chosen this image, we will embed the payload into the file (in this case, the original text file for this chapter). My rationale behind choosing the original text file for this chapter is that it is something you can relate to because you are reading it right now and can appreciate its size. Figure 8-3 shows the same image after it has been processed by the software and has the payload merged into it.

Note that there's no perceptible difference between the original image and the new image, at least visually. However, the file size has increased to 340KB, from its original size of 327KB, which is a minor size difference and would not raise undue suspicion.

Figure 8-2 Original image before being used as a carrier file or covertext

Figure 8-3 Image after being processed through the Invisible Secrets software

This file is now ready to be e-mailed or posted on a website, where someone can later download it and, if they were told ahead of time, extract the file and read it.

Let's talk about something else here—how to keep from giving away our deception. Let's look at the two files and the payload itself. First, if we were to perform this process the right way, we would make sure we erased the original carrier file after we embedded the payload into it, thus creating a new file. The reason for this is that anyone getting access to the drive or system it was created on could compare the two files and see the difference and then figure out something wasn't right. Second, after the payload is embedded into its new carrier, the original payload should be deleted from the drive as well—or at least moved someplace else. Third, to be extra safe, we should make sure the erased file is wiped from the drive in order to thwart file-recovery techniques. This may seem like a lot of work, but being a secret agent ain't easy, nor is effectively covering your tracks.

Tip
When one is working with audio, video, or images, watermarking can be performed to preserve or enforce rights to the content. Watermarking works by embedding information in some form of digital media that the owner or creator wishes to protect their rights on. The actual process that embeds the information does so by putting the information into the media itself, much like for images. What may make it more difficult is that the modification to the carrier cannot be perceptible and must remain totally invisible—unless looked for directly. In the case of images, this means that the modifications have to be invisible. In audio or video files, the modification cannot be such that it interferes with the normal use of the file or leads to corruption or artifacts in the file.

Additionally, the author must decide how durable the watermark should be. The watermark can be durable in the sense that certain alterations to the file will not destroy the watermark in any way, or the watermark could allow itself to be destroyed only under certain circumstances. On the other hand, the watermark may be designed to be fragile, and will be destroyed or removed under certain circumstances.

Steganography in Audio

Of course, images aren't the only suitable carrier for payloads—audio files work just as well. In fact, the method commonly used is known as *low bit encoding,* which is very much similar to what is used during LSB manipulation in image files.

Low bit encoding is effective at storing information, but this comes at the price of increased probability of detection. The method alters the bits at a fundamental level inside the audio file, which means that those with particularly sensitive ears may detect the minor variations in the file and in turn look closer to see if something is being hidden (exactly what we don't want to happen). However, it is just as likely that someone listening may think that the file is of low quality and discard it—whereas the intended recipient will decode the payload.

A secondary method of hiding information inside a file is known as *spread spectrum,* and it can conceal a payload inside an audio file quite effectively. This method works by injecting extra information into a file in the form of random noises that are spread across the full spectrum of audio. This will result is some random background noise, but in the right kind of file (such as a recording of a lecture or concert), such noises may blend in.

Finally, one other method that is useful in hiding information within audio is known as *echo data hiding.* This method exploits the tendency to hear minor or major echoes in some audio files. By using a process to append extra audio to a file, information can be effectively hidden from observation. This method is particularly effective out of all the available methods mentioned here due to the fact that in many cases the adding of echoes to a file can actually result in an improved audio file.

Tip

Just because you hear scratchiness or other artifacts does not mean there is necessarily something hidden within; it could be that you just have a bad recording or corrupted file.

One utility that is particularly interesting at hiding data inside an audio file is MP3Stego, which modifies MP3 files to hide a payload within.

Steganography in Video

In video, steganography information is specially encoded within a video file of some sort and then transported and extracted by a recipient. Much like what was discussed earlier for images, this method relies on imperceptibly altering images within the video so as to make it impossible for the human eye to notice. Adding to the benefit here (for video, over that of images) is that with a moving series of images, the human eye has less time to focus on any specific frame to notice alterations.

There are pros and cons to this method, however. Unlike audio and images, the less information stored as a payload makes detection harder, whereas more information means that the detection process will be more successful at uncovering the payload.

IMHO

Hiding secrets inside of video is not uncommon because it is used to watermark videos and to track ownership, but it is still fascinating nonetheless. Imagine the possibilities involved with hiding secrets inside of a video file and posting such a file on the Web. With the proliferation of video-sharing sites and online file sharing, it would be incredibly easy to post a file somewhere someone could extract the information hidden within.

Steganography in Documents

At this point, you should be able to reason that a payload can be stored in just about any file type, so saying that data can be hidden in documents should come as no surprise. How this type of steganography works is quite simple and incredibly effective—as well as quite obvious. This type of process functions by appending white space and tabs to the ends of the lines of a document.

Consider that the average document contains plenty of white or blank space, such as that between paragraphs or the end of lines. All of these formatting marks appear naturally within the context of any document, so if they have been altered (or added, in some cases) to a document, they would not be noticed or even draw suspicion.

A piece of software that is useful in performing this type of process on documents is SNOW. It was created to hide text in the trailing white space prevalent in documents (Word files, for example).

Null Ciphers

Another excellent method of concealing information is via a null cipher, which is one of the oldest methods of concealing information. This type of process seeks to hide information within large bodies of text without the need for an overly complex system.

As a carrier, spam is excellent for manipulation through a null cipher, because in many cases it's discarded without being read and can easily hide within a folder where spam messages are stored. It's possible to place an entire sentence or even message within a spam e-mail, and it still may not be read by a third party.

In a null cipher, the message to be hidden is encoded into the larger message by replacing every *n*th character with one from the message. More specifically, every *n*th letter of the e-mail forms the contents of the message.

Steganography on Hard Drives

One of the more interesting applications of the process of steganography is using the space on a hard drive itself to hide files. Specifically, this process involves altering how data is stored on a drive as a means to obscure or hide that data. Researchers have found that by manipulating the patterns or the process a hard drive uses to store data, reasonably large amounts of data can be hidden with little hope of detection. In fact, recent research has shown that a 160GB drive could easily store 20MB of data within it, totally hidden from any sort of forensic or other detective mechanism.

Normally, when data is written to a disk, it is placed at the best or most efficient locations between existing data. With the steganographic program, the bits forming a secret message are encoded as cluster differences in cluster locations. For example, two clusters together are interpreted as a "1" and two clusters further apart are interpreted as a "0." Because there would also be a lot of natural fragmentation on the same storage volume as part of normal operation, it would be extremely difficult for anyone else to detect the pattern.

IMHO

I find incredibly fascinating a relatively newly envisioned place to hide data: human DNA. Yes, the building blocks of life itself may be another ideal place to hide information through the use of genetic markers and other tags. Although this method was previously mentioned in a *Star Trek* episode in the 1980s, it looks like it may now become a reality, with information being hidden in DNA strands.

Steganalysis: Detecting Hidden Information

So now that you know the different ways information can be hidden and how this information may be passed off as "innocent," it is time to discuss how to detect such information. Each tool or technique tends to hide information in a slightly different way, depending on the goal in mind and the way the tool or process was designed. For example, tools designed to hide large volumes of data typically break the information down into large blocks and then distribute them through the carrier, whereas data used for watermarking is smaller and spread out over a file, making detection harder. Although the end result is information that is hidden to the human eye (or ear, in some cases), it is still possible to detect the information. Why? Simply put, the process of manipulating a file such as an image or video will always introduce some amount of distortion or overall degradation in the carrier. However, without knowing the process involved or the potential stego-key used, it can be complex or nearly impossible to detect the information hidden within a carrier. This whole process of detection and extraction is known as *steganalysis*.

Steganalysis does not deal with actually decoding the hidden message; that's something we will discuss elsewhere in this book. Instead, steganalysis is concerned with the detection and usage of steganography inside of a file. Steganalysis techniques seek to target files and perhaps allow a third-party to extract the information and decrypt it, if necessary or desired later.

Many methods can be used to detect steganography:

- **Viewing the file and then comparing it to another copy of the file that is known to be original and unaltered** There may be multiple copies of the same image available, so finding the unaltered may be tricky—and in such cases multiple comparisons may need to be done with multiple images. For example, suppose you download a JPEG and your suspect file is also a JPEG, and the two files look similar. However, you notice that one JPEG has a larger file size than the other. This may suggest that the suspect file has information hidden inside of it.

- **Listening to the file** This is similar to the previous method used for trying to manually detect hidden content in picture files. If you are trying to detect hidden information inside of a MP3 audio file, you will need to find an audio file to compare it to that uses the same compression (MP3 in this case).

- **Watching the file** Again, this method is similar to image comparison and can be used to manually detect hidden content in picture files. If you are trying to detect hidden information inside of an MPG or WMV file, you will need to find another file to compare it that's the same format.

Although the techniques described here are not the only ones available, they are some of the more common techniques in use.

Most steganography techniques rely on the careful application of statistical analysis on a suspect file. Ideally, a untouched or unaltered file from some source such as a digital camera is compared with an altered version from the same source. This method will take these files and compare them, looking for any sort of inconsistency between them that may be indicative of a hidden payload. The process can also look for issues that seem out of the ordinary in files, such as those that are compressed or are run through a known algorithm, as is the case with image files such as JPEGs.

Although steganalysis itself covers the process of detecting whether steganography is being used and then extracting the data, the methods involved vary wildly, depending on the medium being used. Although this chapter is not going to cover every method, you should know at a high level how the process works. For our discussion, we will focus mainly on image files as a carrier medium to keep things as simple as possible, and to avoid some complicated math that we just don't need.

In the world of image files, one of the simplest methods for detecting an anomaly indicative of a hidden payload is through the use of histograms and simple comparison. Figure 8-4 shows an image with histograms of the RGB channels on the right.

If you were able to get a copy of both the original file and the altered one, the histograms of each would be different, even though the images look the same to the naked eye. This would be a potential giveaway that the files may require closer examination to see if something is hidden within. This method is one of the reasons why I mentioned earlier that we should delete the original image in order to avoid comparison between the two, which could lead to unwanted detection.

Figure 8-4 Image file showing histograms of the RGB channels

On this last point of hiding the evidence and covering tracks, much needs to be said for us to understand the applications of hiding data. The first point is that smart users of this process should always try to carefully choose their carrier image with special attention to a few points to make the process more effective. In fact, the biggest issue is that choosing the wrong type of image can make for big problems. For example, choosing an image such as a GIF with few colors make hiding data very difficult. The fewer the number of colors in an image, the tougher it is to hide the payload. In fact, the most extreme level of difficulty would come as a result of choosing a binary or 2-bit image, such as is used for diagrams. Figure 8-5 shows an example of a image that would be unsuitable as a covertext.

Tip

GIF images are not the only type of image that can be unsuitable. GIF images are unsuitable generally because of their low color count (256 colors maximum), which cannot be expanded or altered. However, other image types such as JPGs and PNGs could also have a small number of colors in use, which would make them somewhat unsuitable as well.

Of course, what happens when only one file is available? In this case, you can't compare two or more images, so another method must be used, such as noise-floor consistency analysis. Using this method, it may be possible to detect in an image and other file a hidden payload, especially if the LSB in the file has been altered. For example, in an audio file data may be obscured in what is known as white noise or background information in a file. Data must be hidden well enough to fool the ear, but such techniques would not necessarily fool technology or software. In software, the patterns can be

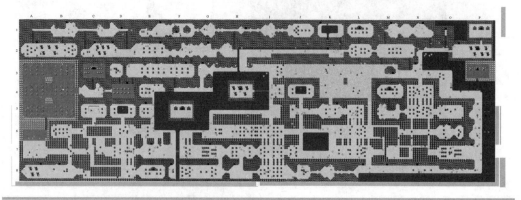

Figure 8-5 A GIF image that would be unsuitable as a covertext

analyzed to look for inconsistencies and detect any alterations that may suggest a hidden payload.

Other Methods

Other methods exist in the field for locating hidden content that borrow from some methods discussed in previous chapters. Let's revisit these techniques and compare them to the techniques in steganalysis.

A cryptanalyst can apply many techniques to recover data from an encrypted format that are similar to those the steganalyst will employ. Let's review each of them so we can make a good comparison:

- **Ciphertext only**   In ciphertext-only attacks, the cryptanalyst knows the ciphertext to be decoded. The cryptanalyst may have the encoded message and part of the decoded message, which together may be used for a known-plaintext attack.

- **Chosen plaintext**   The chosen-plaintext attack is the most favorable case for the cryptanalyst. In this case, the cryptanalyst has some ciphertext that corresponds to some selected plaintext.

- **Chosen ciphertext**   The chosen-ciphertext attack is used to deduce the sender's key. The challenge with cryptography is not in detecting that something has been encrypted, but decoding the encrypted message.

Similar methods are available to those trying to break steganography:

- **Stego only**   A stego-only attack is similar to the ciphertext-only attack, where only the carrier is known and available for analysis.

- **Known cover**   If the original file and altered carrier are known and both are available, then a known-cover attack may be possible, similar to what was shown previously.

- **Known message**   A known-message attack is when the hidden message is revealed at some later date; an attacker may attempt to analyze the carrier for future attacks.

- **Chosen stego**   Even with the message, this attack may be very difficult and may even be considered equivalent to the stego-only attack. The chosen-stego attack is one where the steganography tool and carrier are known.

- **Chosen message**   A chosen-message attack is one where the steganalyst generates a carrier using a steganography tool or algorithm from a known message. The goal in this attack is to determine corresponding patterns in the carrier that may point to the use of specific steganography tools or algorithms. This method is described earlier in this section.

Tools in Use

Many tools can be used to perform steganography. I'll introduce a few to you here so you may better understand the options available:

- **Hiding Glyph** The Hiding Glyph application is used to store a file or group of files within an uncompressed 24-bit BMP image. The benefit of this application is that you can select any image that contains a reasonable variation of color as a carrier and have confidence that it is reasonably free from detection. Furthermore, without one having both the original and altered image, detection becomes almost impossible, not to mention the actual extraction of the information.

- **Vecna** Vecna is a unique Java-based application that can use any image format that can be read by the Java language as a carrier to hide data. Once the information is embedded into the image, the resulting data is output as a PNG file with added Alpha channel information that is used to carry the payload.

- **TrueCrypt** TrueCrypt is a very popular open-source tool for performing encryption of a volume of data, but it can provide an additional layer of protection by hiding a volume inside an already encrypted volume. TrueCrypt can be used to create this initial encrypted volume and then take the free space within the encrypted volume to hide additional data. The manufacturer of TrueCrypt states that this feature gives a measure of plausible deniability because one can easily detect that there is an encrypted volume, but even if they manage to crack the key on the volume and open it up, there is relatively little chance of them detecting the hidden volume, even if they suspect it is actually there. Figure 8-6 shows the TrueCrypt interface, and Figure 8-7 shows the encryption options.

Note
TrueCrypt has the ability to hide not only volumes but whole operating systems from being detected.

- **F5** This application was developed some time ago and has since had some "facelifts" to make it more usable. Basically, F5 is another tool for hiding data, such as hiding TXT or DOC files in JPEG images.

- **MP3Stego** MP3Stego can be used to hide data, as the name implies, within MP3 files of a size proportional to the original data. Basically, the process works like this: We obtain a WAV file, hide our data within it, and then compress the WAV file into an MP3 file. The benefit of this format is that it can be used to easily hide data of any type in a plain and simple-looking MP3.

Figure 8-6   The TrueCrypt interface mounting a volume

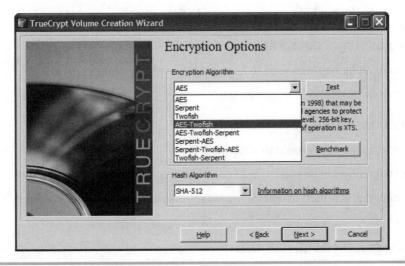

Figure 8-7   The TrueCrypt encryption options

Just envision the possibilities of this process in contrast to the image-based techniques mentioned earlier as one could hide potentially bigger files in an MP3 file. MP3 files and images both represent different ways of distributing hidden data. An image file can be posted on a website where someone would be unlikely to suspect that some secret data is present (for example, posting some secret data in a pornographic image on some website—not exactly the first place you would expect to find hidden secrets). An MP3 file, on the other hand, could have data encoded into it and posted on BitTorrent (for example, a recording of a lecture from a conference could have data coded into it and then uploaded, and chances are if someone downloaded the file they would be bored long before they even suspected there was something hidden).

- **Steganos Suite** This application package is a commercial software suite that includes a toolbox of steganography utilities as well as other tools to cover one's tracks. Steganos Suite offers the ability to either select an existing file and embed data within it or to create an image or sound file to carry the data. In fact, this suite can interface with a scanner or an attached microphone to create the carrier file.

We've Covered

Why steganography?

- Steganography is used to hide data in plain sight.
- Steganography can hide data in any type of file.

History of steganography

- Steganography has been used to hide images in photographs.
- Microdots are a form of steganography.

Applications of steganography

- Steganography can be used to watermark data.
- Steganography can be used to hide data where encryption itself isn't useful.
- Steganography is used to conceal messages instead of encryption or along with regular encryption.

Steganography fundamentals

- Steganography hides information within other information.
- Steganography is not a replacement for encryption.

CHAPTER 9

Applied Cryptography

We'll Cover

- How is cryptography applied?

- Exploring Secure Sockets Layer (SSL)

- Encryption and automated teller machines (ATM)

- Working with digital signatures

- Drive encryption

Up to this point in the text, we have explored the many different areas of cryptography and how it works. Although I can stress the importance of cryptography to you, it is more valuable for me to show you. In this chapter I will do just that.

This chapter contains within it a number of examples of how cryptography is applied in everyday life, and I can guarantee that you have encountered some of the situations discussed here yourself. The situations presented in this chapter are intended stress the importance of cryptography and—along with what you've learned thus far in the book—give you a new appreciation of the art.

Less Theory, More Practical

As you have seen in this book, cryptography is a very complex science with a tremendous amount of daunting details in play. So why use it? Simply put, it is extremely useful to us because it preserves data and information in ways that would be near impossible to do otherwise. Don't be concerned, though: You have learned quite a bit so far, which will enable you to see how all this information is applied.

No matter what the application, the basic information you have learned still holds true, and it is these basic concepts you must remember.

Some of the more simple applications are secure communication, identification,

LINGO
You have learned a lot of the various building blocks used to perform the transformation of information. We can consider these various blocks to be the **primitives** out of which we construct more complex and advanced systems that perform the transformations. Remember the term *primitive* and what it means as a basic building block of a system.

authentication, and secret sharing. More complicated applications include systems for electronic commerce, certification, secure electronic mail, key recovery, and secure computer access. You can see some of these examples here (we will delve into the others a little more in depth later, but I just want to give you a taste first):

- **Secure communications**   This is one of the most commonly encountered uses of cryptography, as you may have already guessed or encountered. We have seen already that two or more parties can communicate with some degree of confidentiality by encrypting the messages between them using an algorithm together with a key that is known only to them. If this is done properly, a third party will not be able to eavesdrop on the communication easily and in many cases they will never be able to decrypt the messages at all. We have also seen that this one issue itself has led to many problems and solutions, such as key management.

- **Identification and authentication**   Although you may not know it, cryptography has played and does play an essential part of confirming who or what someone is or what they claim to be. Remembering back to our discussion of digital signatures, you already have some idea of how cryptography verifies identity. Whether you are connecting to a website, taking money from an ATM, or even using a credit card, cryptography is there. Take, for example, your ATM card, which requires you to use a special code such as a personal identification number (PIN) as an authenticator to establish if you really own the account you are trying to access. Cryptography is also there when you connect to a website such as Amazon, Wells Fargo, or Facebook to identify that party to you.

- **E-commerce**   The whole field of e-commerce could not exist in its current form without cryptography—and some would argue it wouldn't exist at all. E-commerce consists of banking, stock trading, music purchasing, online game purchasing, online shopping, and more. Think about what would happen if cryptography was pulled out of the picture. You might not be able to buy those fancy new clothes online, plane tickets, hotel reservations, or any number of other things.

- **Certification**   Digital certificates are completely instrumental in e-commerce and other areas, to say the least. Certificates are issued for situations involving not only e-commerce, but virtual private networks and other forms of communication.

- **Key recovery and management**   You already know the value of keys in a cryptographic system and how important it is to keep these items safe and sound. In the cryptographic field, keys are addressed in two areas: recovering lost or inaccessible keys, and handling who is issued keys and how they are transferred between these parties.

- **Remote Access** Remote access strategies would not even be possible—at least not safely and securely—without encryption. For instance, passwords can be eavesdropped, forgotten, stolen, or guessed. Many products supply cryptographic methods for remote access with a higher degree of security.

- **Technologies** Cryptography is also found in many common devices, such as cell phones, smartphones, DVDs, CDs, MP3, Digital Rights Management (DRM), and photography, to name a few.

So let's stop discussing encryption and start to look at some of these areas more closely.

Secure Sockets Layer (SSL)

One of the systems that uses (and indeed heavily relies on) cryptography is *Secure Sockets Layer,* or *SSL.* Originally developed by Netscape back in the 1990s, SSL was meant to be a way of allowing web browsers and web servers to transmit and deliver information securely (mainly sensitive in nature). Over the years, SSL has been upgraded, and SSL 3.0 later evolved into what is now known as *Transport Layer Security,* or *TLS.*

You have seen SSL in use when browsing the Web and observed that little lock icon in the browser interface somewhere. You probably also noticed that the address line of browser changes to "https" instead of "http," indicating that your browser is using SSL to encrypt or secure all traffic, which is what the lock indicates. Either of these events should be observed when you go to online banking sites, e-mail accounts, or sites that handle personal data. Additionally, as discussed in Chapter 6, you also get the benefit of verifying the identity of the online resource via its certificate. It's safe to say that SSL is something you should be using whenever there is sensitive information to be passed online. Figure 9-1 shows what the lock icon looks like in Google's Chrome web browser.

The successor to SSL is Transport Layer Security (TLS), which like its predecessor makes use of certification authorities, which you learned about in an earlier chapter. We are now going to utilize certification authorities when talking about SSL and TLS. First, let's look at the process. In this example, you are the client and the server is an entity such as your online banking system:

1. The client transmits to the server information about the SSL version it is able to support, along with information regarding supported ciphers and anything else required to support the connection.

2. The server reciprocates by sending the corresponding information back to the client, along with a copy of the server's certificate.

3. The client receives the information from the server and uses the certificate to authenticate the server. If the authentication checks out, the process continues; if not, the client is informed of the problem.

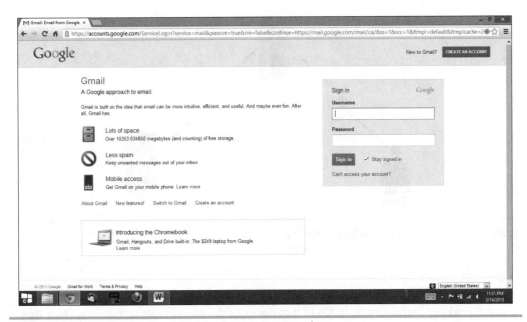

Figure 9-1   Google Chrome with a lock icon visible

4. The client generates a unique secret (known as a pre-master secret) that it encrypts with the server's public key and then transmits the information to the server.

5. The server uses its private key to decrypt the pre-master secret and then performs a series of steps to generate the master secret.

6. The client and server then use the new master secret to generate a special symmetric key that will only be used during the transmission of data to preserve the confidentiality and integrity of information.

7. The client sends a message to the server, informing it that the following information will be encrypted with the session key.

8. The server sends a message to the client, informing it that the following information will be encrypted with the session key.

To better visualize the steps, take a look at Figure 9-2, which illustrates the three parties involved in this transaction.

If we want to simplify this process, we can look at it a different way with our previous lessons about cryptography in mind. Consider in our example that that the client is a web browser and the server is a typical e-commerce site. We can break this down to a very simple interaction, like so: Our web browser generates a randomly selected symmetric

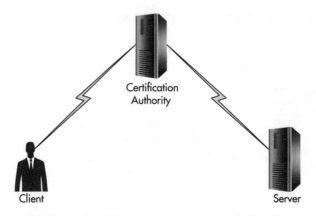

Figure 9-2   The cast of characters in the SSL process

key and then uses the server's public key to encrypt the key. The browser then sends this encrypted key to the server, which in turn decrypts the key with its private key. Once this is done, the two systems can communicate using good old symmetric encryption. Once done, the session is ended and the symmetric key is discarded.

In Actual Practice

In real life, the symmetric key used is chosen randomly and then discarded, but what happens after it is discarded? Basically, the key is returned to the "pool" of keys, much like a bingo ball is returned to the machine after it is picked. The bingo ball may be chosen again, right away, or after a hundred tries or longer—we just don't know. The difference between this and the symmetric key system is that the pool is much bigger, kind of like picking a grain of sand off of a beach and throwing it back afterward.

The way I have shown SSL here probably is most familiar to you in the context of e-commerce, but there are several other areas where it is used that you may not be as familiar with:

● E-mail clients such as those from Mozilla and Microsoft use SSL to encrypt the exchange of passwords and information between client and server.

- VPNs use SSL for the same reason that browsers and email clients do, but in this case they are not only encrypting the authentication process, but the whole VPN communication from end to end.

- Web applications such as portal systems, much like SharePoint and others, also use SSL.

So is SSL the only application of cryptography? Far from it. Let's look at another application in the form of digital signatures.

Digital Signatures

We see digital signatures in use more and more every day, but few actually understand what is behind them. However, you know the elements already. Digital signatures are used today to verify documents, transactions, driver files, and other pieces of software. In today's world, in fact, digital signatures are seeing increased usage as people move from traditional paper documents to electronic documents and electronic transactions of all types.

Before you learn how a digital signature is created, let's examine what it is used for and what it is expected to accomplish.

If we look at a traditional signature versus a digital signature, we see similarities and differences. A traditional signature provides us with some important abilities, including:

- It verifies the identity of the signer because a signature is unique to the individual.

- It states that the signer agrees to the document being signed because the signature is attached to the document and, excluding a forgery, cannot be applied to a new document.

So what does a digital signature provide us?

- It guarantees that the document was actually sent by the sender.
- It guarantees that the document wasn't modified en route.
- It guarantees the authenticity of the document.

Not too different from what we would normally expect from a traditional signature, huh?

Think about how powerful these abilities are in the real world (or, I should say, the digital world). Also consider the fact that we can expand digital signatures to places and applications where traditional signatures fear to tread. Software, drivers, and communications are only a few of the places digital signatures can be used.

In Actual Practice

Ever updated a device driver or your antivirus? If you have, chances are you used something that was digitally signed by the vendor. Consider how problematic it would be if an update for your antivirus application—the very thing that protects you from viruses and worms—was not from an authentic source. Would you want something from a untrusted source on your system being entrusted with keeping your system safe? Probably not.

As an example, let's consider what a digital signature offers to a document. By applying a digital signature to a document, you are accomplishing two of the three of the items on the preceding list. The document is now safe and more secure, as well as having brought non-repudiation and integrity aspects into play. However, it doesn't do anything confidentiality-wise. As you will see, though, digital signatures can be verified quite easily by just about anyone.

In Actual Practice

Digital signatures, as mentioned in our previous discussions of hashing and message digests, are considered legally binding. When I bought my house not too long ago, all of my documents were signed digitally. Except for a small handful of papers that needed to be signed in the traditional way, everything was signed digitally with a few button clicks.

In 2000, President Clinton digitally signed into law the Electronic Signatures in Global and National Commerce Act (E-SIGN Act). This public law states the following:

> …a signature, contract, or other record relating to such transaction may not be denied legal effect, validity, or enforceability solely because it is in electronic form; and (2) a contract relating to such transaction may not be denied legal effect, validity, or enforceability solely because an electronic signature or electronic record was used in its formation.

At the state level, the Uniform Electronic Transactions Act (UETA), passed by 48 U.S. States, provides much the same protections to electronic signatures and records. (The remaining two states have other legislation covering electronic signatures.)

Hashes

From our previous explorations, you already know what a hash is, so we won't explore all the details again. As a quick review, a hash is the compressed and encrypted form of some input; this output is a unique alphanumeric string that will change dramatically even if the littlest bit of information is changed in the input. Hashes are not designed to be reversed and are, in fact, mathematically infeasible to reverse.

Here's an example of a hash using the MD5 protocol:

280130708090bedfe5219234143caea2

And here's another one:

54833f563eac94ce6f2e716058f5e270

I made both hashes from the Microsoft Word document of this chapter, but I only removed a single period to cause the difference seen here to occur. As Mr. Spock would say, "Fascinating."

Obviously, with hashing alone, we have the ability to detect even the most minute changes in a document, which is great. However, what if someone got ahold of the document and the hash itself; they could conceivably generate a new message with a corresponding new hash and then everything would still check out. (Don't worry, we have a way to deal with this, too, so hold on.)

If we wish to add protection against someone re-creating, rehashing, and replacing a message, we must have some other items in play. We need something that would keep the hash from being so easily redone without someone's knowledge. This is possible using public key cryptography and the benefits it provides us.

Go back to our hash for a moment, and think, how can we prevent someone from rewriting the message and replacing the hash? If someone were to do this, there is no way of knowing that the message or the hash came from an illegitimate source or false source, which represents a serious problem. Can we solve this? Yes, with a private key to the rescue.

If we create the document, hash it, and then encrypt the hash with a person's private key, then anyone who identifies the sender and retrieves their public key can decrypt the hash and then verify the message. And remember, only the public key that was assigned to the sending party can decrypt something that was originally encrypted with the sender's private key. This may sound a little backward to how we think of verifying something conceptually. In other words, sending a protected message to a particular recipient starts by encrypting the message with the recipient's public key. Once it is received by the recipient, they use their private key to decrypt the message. In this instance, we want to verify identity, thereby verifying the validity of the carried message. What this translates into is a scenario in which the private key is used for initial encryption; all who have access to the public key can verify the integrity of the sender's message payload as well as the sender himself. Because the private key is only held by the single party who is sending and that person alone, we have now accomplished all three points we stated earlier about digital signatures. Figure 9-3 shows the process of creating a digital signature.

Keep in mind that if any party wants to alter the message, they would, by necessity, need access to the sender's private key.

Therefore, when messages are signed with a digital signature, the following takes place:

- The hash ensures that the message has not been changed in any way without the receiver being able to tell.

- Encrypting the hash with the sender's private ensures that the hash itself cannot be altered.

- Finally, because the hash can only be revealed when decrypted with the sender's public key, both authenticity and non-repudiation are complete.

Powerful technology, huh? This is why many companies and experts are pushing digital signatures as a means to secure messages and files.

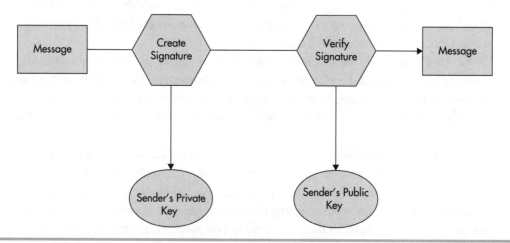

Figure 9-3 Creating a digital signature

Automated Teller Machines

Another place where encryption has a high degree of importance is in ATM systems. You know, those systems from which you withdraw money with a plastic card and a PIN code? Turns out that the card with the magnetic stripe on the back needs to have some way of storing knowledge of the PIN.

Consider the situation involved in withdrawing money from the ATM. A customer puts their card into the system and is prompted to enter their PIN. After selecting the option to withdraw money, they enter an amount that causes the system to check the code for correctness before approving the withdrawal. The verification of the code takes place after the information is sent to and from the bank's own servers for its check. This authorization allows the bank to approve or deny the transaction.

In Actual Practice

In the real world, several layers of complexity may be involved in authentication and authorization in order for the verification to take place. For example, if you go to a bank that's not yours, the information may need to pass through other systems before it can be verified. This aspect is outside the scope of our discussion.

Consider the issues involved with moving financial transactions and authenticating account holders. These types of messages and transactions, by necessity, require integrity protection and safeguards against possible attack and modification. Consider what would happen if an attacker got ahold of a legitimate transaction and altered it to say that he or she was depositing $10,000 instead of the $100 check they actually deposited. Or what would happen if someone intercepted a transaction that withdraws $1,000 and kept replaying it over and over again to get more and more out of the bank. Both bad situations, to say the least.

The bank must take several items into account when securing our bank accounts:

- Securing the PIN
- Protecting against replays
- Storing PIN information safely
- Protecting integrity of transactions

So how is this accomplished? Encryption.

Per the first point, the financial institution must ensure that the customer's PIN is not compromised, so the PIN is encrypted during transmission as well as in the database within which it is stored. In many cases, the algorithm used may be DES or some other algorithm to encrypt the four-digit PIN code. Due to the limitations of some protocols used for encryption, padding may be needed to prevent a party from gaining multiple PIN codes from various customers and seeing patterns.

To make things more secure, banks have added another layer of protection in the form of smartcards. These cards are devices the size of a credit card that contain a private key and a certificate, signed by the card issuer, to confirm their public key value. The ATM can then validate the card by issuing a challenge for the card to sign. As with any system or device that utilizes digital certificates, it is necessary for the terminal to have an authentic copy of the card issuer's public key in order to check the validity of the certificate.

Drive Encryption

One of the more popular applications of cryptography nowadays is *drive encryption,* which serves as a powerful tool for protecting the contents of a hard drive and other storage media, keeping the contents safe, sound, and accessible only by those allowed to view or modify them.

In Actual Practice

In today's world, using drive encryption is not just a good idea, it may be the law in your industry. Companies and organizations that deal with financial data, personal data, or information such as healthcare are legally compelled to use all sorts of encryption (such as drive encryption) to safeguard data, and they can be subject to severe fines and penalties if they do not do so.

Most software and hardware of this type uses on-the-fly encryption technology, meaning that information is encrypted and decrypted before it is loaded or saved to the storage media. Once the information is stored, it cannot be read without providing the correct key, which is usually accessible once a password is provided. After that, the encryption/decryption is performed transparently, without user intervention.

Other than the encryption/decryption process, the storage device—whether it is a hard drive or a flash drive—is accessed the exact same way as it would be if encryption wasn't involved.

We've Covered

This chapter could go on and on with endless examples of how cryptography is used in the real world, but that would be pointless. This chapter sought to acquaint you with some of the places where cryptography is used and why it is important. As you may have noticed, it was easy to put together the primitives (that is, building blocks) established throughout this book and apply them here.

I encourage you to look around at the technology you use and the information you transmit and think about how cryptography may have had a part to play.

How is cryptography applied?

- Cryptography is applied to various technologies in different ways.
- Digital signatures use cryptography.
- Cell phones use cryptography.

Exploring Secure Sockets Layer (SSL)

- SSL is designed to secure transmitted data.
- SSL relies on PKI.
- SSL is used in e-commerce.

Encryption and automated teller machines (ATM)

- Encryption is used in ATM cards.
- Encryption is used to verify credentials.

Working with digital signatures

- Digital signatures use hashing.
- Digital signatures use PKI.
- Digital signatures are legally binding.

Drive encryption

- Bitlocker is used to encrypt hard drives.
- Truecrypt is software designed to encrypt data and hard drives.

CHAPTER 10

Quantum Cryptography

We'll Cover

- What is quantum cryptography?

- The impact of quantum cryptography

- How this new technique will change the field

- How the process works

- How the process differs from previous techniques

Well now, friends, in this chapter we venture into an area that is exciting, complex, and mysterious—quantum cryptography. Unlike previously discussed forms of cryptography, this system leaves behind the purely mathematical and logic-based approaches for new ones that mix in the "magic" from the world of physics and the properties of matter.

Simply put, quantum cryptography is based on our current knowledgebase of the world of quantum physics, where we have developed new cryptosystems that cannot be defeated—or at least not using current methods. In theory, this new system cannot be defeated without the knowledge that both parties possess. So what does it take to implement this type of system? Let's look at the name itself to get an idea. *Quantum* refers to behaviors that happen at the subatomic level involving particles and waves, and we use that knowledge to build an extremely strong cryptographic system.

Before we get into that, let's talk about some situations and why the new approach is so important as well as how it came about and how it works.

So What Is Quantum Cryptography?

Quantum cryptography is a new wrinkle in the world of cryptography—one that introduces fascinating possibilities. The technique is a method used to secure information through the application of quantum mechanics.

Note
The field of quantum mechanics is one the deals with the study of matter at the atomic and subatomic levels as well as the study of energy at these scales. The normal field of physics deals with matter at the macroscopic level, whereas quantum deals with matter at the other end of the spectrum, which is the infinitesimally small. The study of matter and energy at this scale will not only yield a better understanding of matter and energy, but helps explain how activity at this level could impact everyday life. Additionally, the principles learned from our study and application of quantum mechanics opens doors to whole new worlds of cryptographic systems.

This new spin on the field of cryptography seeks to revolutionize the security of data between parties by changing how several core components of traditional cryptography are accomplished.

Note

Sometimes quantum cryptography goes by the name *quantum key distribution,* or *QKD,* which may give you a clue as to how it works.

Quantum cryptography, also known as quantum key distribution (QKD), is a method of secure data encryption and transmission using quantum mechanics. Using QKD, two parties can create a shared random bit string known only to them, which can be used as a key to encrypt and decrypt messages.

Before we get into exactly what this means to us, let's look at the problems associated with traditional cryptography, as described in earlier sections of this book.

Traditional Cryptography: A Quick Review

Up to this point in this text, we have been discussing mostly traditional and classical forms of cryptography as well as public key systems. These systems emphasize protecting the privacy of sensitive information through the use of a key, and they apply the mechanism of information manipulation without regard to the secrecy of the mechanism itself.

We have looked at numerous ways of encrypting information, including the Enigma machine, Caesar cipher, and Vigenère cipher. Each one of these types of systems uses a different mechanism or process to convert plaintext to ciphertext, and back, but the end result and goal are the same: keeping data private. Even with systems such as the Enigma, which was big and clunky by today's standards, the process conceptually is the same.

Notice a constant theme with all the ciphers and systems we have discussed so far in regard to their core function: It is the key. Any system we have covered requires and algorithm and a key to process data from one state to another, with the key being the most critical to the operation. As you've learned, with any system the key is the most critical item needed; in fact, without the proper key it becomes extremely difficult (depending on key strength, of course) to decrypt a message, even if the algorithm is known to the public at large. Also note that the key is critical for maintaining the secrecy of data in both symmetric and asymmetric systems.

Note

Remember that some algorithms can have literally millions of potential keys, which would make finding the correct one extremely tough. This does not include any of the advanced cracking techniques discussed in our code-breaking chapter because these techniques will meet with varying levels of success depending on the design of the system.

Although we have a huge number of algorithms in both the asymmetric and symmetric categories, they all use some form of key. Any algorithm that is considered to be strong will have seemingly limitless numbers of keys available, making an exhaustive search of the keyspace nearly impossible (although still technically possible nonetheless). In the world of quantum cryptography, the way keys are generated and transmitted puts a new "spin" on this paradigm.

In asymmetric or public-key cryptography, two keys are generated that are interrelated mathematically. By using this process, we discovered that anyone who wants to send an encrypted message can use one key to do so, with the other key being kept secret or private. Using this system, someone can send an encrypted message that can only be decrypted by the intended recipient.

In Actual Practice

Some descriptions of public key cryptography use the example of a mailbox. In this example, we would have the mailman in possession of a key that opens the mailboxes of everyone so that he can put the mail in those boxes. The other party would be the individual who owns the mailbox. That person can open their box and would be the only person who could do so.

In traditional cryptography, which we call *symmetric cryptography*, only one key is utilized by all parties involved in the communication. Although all parties will possess the key and be able to use it to encrypt and decrypt, it will not be shared freely. At the same time, the algorithm can be freely shared with everyone, even those not involved in the communication (for all the reasons we mentioned back in the previous chapters). The message itself will remain safely protected in its encrypted form as long as the key is kept secret.

One of the biggest problems with shared-key cryptography is the key. How do two different parties agree on a key safely? If we just look at two parties, we need to figure out how they can agree upon a key and share it with one another without anyone else viewing or capturing it. Of course, if the parties are in close proximity, this is not a problem, but move a ZIP Code or two away, and now it becomes a concern. Additionally, if you wish to change the key regularly, you must have a process in place that is easily repeatable—which again could be problematic for reasons mentioned earlier in the book. Although we have this capability in place for cryptography already, quantum methods solves the problem much more effectively than existing methods.

Logic initially states that with traditional cryptography, we could send a message with the key information, but then how does the message with the key stay protected? Should this message be encoded then, too? If it is encoded, then again the problem becomes one of how to agree upon a key once more. This process illustrates one of the largest problems with shared-key or traditional cryptography. In the case of working with keys, this is one of the many issues with key distribution.

Eavesdropping is one of the great challenges of cryptology: How do we keep unwanted parties from obtaining secret information? After all, if it was okay for just anyone to hear, there would be no need to encrypt a message in the first place.

IMHO

Remember, even though shared-key cryptography has flaws, it is still in major use due to its increased performance over public-key systems when working with bulk data. Quantum cryptography will offer many benefits over current systems, but it is unlikely to phase out current systems "overnight."

If we look at the alternative to the traditional systems we have explored, we have public-key cryptography. As you know, public-key cryptography utilizes a pair of keys known as the public and private key pair, which has advantages over shared-key systems. As we've discussed previously, shared-key systems have the inherent challenge of key transfer.

LINGO
Asymmetric algorithms use public and private keys generated when a user or party joins a system that uses a public-key algorithm.

So why call the keys public and private? Simply put, it is a question of distribution. The public key is published someplace where those who need it can get ahold of it, and the private is held by the person it was originally issued to and kept secret. By using this method of key distribution, we are in effect eliminating the need for the secrecy of the key in transit; the "exposed" key, or public key, travels across the wire and is available to everyone. It is the private key that stays secret, and subsequently stays in possession of the owner. Of course, we can't leave it at that because the keys must be associated to the people they are assigned to in order to be trusted and authentic. How we do this association is something we discuss later, so let's just concentrate on the algorithms at this point.

What you should be asking right now is, how does the two-key system work? First of all, the two keys are linked mathematically to one another, which is an important detail. Although in theory it may be possible to derive a private key from the public key, we can conquer this problem by engineering a system in such a way that deriving one key from another is difficult to do. This can be done in a number of ways, but one of the more common ways is to rely on a complex mathematical equation that is easy to perform one way and not the other. However, what if we had another way of handling key management?

LINGO
Remember, public-key cryptosystems are examples of **zero-knowledge proof**, which is a fancy way of saying that you have a means of verifying something is true without having direct knowledge. Consider this: You can verify someone has a private key by using the correct public key to reverse whatever they have done with the private. Because both keys are mathematically related, one key can reverse anything done with the other without the private key needing to be revealed.

So this system may seem ideal considering that we no longer have to worry about key distribution, right? Well, young padawan, we must look at another matter relating to the keys. When we talk about this problem, first consider that to achieve the same level of strength between asymmetric and symmetric systems, we need to have a 2,034-bit key on average for asymmetric, whereas in symmetric we need only a 128-bit key. Additionally, because of the way the algorithms work, asymmetric systems can be at least a factor of 1,000 times slower than symmetric systems. It is for this reason specifically that asymmetric is used where small amounts of data are present and not where large or bulk data is expected.

One of the biggest problems with public-key systems is that it relies on high-order mathematical operations and the sheer size of the numbers used to transform the message along with the algorithm. The numbers generated and used can easily reach extremely large proportions, which can make them both strong and extremely hard to handle by modern computing systems. What's more, they can be made so that in order to understand each bit of output data, you have to also understand every other bit as well. This means that to crack a 128-bit key, the possible numbers used can reach upward of 10^{38} power. That's a lot of possible numbers to find that one correct key needed to decode a message.

In Actual Practice

Something that I didn't really mention earlier is that the keys used in modern cryptographic systems are so extremely large that it would take a billion computers working in parallel, with each processing a billion calculations per second, a trillion years to uncover the correct key. For those who are protecting information with a public-key system, this is great news because it makes code breaking that much more difficult. However, the current computing systems will be replaced with what are known as "quantum computers" in the future; these computers (which exploit the properties of physics on the immensely small quantum scale) will represent a threat to cryptographic strength. Due to their design, these computers will be able to perform calculations and operate at speeds no computer in use could possibly attain under any circumstance. So the codes that would take a trillion years to break with conventional computers could possibly be cracked in much less time with quantum computers, maybe taking the proverbial "blink of an eye" to do the same work.

Finding a Solution via Quantum Mechanics

So how does quantum cryptography address these issues with current cryptographic systems? The solution has been provided via the fascinating world of quantum physics. Through the use of the powerful and unique nature of matter, down at the smallest levels, researchers have found ways to exchange information not possible before. But before you can understand how quantum cryptography works, we must also take a quick look at the field of quantum mechanics. Let me first give you an overview of what quantum cryptography does before we get into how and whys it functions.

So How Does Quantum Cryptography Work?

Quantum cryptography also goes by the name quantum key distribution (QKD), which is essentially just a method of securing data using the power of quantum mechanics. Using this new powerful form of encryption, it now becomes possible for parties to share information to be used as a key that will remain known only to them without fear of eavesdropping.

Although methods such those that have been developed in public key system rely on advanced and complex mathematical functions, they cannot identify or guarantee the security of a key. Because QKD relies on a fundamental property of nature, it is far superior with regard to security.

Note

As with traditional methods, the fundamental cryptographic requirements and operations still remain; quantum cryptography is focused on generating and distributing a key. Once this key is generated, it can be used with any given encryption algorithm during the encryption and decryption process. Although the range of algorithms that can be used is fairly broad, the one that is most commonly used is the one-time pad, because it has been proven secure when used with a secret random key.

Quantum cryptography is radically different from existing methods, to say the least. In fact, it offers an advantage that current cryptographic methods cannot—the ability to detect eavesdropping or someone trying to determine the key. This particular ability owes to something that is fundamental to the field of quantum mechanics—namely, that any attempt to measure a system will alter the system in some way. Applying this to quantum cryptography means that anyone trying to obtain the key must eavesdrop and attempt to recover the key through some means of measurement, meaning that very real and detectable changes to the system will occur. By transmitting important information in this way, it is therefore possible to detect eavesdropping.

So how does this work? I don't promise that this will be simple to explain, and some of you who know quantum mechanics may argue with my description, but that's fine. This is a book on cryptography and not physics, so we will simplify as much as possible to make it accessible for all of us who are mere mortals.

One of the cornerstones of physics is known as the Uncertainty Principle. Simply stated, the principle states that we are limited to what we can know about a quantum system. In layman's terms, it means that we can understand one of two things: either the position of an object or the momentum of an object (*object* in this case being a particle of matter such as an electron). You can know one item or the other, but not both at the same time because measuring one will impact the other in some way.

In Actual Practice

In the physics world, the principle I am describing, rather crudely, is known as the Heisenberg Uncertainty Principle. Werner Heisenberg was a German physicist who won the Nobel Prize for Physics in 1932 for the "Creation of Quantum Mechanics."

If it helps you visualize this a bit better, let's use a variation of one of Heisenberg's famous thought experiments. Imagine, if you will, a pool table that represents the boundaries for our model. In the center of this table is a lone pool ball. As part of our experiment we want to take a picture that shows the position of the pool ball (electron). To take this picture, we will bounce a particle of light off of the pool ball; to represent this particle we will use another pool ball. When we roll one pool ball at the other, no matter how gently, the system is altered when the two touch. In the case of the first pool ball, its position will be altered in some manner by the impact of the second ball. Learning about the ball's position would create uncertainty in its velocity, and the act of measurement would produce the uncertainty needed to satisfy the principle.

Another physicist by the name of Schrödinger also had a famous experiment commonly known as Schrödinger's Cat. In this experiment, a box with a cat inside is placed in front of the observer. Until the observer actually opens the box, the cat is both alive and dead at the same, but once the box is opened the cat is either alive or dead. The outcome in this experiment is affected by the observer and only occurs once an observation is made; until then, all possibilities exist. Figure 10-1 shows Schrödinger's Cat experiment.

Note

In the physics world, when all possibilities exist like they do in Schrödinger's example (alive or dead) prior to observation, this is a state of "superposition." This is an interesting concept, to say the least, if applied to real-world situations we can relate to. For example, if I was standing at the end of a long hallway with ten closed doors, we could use these doors to represent all the possible choices you could make. If you came up to me (and I had my back to the hallway) I could tell you to open and go through one of the ten doors. If I didn't turn around to look and observe which door you went through, a superposition would exist where you went through all 10 doors because I had not made the observation to determine which one you went through.

Objects can exist in this so-called "superposition" until we observe them directly to tell which event happened. Once that observation is made, reality (or at least our reality) collapses around that event and the other possibilities are inaccessible to us.

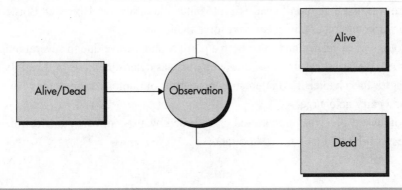

Figure 10-1   Schrödinger's Cat experiment

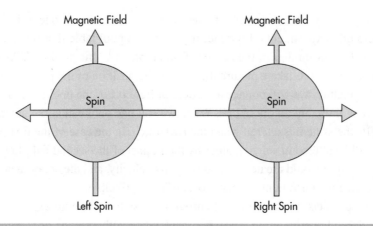

Figure 10-2 Spin of a photon

So let's go a little deeper into this and talk about photons. Although many of us think of photon torpedoes from *Star Trek* when we hear the word *photons,* the term actually refers to a particle. Specifically, the photon is a measure of light that has no mass that can exist in many different states at once (something known as a *wave function).* Essentially what we are saying is that a photon spins in all directions at the same time, and is said to be in an unpolarized state. Figure 10-2 shows photon spin in action.

In Actual Practice

Light is made of particles known as photons, and these photons were at the center of a fundamental argument in physics. For years, physicists argued that light was either a particle or a wave. In one camp, we had those who thought light was made up of particles, and in the other camp, we had those who thought it was a series of waves. The problem was that light didn't neatly fit into either classification. However, Einstein was able to work with other physicists to resolve the issue.

Photons were determined to be both a particle and a wave due to several unique properties. We won't get into how and why this was determined; we will simply accept this fact for this chapter. Two interesting properties of photons are that they have no mass and carry no charge.

Photons are also what are emitted or absorbed by an atom when an electron changes its orbit (but let's not go too far).

(continued)

In case you're wondering, the supercool technical description of a photon is "a discrete bundle or quantum of energy." According to the laws of science, photons are always on the move, and when placed within a vacuum, they exhibit a constant speed (the speed of light) to all who observe them.

My brain hurts....

When we use photons for encryption, we can take advantage of this wave function property and Heisenberg's principle. In current implementations of quantum cryptography, photons are generated using light-emitting diodes (LEDs) to create unpolarized light. Because LEDs have the ability to create a photon at a time instead of an explosion of photons, this allows us to implement our system. Via the use of what is known as a "polarization filter," a photon can be induced to take on only one of the states mentioned earlier, thus making it polarized. For example, we could use a filter to polarize all the particles to have a horizontal spin instead of a random spin.

By polarizing the photons in such a manner, we no longer have the ability to measure them accurately again unless we use the same type of filter. If we were to use a vertical filter instead of a horizontal one, the photon either won't be passed through or it will be altered. If the photon is altered by the filter, any information attached to the particle is lost. Figure 10-3 shows the transmission process of photons with information attached.

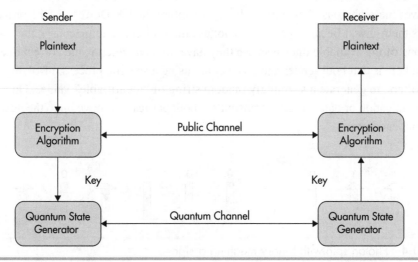

Figure 10-3   The data-transmission process with key exchange

Next comes the most important detail, which I'm sure you're wondering about: How we can use a particle to carry information, which is the cornerstone of quantum cryptography? For that answer, let's take a look at a few more things.

Photons as Information Carriers

You already have learned about photons, and the property called "spin," as well as polarization, but how do photons carry information about a key? In other words, how do we use the spin of a photon to convey information about a key?

Quantum cryptography uses photons to transmit keys. Once a key is transmitted, coding and encoding using the normal secret-key method can take place. But how does a photon become a key? How do you attach information to a photon's spin?

We now need to examine binary code, but don't worry: We are not going to do any binary math or anything like that. As you may know, binary is simply 1's and 0's in computer speak, with a string of 1's and 0's representing an actual message. For example, 101110100001111101 could represent "Master Sword" in plain English. Because a photon can have one of several unique spins, it is a simple matter for us to assign a 1 or 0 to these spins and then interpret them accordingly. When one party transmits the photons, they simply pass the photons through randomly chosen filters and then record the results in turn. It is in this way that the transmitting party will know what results the receiving party should obtain. Figure 10-4 shows binary code assigned to a photon.

Let's envision a simple thought experiment for a moment—one where two parties (labeled A and B) are communicating. When party A transmits photons using a special LED, they will be passed through an UP, DOWN, LEFT, or RIGHT filter. When party B receives these photons, they will randomly use either the UP, DOWN, LEFT or RIGHT filters themselves. Because party B cannot use these filters simultaneously, they simply use one of the available ones because they have no idea which is the correct one. The intent here is that both sender and receiver are using a specific process, involving photons and filters, to generate a seemingly random string of "identifiable" values. Once the communication or data has been transmitted, both parties can move on to the next phase without encryption.

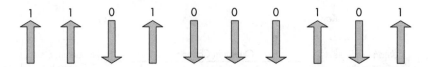

Figure 10-4   Photon spin with binary meaning assigned

This next phase is unencrypted due to the way the information has been transmitted in the previous step. In this step, party B contacts party A and informs them of the filters they used and in which sequence. This is where party A will tell party B which filters are correct and which are not. So why is this unencrypted? Well, simply put, nothing can be gleaned from this process by a third party because there is not enough information to determine what is going on without knowing the original measurements and the photons involved. Eavesdropping on this information would be like hearing me tell my best friend he had the right combination to my gym locker, but at no point does either of us say the actual combination (kinda useless to anyone listening, huh?).

Their conversation may sound a little like this:

B: Up A: Correct
B: Up A: Incorrect
B: Down A: Correct

Note that A is not providing information on the measurements, only the type of filter actually used at each step. By performing the negotiation, party A isn't saying what the measurements are—only the type of filters used. Therefore, a third party listening in on their conversation can't determine what the actual photon sequence is—only that it is one of many possibilities. Although B will know which measurements are correct, a third party will not know and therefore will be unable to decode the message.

To understand this a little better, look at the following example:

1. A sends a photon as UP.

2. B uses a DOWN filter to measure the photon.

3. B will inform A that they used DOWN to measure the photon.

4. A will answer incorrectly.

There will also be points where the conversation will look like this:

1. A sends a photon as DOWN.

2. B uses a DOWN filter to measure the photon.

3. B will inform A that they used DOWN to measure the photon.

4. A will answer correctly.

Once this process has taken place, all of the incorrect answers will be discarded on party B's side. Once this has been completed, both parties will now have identical strings of polarized photons. Although initially both parties will be left with what is ultimately a set of photons, applying the proper algorithm will convert the spin of the photons into 1's and 0's.

Simply put, this now means that what was a string of photons is now something like this:

011101110110100101110011011001000110111101101101001000000110001101101
1110111010101110010011000010110011101100101001000000111000001101111101
11011101100101011100100

This, in turn, can now be converted into language or whatever it originally happened to be. In our case, the message would translate to:

wisdom courage power

Simple, huh?

But What About Eavesdropping?

One of the main goals of quantum cryptography is to eliminate the threat posed by eavesdropping. Whereas this has always been a problem in traditional cryptography, you will see that in the world of quantum it becomes a non-issue.

First, let's briefly look at how current cryptographic systems work. In the current systems, a third party, whom we will call Eve, is the one who will perform the eavesdropping (I know, real creative, huh?). Eve will passively obtain the message by listening in using some method, and then she will later on attempt to decode the message using some form of code breaking or cryptanalysis. Figure 10-5 shows the eavesdropping process.

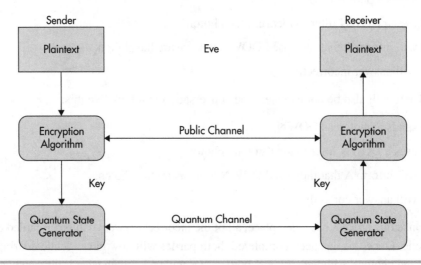

Figure 10-5 The eavesdropping process

In the world of quantum cryptography, we quickly learn that this ceases to be a problem due to the "magic" of the underlying science. As you saw previously, the Heisenberg Uncertainty Principle comes into play when that pesky snoop Eve comes sniffing around again.

Let's see how this works:

1. A sends B a series of polarized photons.

2. Eve sets up her own filter somewhere to intercept the photons.

3. Not knowing which filters are correct and incorrect, Eve does not know which ones to use.

4. Eve randomly measures polarization of the photons.

5. Eve then passes the same photons on to B using a similar LED as before.

6. Because Eve measured the photons, the sender and receiver will be alerted to her presence.

After Eve has measured the photons by randomly selecting filters to determine their spin, she will pass them down the line to Bob using her own LED with a filter set to the alignment she chose to measure the original photon. She does this to cover up her presence and the fact that she intercepted the photon message. But due to the Heisenberg Uncertainty Principle, Eve's presence will be detected. By measuring the photons, Eve inevitably altered some of them.

In practice, after the photons have been transmitted and A and B have had their discussion about filters, much like before, the truth would emerge. Because Eve intercepted the message and altered the photons by her interactions, when party A and B go through their "correct" or "incorrect" back and forth, the filters won't match up, and the eavesdropping would thus be revealed. The differences in their measurements would reveal that a third party has altered the information and that the message was compromised.

A and B could take measures to further protect the data if they so choose by performing a parity check. Specifically, they would check some of the exact results obtained during the transmission to see if they match up with one another. If the chosen samples match, then the message would be considered safe and uncompromised.

The two could discard these discussed measurements and use the remaining secret measurements as their key. If discrepancies are found, they should occur in 50 percent of the parity checks. Because Eve will have altered about 25 percent of the photons through her measurements, they could reduce the likelihood that Eve has the remaining correct information down to a one-in-a-million chance by conducting additional parity checks.

So There Have to Be Problems, Right?

Every new innovation comes with new problems, despite all the neat benefits it offers—and quantum cryptography is no exception. One of the bigger problems tends to be distance—at least right now it is.

Originally, the quantum cryptography system as envisioned in 1989 was able to transmit information over a short distance of 36 centimeters. At this time, distances of 150 kilometers have been reached, which is impressive, but far short of what is needed to be practical. To be useful, the range needs to be substantial. In fact, in theory it should be, but the real world for now poses a limitation.

In the real world, the distance of transmission is so shortened due to environmental interference. Much like Eve in our earlier example, who makes changes to the photons by interacting with them, particles in the real world will get in the way of the photons, thus causing issues. In fact, the photons will bounce off of particles in the environment, and this will impact or affect the polarization they were transmitted in, meaning the information they carry will be altered. Additionally, the longer a photon travels, the more likely it will bump into something along the way.

Recently, a group of Austrian researchers solved (or started to solve) this problem by using Einstein's work as a guide—something called "spooky action at a distance." This observation of quantum physics is based on something known as the entanglement of photons. What this refers to is the ability for photons to become dependent on one another after having some interaction. Although we won't worry about the nature of this entanglement and the specifics of how it happens, we can get into the basics. Entanglement doesn't mean that particles become physically linked; instead, it means that they become connected in some way that is not currently known to science. When a pair of photons becomes entangled, the two will have the opposite spins of each other. If one particle is measured, then the other's spin can be accurately inferred. Want know why we call this "spooky"? When these particles are moved apart, whether it is a few feet or a much, much further distance, they still will be linked—distance doesn't seem to matter. This is much like me and my girlfriend—no matter where I am in the world, if I am happy, she is mad at me (probably because I forgot our anniversary or forgot to take out the trash). Figure 10-6 shows a rough illustration of this relationship (not the girlfriend issue).

How does this solve the distance problem? Well, simply put, if photons are entangled and the position of one can be determined by measuring its partner, no matter how far the distance between them, then we can easily send information over long distances without having to worry about the interference of those pesky particles in the environment.

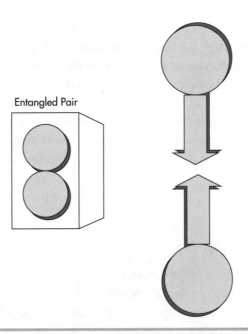

Entangled Pair

Figure 10-6   Quantum entanglement

In Actual Practice

Interestingly enough, a team at the Massachusetts Institute of Technology has taken advantage of another property of entanglement. Using their research, they found that two entangled photons will stay linked with a change in one photon being reflected in its opposite. Through careful measurements, they were able to measure a property of a photon and make a well-informed assumption as to what the other properties such as spin would be. By using this method instead of measuring the spin directly, the researchers found that the photon is not adversely affected, so the eavesdropping is impossible to detect.

The method is not ready for the "big time" yet, but the team at MIT suggest it could be perfected and therefore become a threat. However, as we have seen so many times before, technology evolves and countermeasures will be found.

What you have seen here is that traditional systems rely on computational and other systems to make them tough to break. Although these systems work pretty well, the downside is that they cannot absolutely guarantee the security of a key, nor can they fully prevent eavesdropping. Therefore, quantum cryptography is magnitudes more secure than any current method.

Similarly, as with many existing systems, this new form of cryptography is used to generate and later disseminate a key. The algorithm most commonly used with quantum cryptography is the one-time pad, because it has been proven secure when used with a secret random key.

In Actual Practice

Quantum mechanics, and more specifically, cryptography, are already present in the voting systems used in democratic nations, essentially providing substantial protection to the security of the ballots themselves. When the security of the ballots is compromised, so too is the individuals' right to choose their leaders.

The Swiss manufacturer Quantique developed a system known as "U-sing" that was used in 2007 during parliamentary elections. Information during this election was transmitted using an algorithm that utilized a key generated by quantum cryptography. Due to the magic we have seen so far, this system is nearly unbreakable and therefore the secret ballots remain just that—secret.

We've Covered

Quantum cryptography holds major promise and wonder, and will definitely revolutionize the whole idea of secure communications. By leveraging the seemingly mystical and complex properties of quantum mechanics over the traditional mathematical-based approaches, a new level of performance and power is reached. Some systems currently exist that can use this science, and more are becoming available each day, along with regular improvements and upgrades. Expect that within the next few years quantum-based systems will start encrypting some of the most valuable secrets of government and industry.

What is quantum cryptography?

- Quantum cryptography is a key exchange system.
- Quantum cryptography is a faster, more powerful form of cryptosystem.

The impact of quantum cryptography

- It will change the complexity of current cryptosystems.
- It will require a reevaluation of current cryptosystems.

How this new technique will change the field

- It will be much faster.
- It will allow for much longer keys.

How the process works

- Relies on the details of quantum mechanics.
- Uses processes such as quantum entanglement.

How the process differs from previous techniques

- Is much faster than current methods.
- Can create near unbreakable cryptosystems.

CHAPTER 11

The Future of Cryptography

We'll Cover

- Future applications of encryption

- Future directions of encryption

- Encryption and the law

This book has covered a lot of ground on the subject of encryption. Although a few things have been left out, we have covered the fundamentals needed to get you off and running. What we need to do now is look forward and see where encryption and cryptography go from here.

Where Are We Now?

Cryptography has been around as long as mankind's ability to communicate. Much like communication technologies, cryptography has revolutionized human existence—and will continue to do so in its future forms, such as quantum cryptography.

In the mid-1800s the telegraph was invented, and not too long after the first transatlantic telegraph was sent by the Governor of Utah. The date was October 24, 1861 and the telegraph read as follows:

> "Utah has not seceded but is firm for the Constitution and the laws of our once happy country."

A short two days after this message, the Pony Express ended its short existence and a new age of communication started. Not too long after that, people not in government or the military came to expect private communication, and cryptography became the answer to a lot of questions.

As you know by now, cryptography has a complicated and unique language all its own. Although it may have looked complicated to you at first, it got easier along the way. Terms that were once intimidating and overwhelming, such as keys, algorithms, and ciphers, have been brought down to size and are now understandable to you. Give yourself a pat on the back—you have come a long way.

In this book, you learned that encryption is used in the following areas:

- **Hard drives** In today's world, with the abundance of portable computing devices such as laptops that are easily stolen, drive encryption has become huge. Systems that protect hard drives ensure that the thief cannot view information on the system that they are not authorized to see, thus keeping it confidential.

- **Digital signatures**   An increasing amount of e-mail is being digitally signed to validate the identity of the sender and to verify that the information has been sent as the sender intended it to be.

- **E-commerce**   For the last decade, an increasing number of transactions, such as banking and shopping, have taken place online. Without encryption offering the protection needed to keep these transactions secret and authentic, e-commerce would not be possible—or at least not in its current form.

- **Cell phones**   Cell phones make widespread use of cryptographic technologies to authenticate devices and to protect data and other items.

- **Digital Rights Management**   DRM is designed to preserve the rights of an author, creator, or publisher of a work by keeping the copyright and other rights intact.

- **Communication**   Technologies such as SSL and TLS protect the confidentiality and integrity of information in transit.

As you now know, this is just a small sampling of the applications of today's cryptographic technologies. At this point you should be looking at current technologies and applications with a new perspective that includes the concepts we have discussed.

The function of cryptography is almost always to protect data. This is important to remember because the amount of information being generated (and later maintained) is increasing exponentially, with typical companies doubling the amount of information they currently possess every 18 months (and some at an even faster rate). It is no surprise that, as a result of this ever-increasing and deepening pool of data, encryption has become the foundation upon which enterprise-level storage and security systems are built. In fact, industries such as finance and health care have had to invest heavily in getting more advanced and specialized equipment to perform encryption and provide the heightened security being demanded.

I have made mention of health care and finance many times in this book. I can't emphasize enough that these fields have had increasing need to improve security due to numerous issues and to meet regulations such as the Health Insurance Portability and Accountability Act (HIPAA).

I would also like to point out that encryption has, for a long time, been a part of auto manufacturing and design. With new technologies such as wireless key fobs, Bluetooth, and GPS being integrated into cars, along with the long-present computers, introducing encryption into the equation has become a necessity.

Also consider for a moment that encryption is used in home entertainment systems such as the Nintendo Wii U, PlayStation, and Xbox. These all have encryption built in to their makeup, not to mention the games and movies they play. Additionally, the TV you watch these media on also incorporates encryption.

What do each of these fields show us? They show us that the application of encryption is everywhere and will only increase as information increases and as the features present on systems grow.

In today's world, the protection of sensitive data is one of the most critical concerns for organizations and their customers. Due to growing regulatory pressures, businesses have to protect the integrity, privacy, and security of critical information. As a result, cryptography is emerging as the foundation for enterprise data security and compliance, and it's quickly becoming the foundation of security best practices. Cryptography, once seen as a specialized, obscure discipline of information security, is finally coming of age.

Again, the field of cryptography is not new and has existed for as long as mankind could communicate. All sorts of organizations—from banks to health care companies to those that work with national security concerns—have found that encryption is a useful and necessary component of their security strategy. Today, the use of cryptographic methods is growing as the demand to exchange and store increasing amounts of information rises. To put it simply, cryptography and cryptographic technologies have become hot areas in the high-tech field, and this trend is expected to grow even more over the coming years.

In Actual Practice

Already debuting on the scene and expected to become a major force in the next few years is the technology quantum cryptography. Quantum cryptography is a solution that meets the needs for increased computing power, security, and performance.

Personal Data Requirements

One of the areas that is expected to make an increasing use of cryptography is e-commerce in order to meet ever-increasing legal requirements such as the Payment Card Industry Data Security Standard (PCI DSS). This area has only become more urgent in the wake of several high-profile security breaches of companies such as T.J. Maxx, Sony, and Best Buy, resulting in the loss of personal data and lawsuits on behalf of angry customers. Protecting information such as credit card data and other personal information is not going to decrease anytime soon, and will only increase as more systems are integrated and data is shared among systems and vendors.

A couple of high-profile examples over the last few years have only solidified this point. The clothing retailer Gap Inc. was forced to notify over 800,000 job applicants that their personal information, including social security numbers, was potentially compromised when a laptop was stolen containing the sensitive data. The Registered Traveler Program in the United States had a similar problem when a notebook containing applicant information was stolen and recovered four days later. It was revealed during the investigation that the notebook did not utilize any sort of encryption to protect the data on the hard drive, meaning the data was potentially compromised.

In Actual Practice

In the latter case of a notebook getting stolen with Registered Traveler Program information stored on the hard drive, the fallout was massive, to say the least. According to reports, someone entered the Clear offices (that is, the administrators of the program) in San Francisco Airport and stole the computer. It was reported at the time that the system contained over 33,000 applicants' information, including names, addresses, birthdates, and in some cases, driver's license and passport numbers.

Adding to this problem was the fact that in the wake of the theft, the program was shut down temporarily by the Transportation Security Administration (TSA) while an investigation was performed. The TSA stated that the program would only be opened to new applicants once they had assurances on the security of the program overall. Interestingly enough, the investigation of the security breech also uncovered the fact that the administrators of the program did not implement basic security procedures on many of the systems used to store the information at corporate data centers. All of these issues combined resulted in some serious oversight by the TSA.

What we can see from both these cases is that encryption along with other advanced security measures will play an important role in all future measures. Encryption for many types of data is becoming the last and most aggressive line of defense in protecting organizations' information. Because devices will become even more mobile and portable in the future, it is easy to see that encryption will have to play a more important role to protect lost or stolen devices from being accessed by third parties by rendering the information and devices useless and unreadable without the key used to unlock them.

What About the Law?

The role that the law plays in cryptography is something that will affect both current and future developments. As stated before, the incredible volume of personal data (as well as other types of data) on devices and services such as cell phones, e-mail, and file transfers could end up in the wrong hands and potentially bring down or ruin a company or individual.

Governments, as well as corporations and individuals, have determined that privacy is tough to preserve in today's society. Fortunately, encryption provides a powerful and effective way of preserving privacy. Over the last several years, the actions taken by various governments have shown that the demand for privacy is increasing, and cryptography is playing a high-profile role in the solution.

The Law and Encryption

In the last few years, several legal developments have arisen that challenge the role of cryptography and the use of encryption—developments that pose as big a threat to encryption as code breakers.

Two examples in the United States involve cryptography and the Fourth and Fifth Amendments to the U.S. Constitution, which are part of the Bill of Rights. For reference, here are the contents of these two amendments:

Note

There are many examples of how the law and the field of cryptography have been both at odds and in concert with one another, but in this text I will use examples that are U.S.-centric. I don't do this to ignore other countries or trivialize their legal system; I just cannot speak knowledgeably enough about the role of law and encryption in other countries.

- **Fourth Amendment**   The right of the people to be secure in their persons, houses, papers, and effects, against unreasonable searches and seizures, shall not be violated, and no Warrants shall issue, but upon probable cause, supported by Oath or affirmation, and particularly describing the place to be searched, and the persons or things to be seized.

- **Fifth Amendment**   No person shall be held to answer for a capital, or otherwise infamous crime, unless on a presentment or indictment of a Grand Jury, except in cases arising in the land or naval forces, or in the Militia, when in actual service in time of War or public danger; nor shall any person be subject for the same offense to be twice put in jeopardy of life or limb; nor shall be compelled in any criminal case to be a witness against himself, nor be deprived of life, liberty, or property, without due process of law; nor shall private property be taken for public use, without just compensation.

So let's take a look at the Fourth Amendment and how cryptography is involved. Legal experts at George Washington University have cited several cases that could impact or relate to security:

- **United States v. Scott**   The court ruled that shredded documents could be reconstructed and used as evidence in legal proceedings.

- **United States v. Longoria**   A circuit court ruling dictated that criminals using a different language for the express purpose of concealing a crime could have those conversations translated and submitted as evidence in legal proceedings.

- **Commonwealth (Pennsylvania) v. Copenhefer**   The Supreme Court of the State of Pennsylvania determined that deleted files on a hard drive could be forensically recovered and used as evidence in court.

In these cases, it has been suggested that encryption could be impacted as the next logical step—because an action such as talking in a different language to conceal secrets or shredding documents could be considered the same as hiding information via encryption. What this means is that expectations of privacy can be "stripped" away via the law if needed.

Note

Take note that in the cases cited here and in countless others, a warrant was not sought necessarily (or at least the cases do not make note of such). Although I am not, by my own admission, a legal expert, it does show that a lack of warrant does not mean that privacy can be preserved.

As mentioned in an earlier chapter, the use of encryption can be viewed in many cases as implying that illegal or illicit activities are being concealed. We, of course, know that this is not the case, and encryption technologies are something that can be applied to protect any sensitive information—legitimate or otherwise.

The hope by legal experts and technology experts is that their fourth amendment rights pertaining to unlawful search and seizure will be consistently and reliably applied to modern technology. It is hoped that the application of such technology will be treated in the same way that the use of locks and keys are now. Specifically, locks can be used to protect legal or illegal material, and only when due process is followed and reasonable cause proven can entrance be granted.

The Fifth Amendment has also come up in the cryptography debate in the last few years. Specifically, the Fifth Amendment states, in part, that individuals cannot incriminate themselves, in essence providing witness against themselves. However, in a recent case in Colorado, a female defendant charged with bank fraud was ordered to provide the keys needed to decrypt a hard drive and potentially recover evidence that would be used against her. In this case, it was unsuccessfully argued that the Fifth Amendment provided protection against this action.

In another case, the defendant was ordered to provide the keys to decrypt a hard drive after U.S. border agents determined that he had child pornography on the system. In this case, the agents saw the system turned on with the content visible, all during a routine traffic stop.

In both cases, the Fifth Amendment was called into question. These cases are still working their way through the system, and their outcomes may impact cryptography and its application in the future.

Note
I wish to express that in the cases cited here, I in no way condone any of the alleged crimes. I use these cases only as a teaching point, not to defend or prosecute anyone.

Military, Government, and the Individual

Another interesting development is government regulation of cryptographic technologies. This area is intriguing because the fight for stronger cryptographic technologies and increasingly "unbreakable" systems has been in favor of the U.S. Government. Laws have been passed preventing the export of certain systems, as well as the use of certain technologies by civilians.

One area that has been contested between the government and individuals/companies is the disclosure of keys. Keys, as you know, are the most important part of the system to keep protected. Although some discussions have been made over the years about whether or not items such as keys should be disclosed in specific cases, few laws exist covering this topic, and there are none currently in the United States.

Key Escrow

Another issue that may be decided in the near future is *key escrow,* which is essentially where a third party holds copies of keys and can provide them when needed. As you know, if a third party has possession of the keys used to encrypt and decrypt, the process is considered a little less secure than if only the keys were restricted to only authorized parties.

One such example of government involvement in encryption and key escrow is the case of the Clipper Chip. In 1993, the U.S. Government was pushing a system known as the Clipper Chip, which used a symmetric encryption system known as Skipjack. Due to the way the system was positioned and promoted, it was forbidden from being analyzed by experts, so its strength and power could not be independently verified.

This system relied on the key escrow system as an integral part of its operation. In practice, the chip would be installed in an electronic communication device and would be used to encrypt communications. Before the chip was provided to vendors to install in their devices, a set of keys would be generated, copies of which would be held in escrow by the government. The idea was that if criminal activity or other malicious actions were suspected, a warrant could be obtained and the communications decrypted.

The system met with much backlash, however, as many groups such as the Electronic Frontier Foundation (EFF) came out against the device. The reasons cited were that the system could not be scrutinized by experts. A second reason was that U.S. companies could be forced to use the technology, but devices manufactured outside the U.S. would not be effected by such issues.

Ultimately, the plan was scrapped in 1996 and the Skipjack algorithm was released to the public.

Interestingly enough, then-Senators John Kerry and John Ashcroft opposed the program and its implementation. Senator Ashcroft is on record as believing that the program overstepped boundaries that the government should not be allowed to cross, a point that some may find humorous considering Ashcroft authored the USA Patriot Act sometime later… but this isn't a political book.

In Actual Practice

The U.S. Government (as well as several other governments) has not completely given up on ideas like the Clipper Chip, but none have met with much success. I don't point this issue out to make you paranoid or to make myself seem like a tinfoil-hat-wearing crazy person, but the reality is that such plans and schemes do exist.

Embedded Cryptography

Cryptography was once the domain of mathematicians and computer science specialists, but in today's world, the technology is readily available and is, in fact, embedded into devices. Laptop computers, wireless access points, and even devices we don't think of as being part of a typical IT infrastructure, such as vending machines, parking meters, gaming machines, and electronic voting terminals, have encryption embedded.

In the future, this will become even more common, with individuals and organizations getting increased access to military-grade (and even more advanced levels of) cryptography. This increased proliferation of powerful encryption promises to frustrate law enforcement and other entities, but at the same time offers greater protection of information.

We've Covered

Cryptography has been around as long as mankind's ability to communicate. Cryptography, much like communication technologies, has revolutionized human existence—and will continue to do so in the future through quantum cryptography and other forms.

However, despite all the challenges, both technical and legal, at the end of the day the goal is the same: to protect information. Cryptography is a technology that will be increasingly relied on in the future to offer protection that is otherwise difficult to provide.

Future applications of encryption

- Quantum cryptography will supplement or replace current techniques.
- Cryptography will always be used to protect the confidentiality and integrity of information.

Future directions of encryption

- Quantum cryptography is a future evolution of cryptography.
- Cryptography will be used in many future technologies and devices.

Encryption and the law

- Cryptography has clashed with the First, Fourth, and Fifth Amendments.
- Cryptography has been used to conceal evidence.

GLOSSARY

acceptable use of computers   Defines what activities are acceptable on computer systems owned by the organization.

access attack   An attempt to gain information that the intruder is not authorized to see.

access control   A mechanism used to restrict access to files, folders, or systems based on the identification and authentication of the user.

accountability   The process administration uses to account for an individual's activities and to assign responsibility for actions that have taken place on an information system.

Address Resolution Protocol (ARP) spoofing   A tactic used to forge the MAC address of a system to get packets directed to the attacking computer.

administrative practices   Practices that fall under the areas of policy, procedure, resources, responsibility, education, and contingency plans.

advanced persistent threat (APT)   Generally considered to be a hacker or group of hackers with significant resources, who are targeting specific enterprises. The APT uses exploits that may never have been seen before and compromises systems with the intent of keeping control of them and making use of them for some time.

agents   The people or organization originating a security threat.

anomaly   Something that is out of the ordinary or unexpected.

anti-malware system   A system designed to detect and remove malicious software.

application layer firewall   A firewall that enforces policy rules through the use of application proxies.

asymmetric encryption   An encryption system that uses a different key to perform encryption and decryption functions.

audit   One, a formal check to determine policy compliance, typically performed either by internal auditors at a company or organization or by an independent third party. Two, a function in an operating system that provides administrators with a historic record of events and activities that occurred on an information system, for future reference.

availability   The degree to which information is available when it is needed by authorized parties. Availability may be measured as the percentage of time information is available for use by authorized websites. For example, a business website may strive for availability above 99 percent.

backup   Copies of critical information that are archived in the event of a system crash or a disaster.

backup policy   The policy an organization has in place that documents how backup operations will be conducted.

Balanced Scorecard (BSC)   A performance measurement framework that is intended to enrich traditional financial performance measures with strategic nonfinancial performance measures, thereby providing a more balanced view of organizational performance. Developed in the 1990s by Drs. Robert Kaplan (Harvard Business School) and David Norton. (For additional information, see www.balancedscorecard.org.)

best practices   A set of recommendations that generally provides an appropriate level of security. A combination of those practices that proved to be most effective at various organizations.

biometrics   The use of something related to the human body—for example, fingerprints, retina/iris prints, palm prints, hand geometry, facial geometry, or voice recognition—to authenticate an individual's identity for access.

black bag job   A nighttime operation that leaves no evidence of your forensic imaging.

black swan event   An event that is highly improbable and therefore likely to end up at the bottom of the list of priorities to address. See *The Black Swan: The Impact of the Highly Improbable,* by Nassim Taleb (Random House, 2010) for further reading on the theory of black swan events.

botnet   A malicious botnet is a network of compromised computers used to transmit information, send spam, or launch denial-of-service (DoS) attacks. Essentially, a malicious botnet is a supercomputer created by and managed by a hacker, fraudster, or cybercriminal.

brute-force attack   An attempt by a hacker to gain access to a system by trying to log on to one or many accounts using different combinations of characters to guess or crack a password.

buffer overflow   The process of overwriting memory in such a way as to cause an attacker's code to be executed instead of the legitimate program, with the intent of causing the system to be compromised or allowing the attacker to have elevated privileges to the system.

certificate authority (CA)   A central management entity that issues or verifies security credentials.

chain of custody   A document listing in whose possession and control an item was, and when.

change control procedure   The process used by an organization to verify the current system configuration and provide for the testing and approval of a new configuration before it is implemented.

charter   A document that describes the specific rights and privileges granted from the organization to the information security team.

ciphertext   Information after it has been obfuscated by an encryption algorithm.

cloud computing   As defined by the National Institute of Standards and Technology (NIST), a model for enabling ubiquitous, convenient, on-demand network access to a shared pool of configurable computing resources (such as networks, servers, storage, applications, and services) that can be rapidly provisioned and released with minimal management effort or service provider interaction.

communications security   The measures employed to secure information while it is in transit.

compliance   A process that ensures that an organization adheres to a set of policies and standards, or the adherence to such standards. Two broad categories of compliance are compliance with internal policies (specific to a particular organization) and compliance with external or regulatory policies, standards, or frameworks.

computer security   The means used to protect information on computer systems.

computer use policy   Specifies who can use the organization's computer systems and how those systems can be used.

confidentiality   The prevention of disclosure of information to unauthorized parties.

consultant   A subject matter expert who is contracted to perform a specific set of activities. Typically, a statement of work outlines the deliverables to be completed by the consultant and the deadlines for each deliverable.

core competencies   The fundamental strengths of a program that add value. They are the primary functions of a program and cannot or should not be done by outside groups or partners.

countermeasures   The measures undertaken by an organization to address the identified vulnerabilities of the organization.

cryptanalysis   The art of analyzing cryptographic algorithms with the intent of identifying weaknesses.

cryptographer   An individual who practices cryptography.

cryptographic checksum   A binary string created by running the binary value of the software through a cryptographic algorithm to create a result that will change if any portion of the original binary is modified.

cryptography   The art of concealing information using encryption.

data cleansing The actions performed on a set of data to improve the data quality and achieve better accuracy, completion, or consistency.

Data Encryption Standard (DES) A private key encryption algorithm developed by IBM in the early 1970s that operates on 64-bit blocks of text and uses a 56-bit key.

data leakage prevention (DLP) A mechanism for examining network traffic and detecting sensitive information.

data loss prevention DLP systems are typically network appliances that review all network traffic on your external network, looking for signs of improper data being sent outside the company.

dd image Also called a "raw image," this is a computer forensic image of a system in which the data from the storage device is housed as a single file or multiple files, but without any type of container that stores checksums or hashes.

decryption The process used by encryption systems to convert ciphertext into plaintext.

default allow A policy in which any traffic is allowed except that which is specifically denied.

default deny A policy in which any traffic is denied except that which is specifically allowed.

defendant In a lawsuit, the person and/or company who is being sued by the plaintiff or who is being tried for a criminal act.

defense in depth An architecture in which multiple controls are deployed in such a way that weaknesses in one control are covered by another.

denial of access to applications The tactic of denying the user access to the application that displays the information.

denial of access to information The tactic of making information the user wants to see unavailable.

denial of access to systems The tactic used by an attacker to make a computer system completely inaccessible by anyone.

denial-of-service attack The process of flooding a server (e-mail, web, or resource) with packets to use up bandwidth that would otherwise be allocated to normal traffic and thus deny access to legitimate users.

deperimeterization The current state of most perimeters—full of holes that reduce or eliminate the effectiveness of the perimeter.

Diffie-Hellman key exchange   A public key encryption algorithm developed in 1976 to solve the problem of key distribution for private key encryption systems. Diffie-Hellman cannot be used to encrypt or decrypt information, but it is used to exchange secret keys.

digital signature   A method of authenticating electronic information by using encryption.

digital signature algorithm   An algorithm developed by the U.S. government as a standard for digital signatures.

dirty data   Data that has unacknowledged correlation or undocumented origins or that is biased, nonindependent, internally inconsistent, inaccurate, incomplete, unsuitable for integration with data from other important sources, unsuitable for consumption by tools that automate computation and visualization, or lacking integrity in some other respect.

disaster recovery   The processes and procedures to protect systems, information, and capabilities from extensive disasters such as fire, flood, and extreme weather events.

disaster recovery plan   The procedure an organization uses to reconstitute a networked system after a disaster.

discovery   A phase in litigation between two parties. During discovery, plaintiffs and defendants are allowed to ask each other for documents they believe responsive to their claims or defenses.

Distributed File System (DFS)   Microsoft uses the term to describe its implementation of this technology within Windows servers. Multiple systems appear to have local storage, which is actually mapped across multiple systems in the network.

DMZ (demilitarized zone)   A network segment containing systems that can be directly accessed by external users.

DNS (Domain Name Service) spoofing   A tactic that allows an attacker to intercept information from a target computer by exploiting the DNS by which networks map textual domain names onto the IP numbers used to actually route data packets.

dumpster diving   The act of physically sifting through a company's trash to find useful or sensitive information.

dynamic network address translation   The process used to map multiple internal IP addresses to a single external IP address.

eavesdropping   The process of obtaining information by being positioned in a location at which information is likely to pass.

egress filtering   Filtering traffic that exits through a perimeter.

Elgamal   A variant of the Diffie-Hellman system enhanced to provide encryption, with one algorithm for encryption and another for authentication.

elliptic curve encryption   A public key encryption system based on a mathematical problem related to elliptic curves.

e-mail policy   Governs employee activity and use of the e-mail systems.

emissions security   The measures used to limit the release of electronic emissions.

encryption   The process of changing plaintext into ciphertext.

encryption algorithm   The procedures used for encrypting information.

event   In the context of security risk, this is the type of action that poses a threat.

evidence drive   Also called the "original evidence," this is the hard drive being imaged, versus the storage drive to which we are writing the evidence.

failover   Provisions for the reconstitution of information or capability. Fail-over systems are employed to detect failures and then to reestablish capability by the use of redundant hardware.

false negative   A result that indicates no problem exists where one actually exists, such as occurs when a vulnerability scanner incorrectly reports no vulnerability exists on a system that actually has a vulnerability.

false positive   A result that indicates a problem exists where none actually exists, such as occurs when a vulnerability scanner incorrectly identifies a vulnerability that does not exist on a system.

Faraday cage   A device that blocks electrical fields, including radio waves used for cell phones and tablet devices to communicate.

file carving   Techniques used to recover full or partial remnants of files from the unallocated space of the disk or within large files.; involves removing pieces of data from a large set and putting it aside, much as you would carve a turkey, taking the meat but leaving the bones.

findings   The results of your investigation, or what your review of the evidence revealed.

firewall   A network access control device (either hardware or software) designed to allow appropriate traffic to flow while protecting access to an organization's network or computer system.

first-party knowledge   You personally witnessed and have knowledge of the event to which you will be testifying. If you heard the information from another party, then repeating it in court would be considered hearsay because you did not personally witness it.

forensic artifact   A reproducible file, setting, or system change that occurs every time an application or the operating system performs a specific action.

forensic image   A bit-for-bit copy of the data from the entire contents of a piece of digital storage—that is, areas of the storage medium in use and not in use. Typically a forensic image is accompanied by a hash that allows the analyst to verify that the contents have not changed.

forensically sound method   A method that does not alter the original evidence; some kind of write protection exists to prevent or intercept possible changes to the disk.

GOST   A Russian private-key encryption algorithm that uses a 256-bit key, developed in response to DES.

hacker   An individual who breaks into computer systems.

hacktivism   Process of hacking a computer system or network for "the common good."

hash   A mathematical algorithm that converts data of any length to a fixed set of hexadecimal characters that represent that data.

hierarchical trust model   A model for trust in a public key environment that is based on a chain of authority. You trust someone if someone higher up the chain verifies that you should.

honey pots   Used in research and intrusion prevention systems, honey pots are usually virtual machines that are configured insecurely to lure an attacker in. The attacker's actions are recorded outside of the honey pot and their methods are analyzed.

hot site   An alternative location for operations that has all the necessary equipment configured and ready to go in case of emergency.

identification and authentication   The process that serves a dual role of identifying the person requesting access to information and authenticating that the person requesting the access is the actual person they say they are.

incident response procedures (IRP)   The procedures an organization employs to define how the organization will react to a computer security incident.

information classification standards   Standards that specify treatment of data (requirements for storage, transfer, access, encryption, and so on) according to the data's classification (public, private, confidential, sensitive, and so on).

information control   The processes an organization uses to control the release of information concerning an incident.

information policy   The policy used by an organization that defines what information in an organization is important and how it should be protected.

information security   One, the measures adopted to prevent the unauthorized use, misuse, modification, or denial of use of knowledge, facts, data, or capabilities. Two, the protection of information and information systems from unauthorized access, use, disclosure, modification, or destruction. Also commonly referred to as data security or IT security.

ingress filtering   Filtering traffic that enters through a perimeter.

in-house counsel   A lawyer or lawyers who work in your company. Most large companies have legal departments, and the head of the department is called the general counsel.

integrity   The prevention of data modification by unauthorized parties.

intercept of a line   Identifies the point at which the line crosses the vertical y axis. An intercept is typically expressed as a single value b but can also be expressed as the point $(0, b)$.

interception   An active attack against information by which the intruder puts himself in the path of the information transmission and captures the information before it reaches its destination.

IP spoofing   A tactic used by an attacker to forge the IP address of a computer system.

IPSec (Internet Protocol Security)   A protocol developed by the Internet Engineering Task Force (IETF) to provide the secure exchange of packets at the networking layer.

ISO 27002   The document published by the International Organization for Standardization (ISO) to serve as a guideline for organizations to use in developing information security programs.

JSON   JavaScript Object Notation is a mix of XML and JavaScript used to transfer data between a web browser and a web server without having to reload a web page. Ajax uses JSON in websites we've come to know as Web 2.0.

key   The data input into an algorithm to transform plaintext into ciphertext or ciphertext into plaintext.

litigation   A lawsuit; a legal proceeding in court that occurs when a plaintiff sues a defendant.

live forensics   The act of performing a forensic examination or acquisition on original evidence, particularly a computer hard drive that is powered on and running.

MAC duplicating   The process used by an attacker of duplicating the Media Access Control (MAC) address of a target system to receive the information being sent to the target computer.

malicious code   Programming code used to destroy or interfere with computer operations. Generally, malicious code falls into three categories: viruses, Trojan horse programs, and worms.

malware   Malicious software written to cause harm to the victim's computer system by theft of personal information, proliferation of itself, providing remote access to the user's system, or destruction of data, among other things.

man-in-the-middle attack   Also known as "interception," this type of attack occurs when the intruder puts himself in the middle of a communication stream by convincing the sender that he is the receiver and the receiver that he is the sender.

masquerading   The act of impersonating someone else or some other system.

MD5   Message Digest Algorithm 5 is a 128-bit hash value that uniquely represents a data set of any size that was computed using it. Every time a piece of data is computed with the MD5 algorithm, it will have the same value unless the data has been changed. MD5 is commonly used to check data integrity.

metrics project distance   The amount of a change you want to achieve in your target measurement by the end of the metrics project.

metrics project timeline   How long you want to spend to achieve the metrics project distance.

mission statement   A statement that outlines an information security program's overall goals and provides guidelines for its strategic direction.

modification attack   An attempt by an attacker to modify information that he or she is not authorized to modify.

narrative   A method of organizing the facts of your investigation into a story rather than just listing details. A narrative provides nontechnical details such as the timing of an action—for instance, when the suspect deleted his data after he was put on notice.

network address translation   The process of translating private IP addresses to public IP addresses.

network behavior analysis   An anomaly detection mechanism that watches the flow of traffic on the network. Flow information is acquired from routers and switches or from a device directly connected to the network.

network credentials   Such things as the username and password required to log in to a company computer as the administrator, for example, or the password to network routers and security appliances.

network forensics   A monitoring mechanism that collects all traffic that flows across the network in front of the collection point.

network intrusion detection system (NIDS)   A monitoring system that sits "out of band" and watches network traffic looking for indications of an attack.

network intrusion prevention system (NIPS)   A layer 2 network control that sits inline with traffic and watches for indications of an attack. When an attack is identified, the traffic can be blocked.

network-level risk assessment   The assessment of the entire computer network and the information infrastructure of an organization.

network security   The measures used to protect information used on networked systems.

objective desired direction   The direction in which you want the metrics project measurement to go to achieve the benefits of an information security metrics program, especially the benefit of improvement.

offshoring   Contracting work to resources in a different country (either third party or in house).

one-time pad (OTP)   The only theoretically unbreakable encryption system, this private key encryption method uses a random list of numbers to encode a message. OTPs can be used only once and are generally used for only short messages in high-security environments.

online analytical processing (OLAP)   A specific type of data storage and retrieval mechanism that is optimized for swift queries that involve summarization of data along multiple factors or dimensions.

orange book   Also known as the *Trusted Computer System Evaluation Criteria (TCSEC)*, this book was developed by the National Computer Security Center for the certification of computer systems for security.

orchestration   The administrative oversight that ensures the workflow is executed as specified. It includes functions such as signing off on a metric definition, deployment of its implementation, scheduling its calculation at regular intervals, and executing and delivering updates. *See also* workflow.

organization-wide risk assessment   An analysis to identify risks to an organization's information assets.

original evidence   The source of a case's evidence.

outside counsel   A law firm retained by a company that desires a third-party opinion regarding a decision, also typically retained to represent the company in litigation.

outsourcing   Contracting work to a third-party vendor.

packet-filtering firewall   A firewall that enforces policy rules through the use of packet inspection filters.

penetration test   A test of the capability of an organization to respond to a simulated intrusion of its information systems.

perimeter   The boundary of a network or network zone.

physical security   The protection of physical assets by the use of security guards and physical barriers.

ping of death   An ICMP echo-request packet sent to the target system with added data with the intent of causing a buffer overflow or system crash.

plaintext   Information in its original form. Also known as "cleartext."

plaintiff   The person and/or company who has initiated the lawsuit against the defendant. There is usually only one plaintiff, except in a class action lawsuit.

policy decision point   A control that determines a policy violation has occurred.

policy enforcement point   A control that performs an enforcement action.

policy review   The process used by an organization to review its current policies and, as necessary, to adjust policies to meet current conditions.

prioritization   An exercise in determining relative importance of tasks, projects, and initiatives.

private class addresses   Non-Internet routable IP addresses defined by RFC 1918.

private key encryption   An encryption process requiring that all parties who need to read the information have the same key.

privilege   The status of a document or communication between the attorney and the client (attorney-client privilege). Any e-mail, documents, or other communication between and attorney and a client is considered privileged by default and is exempt from discovery unless a judge rules otherwise.

project management   Defining an end goal and identifying the activities, milestones, and resources necessary to reach that end goal.

project scope   Indicates project coverage, typically by identifying the different regions, different networks, and/or different groups of people the project encompasses.

proxy   A security device used to apply policy to web traffic.

public classification   The least sensitive level of information classification; information that is already known by or can be provided to the public.

public key encryption   An encryption process that requires two keys: one key to encrypt the information and a different key to decrypt the information.

quantum cryptography   An encryption system that uses the power of quantum mechanics instead of traditional methods.

quartiles   Division of all of the observations into four equal groups, which hold the lowest one-fourth of all observed values (first quartile), the highest one-fourth of all observed values (fourth quartile), and the two middle fourths, one-fourth above and one-fourth below the median value (or the value that divides the set of observations into two equal halves).

RASCI   A project management methodology for assigning roles in projects that involve many people and teams. Each letter in RASCI stands for a different type of role—Responsible, Approver, Supporter, Consultant, and Informed—each with corresponding responsibilities.

raw image   Also called a "dd image" (for the dataset definition command, dd). A computer forensic image of a system in which the data from the storage device is housed as a single file or multiple files, but without any type of container that stores checksums or hashes.

red book   Also known as the *Trusted Network Interpretation of the TCSEC*, this document provided guidelines for system security certifications in a networked environment.

regular expression   A mechanism to match patterns within text.

remote login (rlogin)   Enables a user or administrator to log in remotely to a computer system and to interact as if they were logging in on the actual computer. The computer system trusts the user's machine to provide the user's identity.

repudiation attack   An attack in which the attacker targets the accountability of the information.

Request for Proposal (RFP)   A document that an organization uses to solicit proposals for a project that has specific requirements. The organization can then use the responses to the RFP to evaluate and compare the proposals of multiple vendors.

Rijndael   The algorithm used for the advanced encryption standard. This private key cipher uses blocks and keys of 128, 192, and 256 bits.

risk   The potential for loss.

rootkit   A collection of tools used by hackers to cover their intrusion into a computer system or a network and to gain administrator-level access to the computer or network system. Typically, a back door is left for the intruder to reenter the computer or network at a later time.

router   A device used to route IP traffic between networks. Although a router can be used to block or filter certain types of traffic, its primary purpose is to route traffic as quickly as possible.

RSA   Rivest, Shamir, and Adleman developed this public key algorithm that can be used for both encryption and decryption. RSA is based on the difficulty of factoring large numbers.

sacred cow   An idiom for a practice that is implemented simply because it is "how it's always been done," without regard for its usefulness or whether it can help achieve a target goal or outcome.

scan   An attempt to identify systems on a network. A scan may include actions that attempt to identify the operating system version and the services running on the computer system.

script kiddies   Individuals who find scripts on the Internet and use those scripts to launch attacks on whatever computer system they can find (considered a derogatory term).

security appliances   Any type of dedicated system that is made to secure the company's network, such as firewalls, content filters, data leakage prevention systems, and so on.

security information and event monitoring (SIEM)   A system that gathers security logs from many sources and correlates the events to be able to focus on events of importance.

security policy   Defines the technical controls and security configurations that users and administrators are required to implement on all computer systems.

separation of duties   The partition of activities of configuring a policy enforcement function from the activity of verifying the compliance of the function.

SHA-1   Secure Hashing Algorithm 1 is a 160-bit value; unlike MD5, it has no known current weaknesses. The SHA-1 hash and the MD5 hash provide additional validation that the data has not been altered. If even a single byte of data is changed, the resulting hash will change.

single-factor authentication   The process administration might use with a single authentication method to identify the person requesting access to information. Using a password is a single-factor authentication.

site event   A disastrous event that destroys an entire facility.

slope of a line   A value that represents how fast the y values are rising or falling as the x values of the line increase.

Slope of line = $(y_2 - y_1) / (x_2 - x_1)$, where (x_1, y_1) and (x_2, y_2) are any two points on the line.

Smurf attack   This type of attack sends a ping packet to the broadcast address of a large network and spoofs the source address to point the returning information at the target computer. The intent is to disable the target computer.

sniffer   A computer that is configured with software to collect data packets off the network for analysis.

snooping   The process of looking through files and papers in hopes of finding valuable information.

social engineering   The use of nontechnical means (usually person-to-person contact) to gain access to information systems.

SQL injection   An attack that targets applications that take input and use the input in a SQL query.

stack   Controls switching between programs that tell the OS what code to execute when the current code has completed execution.

stakeholders   Leaders responsible for critical decision-making and key supporters who will drive change throughout the organization.

static network address translation   The process used to map internal IP addresses to external IP addresses on a one-to-one basis.

steganography   The science of hiding data in plain sight; the most popular method is hiding data within pictures.

substitution cipher   One of the oldest encryption systems, this method operates on plaintext, one letter at a time, replacing each letter for another letter or character. Analysis of the frequency of the letters can break a substitution cipher.

suspect   The person whose activities we are examining; this does not imply that we believe the person is guilty, but merely that he or she is the focus of our examination.

symmetric encryption   A system of encryption where the same key is used to encrypt and decrypt.

SYN flood   A denial-of-service attack in which the attacker sends a large number of TCP SYN packets to the target computer to render the computer inaccessible.

target   The aspect of an organization's information system that an attacker might attack.

technical practices   Practices that implement technical security controls within an organization.

threat   An individual (or group of individuals) who could violate the security of an organization.

threat analysis   A method of identifying and categorizing threats to an organization. This type of analysis identifies individuals and groups who have the motivation and capabilities to cause negative consequences to an organization.

traffic and pattern analysis   The process by an attacker of studying the communications patterns and activities of a target to discover certain types of activities and information.

Triple DES (TDES)   An enhanced version of the Data Encryption Standard (DES) that uses DES multiple times to increase the strength of the encryption.

Trojan horse   Malicious code that appears to be a useful program but instead destroys the computer system or collects information such as identification and passwords for its owner.

two-factor authentication   The process implemented by administration that employs two of the three authentication methods for identifying a person requesting access to information. An example of two-factor authentication would be using a smartcard with a password.

Twofish   A private key encryption algorithm that uses 128-bit blocks and can use 128-, 192-, or 256-bit keys.

uninterruptible power supply (UPS)   A battery-powered device that serves two purposes: It provides battery power in case the circuit loses power, and it prevents your workstation from powering off while you are doing something important, such as capturing a forensic image.

use policy   The policy an organization develops to define the appropriate use of information systems.

virtual private network (VPN)   A communication method that uses encryption to separate traffic flowing over an untrusted network.

virus   Malicious code that piggybacks on legitimate code and, when executed, interferes with computer operations or destroys information. Traditional viruses are executed through executable or command files, but they can also propagate through data files.

VPN server   A server that serves as an endpoint for a VPN connection.

vulnerability   A potential avenue of attack.

vulnerability scan   A procedure that uses a software tool to identify vulnerabilities in computer systems.

vulnerability scanning   The process of looking for and identifying vulnerabilities intruders may use as a point of attack.

wardialing   An attempt to identify phone lines that connect to computers by dialing a large amount of phone numbers to see which ones return a modem tone.

web application firewall   A security device that operates on the content directed at a web application.

web root   The first folder in the hierarchy from which the web server will return data.

web server   The server that provides web pages to web clients. The amount of systems and processing involved in generating a web page depends on the developers and the underlying code that exists in the page.

web of trust model   A model for trust in a public key environment based on the concept that each user certifies the certificates of people known to him or her.

Windows Explorer   The graphical user interface with which you access your PC desktop when using the Windows operating system. If you are viewing files and folders through My Documents, My Computer, or other Windows areas, you are using Windows Explorer.

Wired Equivalent Privacy (WEP)   A protocol designed to protect information as it passes over wireless local area networks (WLANs). WEP has a design flaw that allows an attacker to determine the key by capturing packets.

witness   A person called upon to testify in a court of law or in a deposition. Anyone can be a witness if they have information relevant to the case and have first-party knowledge of the information.

work product   A legal term that refers to documents, spreadsheets, databases, forensic files, notes, and so on that you produce during your investigation. If your investigation is under direction of an attorney, your work product may be excluded from being produced during litigation.

workflow   A collection of rules that govern the relationship of steps required to complete a process. Relationships might include sequence order, branching conditions, looping, and number of repetitions.

worms   Programs that crawl from system to system without the assistance of the victim. They make changes to the target system and propagate themselves to attack other systems on the network.

zombies   Computers on the Internet that have been compromised and the programs that have been placed on them to launch a denial-of-service attack either at a specific time or on demand.

Index

Stop Hackers in Their Tracks

Hacking Exposed, 7th Edition

Hacking Exposed
Malware & Rootkits

Hacking Exposed Computer
Forensics, 2nd Edition

Hacking Exposed Wireless,
2nd Edition

Hacking Exposed:
Web Applications, 3rd Edition

Hacking Exposed Linux,
3rd Edition

IT Auditing,
2nd Edition

IT Security Metrics

Gray Hat Hacking,
2nd Edition